POST-SOVIET

POST-SOVIET CHAOS
Violence and Dispossession
in Kazakhstan

Joma Nazpary

Pluto Press
LONDON • STERLING, VIRGINIA

First published 2002 by Pluto Press
345 Archway Road, London N6 5AA
and 22883 Quicksilver Drive,
Sterling, VA 20166–2012, USA

www.plutobooks.com

British Library Cataloguing in Publication Data
A catalogue record for this book is available from the British Library

Library of Congress Cataloging in Publication Data
Nazpary, Joma.
  Post-Soviet chaos : violence and dispossession in Kazakhstan/
Joma Nazpary.
    p. cm.
Includes bibliographical references and index.
  ISBN 0–7453–1503–8 (hbk) — ISBN 0–7453–1597–6 (pbk)
  1. Kazakhstan—Social conditions—1995– 6.
Post-communism—Kazakhstan. 3. Alienation (Social
psychology)—Kazakhstan. 4. Capitalism—Kazakhstan. 5.
Women—Kazakhstan—Social conditions. I. Title.
  HN670.23.A8 N38 2001
  306'.095845—dc21
                                                              2001000156

ISBN 0 7453 1503 8 hardback
ISBN 0 7453 1597 6 paperback

Designed and produced for Pluto Press by
Chase Publishing Services, Fortescue, Sidmouth EX10 9QG
Typeset from disk by Stanford DTP Services, Towcester
Printed in the European Union by TJ International, Padstow, England

CONTENTS

ACKNOWLEDGEMENTS

My foremost gratitude goes to those people in Almaty who helped me in conducting the research which led to the writing of this book. Although I cannot mention any name for ethical reasons, this book would not have seen the light of day without their generous support. Many children, men and women, from different walks of life and from different ethnic backgrounds sheltered me, included me in their circles of reciprocity, protected me against dangers, shared with me knowledge and taught me how to find my way in the social-cultural labyrinth. I hope this book will convey their feelings about their plight to the reader and thereby encourage her/him to take part in the struggle against the global capitalism, which is the prime cause of such a plight.

I am also grateful to the following people: Nancy Lindisfarne advised me on my research at different stages; her intellectual and moral support was indispensable. John Gledhill made thorough and thoughtful comments on an earlier draft. Sarah Ashwin also read an earlier draft and made stimulating comments. Caroline Humphrey, Stuart Thompson and Richard Taper have also made critical comments on various chapters. Jonathan Neale carefully edited an earlier draft. Fiona English taught me how to improve my English and her sympathetic attitude towards my research was a great moral support.

I also have received moral, intellectual and editorial support from Bernice Alcock, Jeanne Cannizzo, Vahid Ghazanfari, Celyan Heaton, Tim Ingold, Hoshang Noraiee, Lena Ryen, and Andrew Turton.

I am also very grateful to the members of the Department of Social Anthropology, the University of Edinburgh and the Royal Anthropological Institute for awarding me the Leach/RAI fellowship to complete this book.

Finally, many thanks to Pluto Press, particularly Roger Van Zwanenberg for his enthusiasm and encouragement.

NOTE ON TRANSLITERATION

I have used the modified Library of Congress Transliteration, used in *The Slavonic and East European Review*.

GLOSSARY

aul	smallest unit of the Kazakh traditional society; a group of nomadic families who moved together
bardak	chaos (lit. brothel; metaphorically: extreme disorder)
bednye	poor/dispossessed
blat	personal influence
Buryats	a minority group of Mongolian origin, living in the Russian federation
Chengizid	assumedly descendants of Genghis Khan
CIS	Commonwealth of Independent States
dikii kapitalism	wild capitalism
Eighth of March	International Women's Day
glasnost	openness
INGO	International Non-Governmental Organisation
Karavan	local Almaty newspaper
Khoje	assumedly descendants of Mohammed
kolkhoz	collective farm
Komsomol	the League of Communist Youth (Soviet)
liubovnitsy	mistress(es)
mejles	parliament
menbet	rural, provincial (derogatory)
MVD	Ministry of Internal Affairs (Soviet)
narod	the people
novye bogatye	new rich
Nuvroz	New Year
OBEP	Organisation against Economic Crime (Russian abbreviation)
tenge	Kazakhstan currency (from 1995 to 1996 the exchange rate dropped from $1=53 tenge to $1=70 tenge).
verny	faithful
vziatka	bribe
yurt	tent
zhuz	tribal confederation

1   INTRODUCTION

THE AIMS

Most people I met in Kazakhstan described the post-Soviet change as chaos (*bardak*) and described themselves as dispossessed by this change.

Two young Kazakhs describe below aspects of what people called chaos. A young Kazakh man:

> The life stinks here. Everybody has become a Raskolnikov without his conscience. He killed an old woman but went mad for that. In Kazakhstan today you can kill a person for $100 in the morning and in the evening drink the money with a prostitute in a restaurant without having any regret. You will sleep without nightmares. The next day you are prepared to kill anybody again for $100. This is our life. It is not only what our elite and mafia do but everybody has the same mentality. Our people (*nash narod*) are starving but they are building their villas in Medeo,[1] buying their Mercedes and spending money on prostitutes in restaurants.

A young Kazakh woman:

> Before, in the Soviet time, there were moral limits and the authorities looked after them. There were high moral standards and the party took care of them. ... But today people have become like savage animals. They behave according to the law of the jungle. Everybody who is strong hits, rapes, murders and robs everybody else who is weak.

A Russian worker gave an illustration of chaos and dispossession by commenting on the following event. On 9 October 1996, Aleksaner Petreovich Terletskii, a 56-year-old Russian worker, poured a bottle of petrol over himself, and set light to himself and burned to death in front of the office of the Belgian multi-national company Traktebel. The event received high coverage in the Russian-speaking media and great attention in my neighbourhood. The man was working as a driver in one of the Almaty energy stations which were bought by the Belgian multi-national. Somebody had stolen his wallet, which contained his driving licence and his

1

salary. He said to a colleague that he would go to the police station to make
a report. After making the report he went to work, but was told by the
manager of the station that he was sacked for leaving work without
permission. He resorted to the other authorities without any result. Finally,
he became so desperate that he burned himself in protest. As result of this
event Traktebel, already feared and hated in my neighbourhood, was dis-
credited further. People were particularly furious because the man had been
working for the station for a long time and had only two years to go to his
pension. A Russian unemployed electrician, who gave me the news first,
was of the opinion that directors in the privatised companies treated workers
as slaves. Then he added: this is chaos (*Eto bardak*).

Bardak, which literally means brothel, was used as a metaphor for
complete chaos. It was used to describe different elements of the current
situation such as corruption, cynicism, violence, the mafia, lawlessness and
arbitrariness of state officials, the dissolution of the welfare state, the dispossession of a wide range of people from economic and social rights,
alcoholism, prostitution, ethnic conflicts, despair, suicide and fear of the
future. Another key word which was interchangeably used with chaos was
wild capitalism (*dikii kapitalism*). *Bardak* is a metaphor with multiple interrelated meanings. It generally connotes the extreme legal and moral
disorder in the social life. When it is used to describe a field of social
relations it means that the interaction between people is based on illegal
and immoral ways such as chicanery, corruption and use of force. The very
arbitrariness inherent in the current situation is described as an absolute
disorder (chaos). It is used to describe disorder and lack of control in a
person's mind or life as well.

But the chaos is seen by the dispossessed to affect different people in
different ways. Those who are already powerful use these arbitrary methods
to subjugate those who are weaker. The dispossessed used the words poor
(*bednye* (plural), *bednaia* (feminine), *bednyi* (masculine)) and poverty
(*bednost*) to depict their own dispossession and lack of power in general as
a results of the chaos. What the dispossessed describe as 'chaos' are the cir-
cumstances of their plunder: a situation which they think has been
deliberately created by members of the former Soviet elite and a variety of
Westerners.

The aims of this book are to describe and analyse the main elements of
the post-Soviet 'chaos' in Almaty, Kazakhstan, from the point of view of
the dispossessed and their responses to it. All names in this book, except
those publicly known, are pseudonyms.

My focus is the way in which dispossessed people understand and react
to what they term 'chaos' and their own dispossession and the variety of

coping strategies they use. In the following two sections I discuss chaos and dispossession.

CHAOS

In the Russian language, in addition to *bardak*, there is another word for chaos, *khaos*, with its root in the Greek word *xaos*. However, people used rarely *khaos*. *Bardak* differs from *khaos* in two senses: it has stronger implications, meaning total disorder; and it has direct immoral connotations. In a sense *bardak* was described as a Sodom created by the devil himself. The local notions of chaos are different from the notion of the 'new barbarism' proposed by Kaplan (1996). Kaplan, focusing on Sierra Leone, Nigeria and other crisis-ridden countries, argues, from a Malthusian position, that the world has reached an irreversible ecological crisis because of the explosive growth of the population. The resultant scarcity of resources has triggered fierce competition for survival. In this struggle those people who have strong cultures, such as Turks, manage well, but those who have weak cultures, such as Nigerians and the other Africans, are doomed to descend into a new barbarism governed by primordial forces. So the current turbulent situation in parts of Africa and the Balkans is described as a new barbarism caused by the resurgence of irrational primordial forces. Richards (1996) and Richards and Peters (1998), looking at the civil war in Sierra Leone, show that the war and the child-participation in it is far from irrational. The war, Richards says, is a result of the crisis of the patrimonial regime, and children take part in it because the partisan army provides them with self-esteem and a kind of education. Kaplan's voice is that of an imperialist: if irrational people, say in the Balkans or Africa, are doomed to chaos and disorder because of their cultural deficiencies, then order can only be restored and preserved by the intervention of the rational and benevolent West (NATO – headed by the US?). Moreover, the West should keep at bay the irrational civilisations which are a threat to its own rational civilisation (Huntington, 1997). The popular notions of chaos in Kazakhstan situate its origins in the post-Soviet change. The new rich and the world capitalism headed by the US, are blamed for creating the chaos through a joint conspiracy. This kind of conspiracy theory, although not sophisticated, has a core of truth. Moreover, it has important political and ideological implications. It opposes diametrically the idea that Western military and economic intervention will provide a solution to the chaos. By contrast, the very intervention of the West, epitomised by American imperialism, is depicted as the main reason behind the chaos (see chapters 3 and 6). In terms of local conceptions, the chaos is not an expression of the surge of primordial instincts, but a result of the speculative capitalist rationality (the profit-making logic).

Another issue, worth mentioning, is the subjective aspect of the notions of chaos. From the point of view of an observer, the levels of social disintegration, growth of violence, ethnic tensions and other indicators of chaos, in its local descriptions, are, judging from the reports in the media, lower than in many other trouble-ridden countries around the world such as Nigeria, Zaire, Somalia, Pakistan, Indonesia, Afghanistan, Colombia, Peru, etc. However, in spite of this, most people have an acute and exaggerated sense of chaos, talk about it often and express enormous feelings of fear and insecurity. The feelings of a total void which permeates all aspects of life are commonplace. Not only is the present disconnected from the past, but the progression of time has been cancelled altogether. There is no future. Such a description of chaos, although corresponding to a real 'chaos', reflects the particularity of the post-Soviet change. That is, the sudden and brutal emergence of market forces in a non-market society. The breakdown of social trust and the sudden emergence of the random and invisible logic of the market forces accompanied by the alienated and alienating greed for accumulation of capital, bolstered by enormous use of force, create the experience of a very radical ontological disruption (see the conclusions in chapter 3). Thus life and events have become *extremely* contingent and unpredictable, reducing the people's sense of agency. Chaos to a great extent is the lack of ability among the dispossessed to navigate these newly emerged stormy conditions of a predatory capitalism. However, not everybody experiences the introduction of the market as chaos. Those few groups who can ride on the waves and get rich, experience the post-Soviet change as a pleasurable spectacle of wealth, power and consumption (see chapter 6). For the newly dispossessed groups this spectacle is the Sodom, mentioned above.

Moreover, chaos should not be understood as the diametrical opposite of order. Chaos is rather a chaotic order, an arbitrariness resulting from the random tensions between and chaotic articulation of myriads of smaller pockets of order. For example, the people's reciprocal exchange within networks have some order (see chapter 4). Racketeers who extract protections fees from traders in a particular market create a kind of order there (see chapter 3). Or a bully who aims to control a particular neighbourhood may claim to be the guardian of social morality (see chapter 7). So chaos is far from being a meaningless anarchy caused by blind primordial forces. It is rather a chaotic mode of domination in the service of the speculative logic of accumulation of capital in the post-Soviet historical conjuncture. Below I discuss this form of domination at some length.

CHAOTIC MODE OF DOMINATION

The political dimension of this chaos is a chaotic mode of domination, a situation which is created by the ruling elite in response to the current 'crisis of hegemony' (Gramsci, 1971). According to Gramsci such a crisis happens in a situation where the whole of the old system is socially, economically and ideologically in crisis, while the revolutionary forces are absent or not strong enough to transform the system into a new one. This crisis is expressed primarily on the level of political and ideological representations. The traditional political parties lose their support and legitimacy, the old common sense is broken and the ruling classes lose their moral and cultural influence over the population. In such a situation the old ruling groups, who have better cadres and much more experience, reorganise their forces in new guises. Fascism, Gramsci says, was such a device, through which landlords and large industrialists rearranged their forces by manipulating middle class prejudices.

Poulantzas (1983), discussing Gramsci's concept of the crisis of hegemony, argues that fascism is only one form of the exceptional states which may emerge as a response to the crisis of hegemony. While arguing that such forms are contingent upon particular historical conjunctures, Poulantzas distinguished empirically three forms of such states: fascism, Bonapartism and dictatorship. I would like to add to his list the chaotic mode of domination which has emerged as a response to the crisis of hegemony in the post-Soviet republics and elsewhere in the former Soviet bloc. From this point of view the chaotic mode of domination is the way the former communist elites rearranged their forces not only to keep but to extend their power and privileges. The domination in this context is in contrast to the hegemony which is achieved through ideological and moral influence and leadership.

The foremost cause of the crisis of hegemony was the economic stagnation since the late 1960s. The crisis of the system began in the 1970s with economic stagnation. According to Aganbegyan (1988), one of the main proponents of *perestroika* and an economic advisor to Gorbachev, the Soviet economy since 1967 had been in a continuous decline. This was accompanied by the growth of the black market, corruption, mafia-like networks and the general decline of morale. To my knowledge, there is no adequate theory of the crisis of the system. This is because we still lack, to a great extent, an adequate theory on the nature of the Soviet economic system. However, some theorists have pinpointed some of the elementary causes of the stagnation. For example, Ticktin (1992), a main theoretical authority in the field, argues that the Soviet type of the growth was dependent on the extensive use of labour and raw materials. The abundance of labour and raw materials up to the late 1960s guaranteed rapid economic growth. But when these reserves of labour and raw materials were exhausted, sustaining the economic growth required the replacement of the extensive use of production factors with an intensive one. This required the modernisation of machines and the deployment of new technological innovations. The regime's failure to fulfil this task resulted in the stagnation. Castells (1998), on the other hand, argues that the crisis of the Soviet society from the mid-1970s onwards was a result of the inability of the system to transform its industrial economy to one based on information technology. Military competition with the West, resulting in the enormous growth of the defence budget which diverted investment from non-military sectors of the economy, played its part in the stagnation of the system as well.

Besides the economic stagnation, the country experienced a general moral crisis expressed by the workers' indifference to their work, the loosening of professional discipline, the growth of alcoholism, widespread corruption, the prevalence of cynicism, the expansion of the second economy, the loss of the ideological authority of the communist party, the high rate of divorce, the decline of birth rate and the rebellion of youth against the Soviet life-style. All these were symptoms of the breakdown of the social contract between the elite and the people. In order to renew their hegemony the most sensitive part of the elite launched *perestroika* under Gorbachev's leadership. As Kagarlitsky (1988) observed, there were two generally opposed expectations of *perestroika* and *glasnost*. Workers and radical groups expected that these should result in socialist democracy, while the elite wanted a transformation to capitalism. The workers and radical groups failed to become a political force capable of significantly influencing events.[2] On the other hand the elite failed to unite around a common platform. It was fractured along two general lines: conservative/reformists on the one hand and centre/periphery on the other. While both conservative and reformist agreed on the transition to a market economy, they differed with regard to the pace deemed appropriate for such a transition. The conflict between centre and periphery acquired primarily an ethnic character. While two Caucasian republics (Georgia and Armenia) and the three Baltic republics plus Moldova wanted to secede, the rest demanded greater political and economic autonomy from the centre. Indeed, these two conflicts were locked into each other, as a consequence of the fact that the conservatives resisted the demands of the periphery for more autonomy and reformists, while opposing secessionist tendencies, agreed to concede a higher degree of autonomy to the periphery. The intensification of these two conflicts led to the failed coup in August 1991 and the subsequent dissolution of the USSR in December of the same year by Yeltsin and the leaders of Ukraine and Belorussia.

The chaotic mode of domination which emerged as a result of the processes of the disintegration of the USSR had two main phases: 1987–92, and 1992 onwards.

The first was characterised by the disintegration of Soviet society as a moral community into networks of influence on the one hand and networks of survival on the other (1987–92). During this phase the central planning and central distribution of goods and credits had collapsed. The communist party, Komsomol, KGB, MVD, the army and the cultural/ideological apparatus were disorganised. The centre did not exert any authority over the periphery. The local and regional elites reorganised themselves into multiple networks of influence which acted independently of the centre (Humphrey, 1991). Humphrey, who reported on such a situation in provincial Russia described these decentralised power networks as 'suzerainties'. As Humphrey illustrates, a main feature of chaos was the enormous illegal and quasi-criminal power that the collapse of the centre bestowed upon these regional and local networks, whose spheres of influence often overlapped. Acting arbitrarily, they negotiated their relationship through the use of violence, exchange of bribes, tributes and favours. In doing so they spread violence, cynicism and corruption in all spheres of social life. Those who created these networks were the political and managerial elite, the black marketeers and the newlyemerged mafia. An important element of this process was the disintegration of the welfare state. Those lower down the social scale built their survival networks, creating new forms of moral communities (see chapter 4).

The second phase has been marked by the emergence of post-Soviet governmental institutions in independent Kazakhstan and the forging of a new balance of power between the holders of high offices in government institutions on the one hand and members of the networks of influence on the other.

The reinforcement of state institutions subordinated the networks of influence to state officials but did not eliminate them. State officials became supervisors/arbiters *vis-à-vis* these networks. From now on the chaotic mode of dominance was characterised by the intertwined over-centralised arbitrariness of the state officials on the one hand and the centrifugal and anarchic arbitrariness of the members of different informal networks of influence on the other. The way these two levels of arbitrariness are imposed on the population, articulated and adjusted to each other, and also the tensions between them, are significant elements of what people call chaos. The chaos is exacerbated by the fact that the gaps left by these two types of arbitrariness are filled by the violence of numerous groups of unruly hooligans (see chapter 3).

This form of dominance is a result of the fact that the resistance of the democratic forces puts a limit to the centralised arbitrariness of officials of the government. This means that in spite of the fact that the main formal political power is concentrated in the hands of an authoritarian president, he cannot rule as a dictator. The president has subordinated the parliament (*mejles*) and judiciary and his decrees replace the law in many cases (Bremmer and Welt, 1996; Olcott, 1997). Moreover, as Olcott (p. 107) put it:

Nazarbaev also has a broad spectrum of informal or extra-legal powers which accrue from his years in the communist party hierarchy, and from the years which his constituents spent as Soviet subjects. The president has a staff of several hundred who can conduct informal interventions or offer necessary persuasion in situations where the more formal powers are inadequate, or might work too slowly.

Presidential rule provides the general background for the arbitrariness of the state officials. However, such arbitrariness is challenged by the remnants of the democratic forces, which came to the fore during Gorbachev's *glasnost* (openness). In parallel with the disintegration of the Soviet state grew a plethora of free associations, free political parties, INGOs, free press, free opinions. The attitudes of the post-Soviet elite towards these forces is ambivalent. On the one hand the ruling elite has tried to curb this democratic space through closing the oppositional press, harassing journalists and leaders of oppositional political parties, fraud in elections (Bremmer and Welt, 1996: pp. 185–93). Such measures have been challenged by the oppositional forces.[3] On the other hand the regime needs a facade of democracy in order to introduce itself as a democratic break with the Soviet totalitarian regime. Thus it tolerates the activities of NGOs in so far as they do not interfere with the business of state officials and their networks. This imposes a limit on the formal arbitrariness of the regime. As a result the regime is neither a dictatorship nor democratic, it is an authoritarian regime limited by democratic forces. Indeed, the networks of influence extend the arbitrariness of the elite beyond the limits placed on formal power by democratic forces. Such networks, bolstered by state officials, are often involved in illegal deals in the economic sphere.

Tribalism?

Many of the local intellectuals in Kazakhstan, most notably Masanov (1996a and personal communication with the author) see this mode of dominance as a revival of Kazakh tribalism. It is argued that Kazakhs lack a tradition of statehood. Under the Tsarist and the Soviet era while subordinated to the centre they preserved their three tribal confederations (*Zhuz*) (Poliakov, 1992; Masanov, 1996a). Since independence, it is claimed, the Kazakh government has been an alliance of these three *Zhuz* rather than a modern state. The competition for power between the three *Zhuz* creates the current chaos and disorder.

The tribalism theory is questionable on three grounds. First, although the Kazakh elite regional division coincides with the old *Zhuz* divisions, the *Zhuz* no longer exists as a form of social organisation but only as a myth. Although every Kazakh I spoke to is conscious of belonging to one of the three *Zhuz* or *Chengizid* or *Khoje* outside these *Zhuz*, these divisions were important for neither friendship nor marriage, which are the cornerstones of networking (see chapter 4). The students, teachers, academic staff and street traders were indifferent to and unaware of the *Zhuz* of their fellows. *Zhuz* hierarchies and *Zhuz* mobilisation mechanisms have ceased to exist. Second, members of the Kazakh elite and intelligentsia whom I met were far more sophisticated in their modern and global political and social orientation than their Russian counterparts in Kazakhstan. To suggest that these people still conduct their relationships according to the old patronage codes of conduct of sultans, khans and bias is to ignore the century of modernisation that the Kazakh community has gone through.

Third, the chaotic mode of domination is not restricted to Kazakhstan; Russia and other post-Soviet republics without tribal backgrounds have experienced similar situations.

A return to feudalism or the advent of wild capitalism?

In a much broader sense such duality of power structures is a common feature of most of the so-called post-socialist societies (Verdery, 1996a). Verdery considers this duality a return to a type of feudalism. True enough, the anarchic nature of the patronage networks of the elite combined with authoritarian state officials, who use arbitrary methods, including violence for the expropriation of wealth, make the post-Socialist systems of power similar to feudalism. However, the metaphor fails to capture the complex ways in which these mechanisms have become a part of late global capitalism. Thus, in this respect, it seems to me that the local metaphor of wild capitalism, mentioned earlier, is a much more suitable notion. Not only did the Soviet bloc disintegrate into the present state of affairs under the financial, military, technological and ideological pressures of advanced capitalism (Verdery, 1996a; Castells, 1998), it also became a target of the imperialistic dominance of the latter (Gowan, 1996). As Gowan argues, Western powers under the supervision of the IMF and the WB succeeded in transforming the former Soviet block into a raw material producing zone, integrated into the world capitalist system. The expansion of NATO eastward and the involvement of Western advisors, speculators, multinationals, oil barons, sex tourists, sex industry, banking systems and money laundering, mafia, missionaries, spies and financiers are a few of the many signs of the West's active intervention in post-Soviet change.

The case of Kazakhstan is an illustrative example. It is a country which followed IMF policies. In 1997 there were 1,388 joint ventures and foreign firms in the republic (Diugai, 1998: p. 27). Multi-nationals such as Chevron, Mobil, Shell, British Gas, State Oil, and Traktebel are among the main actors in the field (Dittmann et al, 1998: pp. 55, 56). The total number of employees of such enterprises amounted to 77,893. The wages of foreigners working in Kazakhstan was $24 million in 1997 (p. 24). Foreign financial

resources make up 50 per cent of total investment in the Kazakh economy
(p. 23). Foreign direct investment in the republic in 1997 amounted to $2.1
billion (p. 26). The following table demonstrates the share of different
countries in such investment:

Table 1.1: The share of the main foreign investor countries in 1997

Country	Share (%)
Belgium	2
Canada	3
China	5
France	2
Great Britain	15
South Korea	22
Turkey	5
US	29
Virgin Island	2
Others	15
Total	100

(Source: Diugai, 1998: p. 28)

The foreign investment has led to an uneven development and has made
the Kazakh economy dependent on the export of raw material. Oil, iron and
non-ferrous metals account for 80 per cent of exports (Wurzel, 1998: p. 20).
Both foreign investors and government prefer investment in raw material,
because of the quick returns (Wurzel, 1998). The most attractive sectors
for foreign investment are oil, gas, ferrous and non-ferrous metals (Diugai,
1998: p. 26). For example, 44 per cent of total foreign direct investment,
$2.9 billion between 1993 and 1997, went to oil and gas (Ribakova, 1998:
p. 44). In 1996 roughly 85 per cent of foreign direct investment was in oil,
gas, ferrous and non-ferrous metals. The figure for 1997 was 75 per cent
(Wurzel, 1998: p. 17). The foreign investors control strategic sectors in the
economy. For example, the share of joint ventures and enterprises with
major foreign participation in the total oil production exceeded 75 per cent
in 1997 (Ribakova, 1998: p. 44). The dependency of the Kazakh economy
on raw material is evident from the fact that when the prices of raw material
fell in 1998, the GDP dropped dramatically and as a result the government
cut the budget by 20–25 per cent. 57.3 per cent of oil is exported to
countries in Western Europe (Ribakova, 1998: p. 43). 90 per cent of ferrous
metals are exported to countries outside CIS (Ribakova, 1998: p. 48).

The orientation of the economy towards the export of raw materials, combined with economic crisis, has contributed to deindustrialisation. For example, the production of chemical products, mechanical engineering and building material dropped respectively by 31.8 per cent, 53.3 per cent and 29.3 per cent between 1995 and 1998. The output of agriculture fell by half (Wurzel, 1998: p. 17). This pattern of development has created a close link between state officials and investors. Foreigners lend money mainly to the government or under government guarantees. Moreover, the foreign investors, because of high financial risks, try to deal mostly with the government (Diugai, 1998: p. 29). On the other hand, the export of raw material generates tax revenues for the government and the privatisation of oil, gas, ferrous and non-ferrous metals has generated financial resources. The local contacts of these Western agencies are the post-Soviet networks of the political and business quasi-mafia elite under discussion. Members of these networks are not only aping the luxurious life-style of the Western bourgeoisie but launder their monies in Western banks, buy property in the West, visit expensive clubs in the West and send their children to study there, negotiate commercial contracts with the multinationals and have friends and associates among the representatives of multinational and transnational organisations.

The multiple ways in which the local and national networks of power are articulated to 'the global ecumene' of capital indicate that the present chaos is not merely understandable with reference to 'the evil heritage of the Soviet past' as the apologists of capitalism suggest, or merely the corruption of the post-Soviet elites, but also the imperialistic interventions of Western financial, industrial and political agencies. An effect of such imperialistic policies has been the creation of uneven economic structures. Clover and Corzine (1998: p. 1) describe such an economy in Kazakhstan as follows:

> Economic reforms also created two distinct economies. One is export-oriented, and includes privatised oil companies and metal plants, and the banks that finance them. Flush with cash, they are busy issuing ADRs and corporate Eurobonds. In the other economy wages are paid in vegetable oil, vehicle tyres and loaves of bread, if at all. The inhabitants of this economy live in Kazakhstan's 'dead cities' so-named by Mr Kashegeldin,[4] and barter whatever commodity they are paid in to heat their homes.

On a global scale the chaotic mode of dominance in the emerging post-Soviet capitalist economies is a particular instance of the crisis of hegemony which results from the contradictions of late capitalism (Gledhill, 1996; Castells, 1998). Similar modes of domination prevail in many countries in the world of which Afghanistan, Angola, Pakistan,

Mexico and Colombia are just a few examples (Gledhill, 1996; Castells, 1998). One may reject this argument by referring to the fact that the dominant form of capital in the post-Soviet economies is fictitious capital and large parts of these economies which are based on barter are not included in the circuits of the global economy. My reply to this objection is as follows. First, the fictitious capital is the hegemonic form of the capital in the global economy, even in the US it outstrips other forms of capital. Second, world capitalism subjugates the economies of countries such as Russia and Kazakhstan through this form of capital. Third, the dual economies (dollar versus barter economies) are the results of such a sub-jugation. The global networks of fictitious capital, including the banking system, have provided the post-Soviet elite with new opportunities for spec-ulative investment and conspicuous consumption. This in its turn has encouraged the elite to pursue predatory forms of rent-seeking such as the sale of raw material, stealing state property and money, involvement in speculation on state bonds and pyramid schemes, building trade monopolies, bribery and extortion. The very fact that the fictitious capital demands quick and high profits prevents the investment in those sectors of the economy which do not give quick returns. As a result these sectors are ruined or manage their transactions through barter.

The chaotic mode of domination is the political instrument of the imple-mentation of the new liberal economic policies. The core element of such policies was the expropriation of wealth from the majority of the people by the elite and their Western allies. The main mechanisms of such expropri-ation which were mentioned by the dispossessed were: the transfer of state property into private ownership through illegal and legal ways; the disso-lution of the welfare state; the liberalisation of prices; eating up people's savings through the dramatic depreciation of their values; cutting wages and pensions and postponing payments. The expropriation went through two consecutive stages, corresponding respectively to the two stages of chaotic dominance. The first step of expropriation began in 1987 when Gorbachev legalised private business in the form of cooperatives (Castells, 1998). As Castells argues the structural background of this expropriation was the transition to a market economy in the context of a chaos which resulted from the collapse of the central political and economic institution of the Soviet state. The economic chaos was marked by the fact that the underground economy which was already (Grossman, 1985) an important, although subordinate, part of the Soviet economy, became the dominant driver of the distribution of goods and services. The members of the *nomen-klatura* accumulated legendary wealth during a short period through hoarding, bartering and selling goods for much higher prices on the black market. Oil, steel, precious metals and weapons were illegally exported. Foreign goods were illegally imported and sold on the black market. This process of plundering was bolstered by the violence of mafia gangs which filled the vacuum that had been created as result of the disintegration of the coercive apparatus of the state.

The next step in expropriation was the formal privatisation of state property and the liberalisation of prices which occurred after independence. As Clarke and Kabalina (1995) argue in the case of Russia, the collapse of central economic institutions had made managers the *de facto* owners of enterprises. The formal privatisation was intended to give this a legal guise. Now, privatised enterprises became either practically the property of managers through being transferred to cooperatives or were sold for nominal prices to friends and relatives for bribes. So in a very short time a network of rich people was formed.

The accumulation of wealth, according to various local sources, still continues through illegal methods. Tax evasions, fraud in customs fees, creating private monopolies, illegal distribution of credits between friends and relatives, extraction of bribes and tributes are some of the standard methods which are deployed by the new rich groups. Liberalisation of prices, closure of factories, redundancy of workers on a massive scale, cutting and abolishing of welfare services are also carried out on IMF and other Western agencies' instructions. Without the chaotic mode of dominance the stealing of state property and IMF-led economic policies could not be carried out without provoking massive resistance. Only under the condition of chaos where fear of unharnessed violence, cynicism and lawlessness had paralysed the dispossessed, was an unchallenged transformation to IMF-designed 'wild capitalism' possible. Thus, it seems to me that the people are in a sense correct in claiming that the elite conspired to create the chaos with the purpose to plunder. This led to the creation of the dispossessed, which I describe very briefly below.

THE DISPOSSESSED

The result of the expropriation of state property was the rapid accumulation of wealth at one pole and poverty at the other and the creation of the new social categories of the New Rich (*Novye Bogatye*) and the dispossessed (*bednye*).[5] This polarisation is the most profound social change which has occurred as a result of the transformation to 'capitalism'. The new rich are distinguished from the rest of the population not only through their wealth but also their luxurious life-style (see chapter 6) and their transnational networks. Buying luxurious cars, visiting expensive restaurants and night clubs and building pompous private houses are some elements of the consumption pattern of the new rich. Although the local notions of the new rich and dispossessed are very close to a concept of class in a Marxist sense, their class positions are ambiguous. Such ambiguity is due to the fact that the relation of the new rich and the relation of the dispossessed to production have been distorted by the collapse of the production apparatus and the emergence of the market. The new rich collect their wealth not through direct extraction of surplus value but through plunder. On the other hand wages constitute a small part of the incomes of the dispossessed, for survival they rely also on small trade and reciprocal exchange within networks. Humphrey (1996: p. 70), inspired by Marx,[6] defines the dispossessed in the Russian context as follows:

> The dispossessed are people who have been deprived of property, work and entitlements, but in a second sense we can understand them as people who are themselves no longer possessed. That is, they are no longer inside the quasi-feudal corporations, the collective 'domain', which confer a social status on their members and which in practice are still today the key units disposing of property and people in Russia.

Then she proceeds to include the following categories among the dispossessed: refugees, unemployed, economic migrants, demobilised soldiers, abandoned pensioners, invalid and single-parent families, vagrants and the homeless.

The local concepts of the dispossessed in Almaty cover Humphrey's definition but stretch beyond it in two senses: they include categories of people who do not fit into the definition; and, although the dispossessed might have become free from the particular set of Soviet-era patronage obligations, for survival they are forced into a new set of such obligations in their post-Soviet networking practices (see chapter 4). As I discuss the second point in chapter 4 let me explain very briefly the first point here. Although the majority of people categorise themselves as a homogeneous poor (*bednye*) group *vis-à-vis* the new rich, in reality the dispossessed is a heterogeneous category. Not only can one distinguish between different sub-groups among the poor, but the dispossessed are also ethnically differentiated. For an illustration let me introduce a rough classification of the local population according to the level of their wealth which I worked out with the help of a group of local people in my neighbourhood cafe.

1. Garbage seekers (Russian old men and women) and beggars (Tadjik/gypsy women and children, Russian old men and women).
2. Unemployed alcoholics (mainly Russians).
3. Street traders (single mothers, Kazakh migrants from the south, war refugees (Tadjik men and Chechen women)).
4. Pensioners.
5. Urban working class (mainly Russian), civil servants (mainly Kazakh), academics and scientific and technical personnel.

6. Sex workers, suitcase traders (*chelnoki*) and those who work for foreign companies.
7. The lower echelon of high state officials (with bribery as the main source of income), middle rank mafioso and kiosk owners.
8. The new rich (*novye bogatye*): managers of the large enterprises, top ranking businessmen, top ranking state officials and top ranking mafia (mainly men).

Indeed, these groups were further classified by us into four wider categories: extremely poor (*Bomzh*)[7] (groups 1, 2), poor (*bednye*) (groups 3, 4, 5), average (*srednyi*) (group 7) and rich (*bogatye*) (group 8).[8] Group 6 were classified by others as average while they considered themselves as poor.

While Humphrey's definition of the dispossessed coincides with what locals call the extremely poor (*bomzhy*) the locals' own definitions comprise a spectrum which includes groups from 1 to 6. The extremely poor at the bottom of the dispossessed spectrum are either non-locals (Tadjik female war refugees, gypsy women) or Russians (old men and women or Russian unemployed alcoholic men). The main reasons for the over-representation of Russians in this group are the break-up of Russian networks because of massive out-migration (see chapter 4), and the fact that the economic crisis has struck most powerfully at the industrial working class, predominantly male Russians. Being unemployed, although many of them avoid getting involved in the 'demeaning' occupation of street trading, they have lost face by no longer being the breadwinners and have turned to alcohol.

The main bulk of the dispossessed according to the wider local descriptions is composed of groups 3 to 6. Indeed, many of the people who had kept their jobs, and even those who owned apartments, cars, animals and small means of production like small boats, fishing nets and dachas felt dispossessed. People like Aleksander (chapter 4), Bulat (chapter 7), Saken and Amira (chapter 3), the four sex workers and other women (chapter 5), belong to this group.

Some people among group 6 who had sustained or improved their material standards felt dispossessed because of the experience of cultural and professional deprivation or insecurity (see chapters 3 and 6). I will discuss in chapters 3 and 6 the feelings of loss of culture and insecurity common to all the dispossessed.

Although group 7 was considered by most people as wealthy, they themselves usually considered themselves as average. They were neither considered by others or themselves as dispossessed nor part of the new rich. It was group 8 which was accused of dispossessing others of wealth through the stealing of public property.

In spite of the wealth differentiation between the dispossessed, in their anti-elite rhetoric they appear as a homogeneous group, interchangeably called: we (*my*), the poor (*bednye*), the people (*narod*), below (*vniz*), working class (*Rabochii klass*) and labouring people (*Rabotaishchie liudi*). On the other hand the elite is called interchangeably: they (*oni*), bosses (*nachal'niki*), authorities (*nachal'stvo*), leadership (*rukovodstvo*), above (*verkh*), new rich (*novye bogatye*), new Russian (*novye Russkii*).

This strongly articulated polarised consciousness among the dispossessed is not only rooted in a common suffering, although differentiated in degrees, but by the depth of post-Soviet expropriation and the speed with which it has been carried out. In the rest of this book I use these concepts in the same polarised fashion, unless otherwise specified.

STRUCTURE OF THE BOOK

In chapter 2, I describe the historical backgrounds of Kazakhstan and Almaty and my fieldwork practice.

In chapter 3, I deal with some aspects of the chaos as it was described by the dispossessed. First, I discuss some aspects of the process of wealth differentiation such as the privatisation of state property, extraction of bribes and tributes and manipulation of credit. Then I describe the upsurge of violence in relation to wealth differentiation on the one hand and the emergence of the post-Soviet gender and ethnic ideologies on the other. Next I deal with feelings of loss and the ways people denounce the post-Soviet change, by arguing that such change has resulted from a planned conspiracy by the West and the elite.

In chapter 4, I explore reciprocal exchange within networks as the strategy the dispossessed use to cope with chaos. The most crucial point about networks is that as a result of the chaos the erstwhile Soviet 'society' has disintegrated into two types of networks: networks of the new rich (*novye bogatye*) and networks of the dispossessed. While the first networks were formed for plundering public wealth, the second were formed to cope with the harsh conditions of dispossession. While the sum of networking practices constitute the chaos, networks of particular individuals or particular households appear as its antithesis. This is so because while the interaction within networks is based on trust and reciprocity, relations outside them are negotiated through money and violence. However, the wealth of a particular individual or his/her access to the means of violence depend to a great extent on the nature of his/her networks. It is clear that the networks of the dispossessed are not well placed in this respect.

Although these networks have their roots in the Soviet era's networking practices (Poliakov, 1992), they are different. The Soviet era's networks, embedded in the state institutions, were subordinated to collective interests of the state and party. By contrast, the post-Soviet networks of influence, dominating the state institutions, use them in order to accumulate private wealth. A result of this was the abolition of the welfare state.

In anthropological literature 'networks' has two meanings: a set of face to face reciprocal relations; and social relations established between people and institutions through electronic and other means of communication (Hannerz, 1992a: p. 41; Castells, 1996: p. 470). In Kazakhstan while the networks of survival are of the first type, the networks of influence are a mixture of both types. A major result of the post-Soviet openness towards the capitalist world has been the transnationalisation of the networks of the new rich. The dispossessed are not only deprived of such privileges, but the Soviet-era possibilities for long distance communication have diminished dramatically as a result of the combined effects of their poverty and the dramatic increase in the costs of stamps, telephone calls and travel. In spite of this difference, both networks are anchored in local kinship, marriage, friendship and ethnic relations.

In chapter 5, I discuss the economic sexual strategies, practised by young dispossessed women. These strategies are: exchange of sexual service for better-paid jobs; finding sponsors (lovers who provide materially for women); finding rich husbands and prostitution. The post-Soviet change has dispossessed most women (Einhorn, 1993; Molyneux, 1990; Watson, 1993). Women are discriminated against in the labour market and their access to better jobs, wealth and influence is mainly conditional upon their relations with rich and powerful men. Under such conditions, women contribute to family survival, through involvement in street trade, suitcase trade, working on dacha allotments and conserving vegetables and fruits. In addition to these socially recognised strategies of survival, many young women[9] deploy the sexual strategies which are socially stigmatised. The resources accessed through sexual strategies are not considered as part of family resources, and men who provide such resources are not included in family networks. Another important aspect of the sexual strategies is their symbolic significance. Most people consider them as signs of a moral chaos caused by wild capitalism.

While most of these strategies were practised in the Soviet era marginally (Posadskaya, 1992; Waters, 1989; Dobrokhotova, 1984) their massive growth is a post-Soviet phenomenon (Waters, 1989; Bridger et al, 1996). In addition to poverty, the emergence of a consumerist culture is pivotal in pushing young women to adopt sexual strategies. Many who cannot afford to buy expensive Western goods resort to such strategies to obtain the necessary money (Bridger et al, 1996). This has led to a widespread mon-etisation of sexuality and the emergence of a transnational sex industry (Shreeves, 1992; Attwood, 1996; Bridger et al, 1996).

The growth of prostitution in tandem with the growth of pornography and images of femininity created by modelling, advertisements, the tabloid press and soap operas has transformed the Soviet official symbolism of femininity. In the Soviet era the official icon of womanhood was that of a muscular 'heroine worker' in baggy clothes, a tractor driver, or 'heroine mother'. Today these images are replaced by those of women as sexual figures. While this is a global trend (*The Economist*, 14 February 1988, pp. 19–20, 23–5) the responses to it vary culturally (Beller-Hann, 1995; Cox, 1993; Kapur, 1994; Waters, 1989). In Kazakhstan, the widespread commodification of women's bodies has provoked a great deal of violence against them (Zabelina, 1996). First, violence is an important element of the appropriation, sale and consumption of sex. Second, such violence is motivated and justified by the current identity politics. Women who practise sexual strategies are considered to be creators of chaos in terms of reproduction. Moreover, they are condemned for the alleged disgrace their practice inflicts on authentic ethnic and Soviet identities (see chapters 3, 5 and 6).[10]

In chapter 6, I deal with the ideological and cultural responses of the dispossessed towards post-Soviet change. The expropriation of wealth and the monetisation of life are considered by the dispossessed as elements of an overall notion of alien, in opposition to which they imagine an authentic Soviet community and an authentic Soviet culture. Alien consists of alien persons and alien phenomena. The alien person is one who comes from outside CIS territory, is male by gender, is wealthy and propagates prostitution and sexual diseases. Metaphorically, the alien person epitomises the manners and the culture of the new rich, consumerism and sexual promiscuity. Alien phenomena include the expropriation of state property, capitalism, wealth differentiation, the consumerist life-style of the new rich and the monetisation of social relations, particularly sexuality. All these are considered to corrupt their imagined authentic Soviet life-style. This is emphasised through expression of a great nostalgia for the Soviet era, which is idealised as the era of prosperity, security, trust, morality, generosity, stability, predictability of life and social peace. I explain this as selectivity of the collective memory of the dispossessed which plays down the negative aspects of the Soviet era. In addition to this, the notions of an authentic Soviet 'identity' is articulated as the sexual modesty of women by the dispossessed (chapters 3 and 6). This book makes an original contribution to the understanding of identity politics in the post-Soviet context by discussing the ways through which the dispossessed imagine a gendered Soviet identity.

The notion of shared Soviet identity is questioned by the continuing ethnic tensions. In chapter 7 I explore such tensions. I do not discuss ethnicity in general in Kazakhstan or all aspects of ethnic relations but those which relate directly to ethnic tensions. These tensions, which are considered a strong element of chaos, are related to the Kazakhification of the state and the struggle for urban space. The Kazakhification of the state

has two main components: monopolisation of high posts in the state institutions by Kazakhs, and the language policy. Both of these give the Kazakh
elite privileged access to the resources. The tension over urban space also
has two main elements: tension between migrant Kazakhs from *auls* and
urban Russian speakers, including urban Kazakhs, and a tension between
migrant Kazakhs and migrant Muslims from other post-Soviet republics.
Many migrants resort to hooliganism and violence to impose their
domination over urban space. The fact that urban Kazakhs and other
Muslim groups side with non-Kazakhs and non-Muslims against rural
Kazakhs fragments both Kazakh and Muslim identities. Kazakhs claim a
privileged position by evoking a primordial notion of the homeland. They
say that the fact that Kazakhstan is the ancestral land of Kazakhs entitles
them to be the masters of the country. Non-Kazakhs challenge such claims
by evoking a constructionist notion of the homeland. They say all ethnic
groups have built the modern Kazakhstan together and all of them are
equally entitled to its resources.

I conclude the book by making a comment on the main findings of the
book in a comparative perspective.

2 PEOPLE AND PLACES

In this chapter I will discuss the ways I interacted with people in order to collect material for this book, describe a neighbourhood in which I did fieldwork, and present very briefly Almaty (the city) and Kazakhstan (the country) to the reader.

METHOD

The themes of this book emerged out of my participation in people's daily life, observing their practices and discussing with them the meaning of such practices. During my stay in Almaty (July 1995 to October 1996), I interacted with nine networks and in addition with a good number of individuals or families without having access to their networks. For ethical reasons I cannot reveal detailed information about these people which might lead to their identification. However, in the course of this book I refer to many of them, describe their social, ethnic and biographical backgrounds and let them speak for themselves.

Three of these networks were related to the university where I taught: a network of teachers in my department, a network of my women students who worked casually as translators for foreign businessmen and a network of male Kazakh students who extracted tributes from other students. I was introduced to the fourth network by Gulnara[11] who worked at the same university, but the rest of its members did not work there. The other five networks which were related to the neighbourhood where I lived are as follows: a drinking circle of urban men, a network of Kazakh migrants from the south (both men and women), two networks of women urban street traders and a network of four women sex workers. Although only a few individuals in each network confided information to me about their transactions with other people, the rest trusted me enough to tell me their opinions on the current political and economic situation. I established good relations with some families and individuals through the university and the neighbourhood. Indeed, negotiation and establishment of trust was much easier with members of a family than members of a network. Once a member of a family introduced me to the rest they trusted me while in networks I had to negotiate the trust separately with each individual. A friend of a member of a family is usually considered as a friend of the family. By contrast, in networks, friendship with a member of a network does not automatically result in friendship with other members and must be established individually.

In addition to my regular interactions with networks, families and individuals mentioned above I had hundreds of casual discussions with people in the neighbourhood, university and many other places. In addition to the people above, workers on a factory shop floor were another source of information. Although I mixed with people from all walks of life, I was careful to spend more time with the dispossessed and reflect upon their ideas, trying to see things from their point of view. I did so because their voices are not represented either in the local or Western media or academic writings. Thus this book explores the uncharted themes mainly from the point of view of the dispossessed. I deployed a variety of field techniques: participatory observation, informal talks, collecting life stories, recording talks in celebrations, taking photographs and copying videos from celebrations, formal interviews, organising discussion groups, taking part in political and cultural meetings and conducting surveys.

The fact that the daily practices of those people were located in different places (and I followed them, if not to all, to a good number of such places) gave a multi-sited character to my field work practice. Related to this, I defined the field as a network of places linked to each other either through the actual movement of people within and between them or through the meaning they invested in them. A neighbourhood, a university, a shop floor in a factory, two villages, a cafe, a club and some other places were some important elements of such a network. The neighbourhood was the central node in this network, because people from it were involved in all other places. Therefore I describe it briefly below.

The neighbourhood
The neighbourhood consisted of residential houses, five kiosks, three shops and an illegal market, a cafe-bar, a restaurant and a culture house (*dom kul' tury*). There were three types of residential houses each built in a different historical period. The first type, built during the 1930s and earlier, consisted of a row of 13 one-storey houses; the owners were Russians. As far as the modern infrastructures were concerned, these houses only had electricity and sewerage. Because of their lack of central heating, central gas, hot water and telephone lines, they were not popular. Most of the owners had rented rooms to Kazakh or Tadjik migrants, mainly street traders. After Almaty became the capital of Kazakhstan in 1929, it underwent considerable expansion and modernisation. The new yellow houses built in the 1950s marked the new status of the city. These houses, which were four- or five-storey houses, had amenities which the first houses lacked. The state shop, opened in 1962, was a shopping centre not only for our neighbourhood, but for other neighbourhoods as well. These houses,

which were given in the 1950s to those who worked as state and party func-
tionaries, were now inhabited by their children or grandchildren. Unlike the
first group of houses, the majority of owners were Kazakhs. The majority
of buildings, the third type of houses, were built in the 1960s and early
1970s. These houses, which were called Khrushchev houses
(*khrushchevskii doma*), were five-storey cement houses. Most of these
buildings were given to different organisations, which in their turn distributed them to their own staff. Although Russians made up a considerable
portion of the owners of these houses, they came from diverse ethnic backgrounds. The residents in the neighbourhood were mainly workers in
industrial enterprises like the energy sector, furniture factories and machine
industry, but other residents were teachers, university lecturers, police and
army personnel, clerks and traders. Most of the people in the neighbourhood considered themselves poor, five families considered themselves
average, of which two were considered rich by others. A considerable
number of extremely poor (*bomzhy*) people, most of whom were Russian
alcoholics, gypsies or Tadjik and Uzbek female beggars, were present in
the neighbourhood.

The ethnic combination of the neighbourhood was very complex. I could
not map it exactly because 42 families refused to answer my questions or
did not open the doors. Although most of those who opened their doors but
did not answer my questions had Mongolian features, it was impossible for
me to discover their ethnicity.[12] From the families who answered my
questions and other enquiries the following picture emerges:

Table 2.1: Approximate ethnic mixture of the neighbourhood

Ethnicity	Number of families
Chechen	1
Cherkes-Ukrainean	1
Dungan	1
German	2
Georgians	1
Greek-Uigur	1
Jewish	2
Kazakh	15
Korean	3
Polish	2
Russians from Russian ancestors	20
Russians from mixed Russian and non-Russsian ancestors	13

Table 2.1: *continued*

Ethnicity	Number of families
Russian-Armenian	1
Russian-Chinese	1
Russian-Irish[13]	1
Russian-Kazakh	2
Russian-Tatar	3
Russian-Ukrainian	17
Russian-Belorussian	12
Russian-German	1
Russian-Polish	1
Russian-Jewish	2
Russiam-Uigur	1
Tatar	2
Tatar-Kazakh	1
Uigur	4
Ukrainian-Kazakh	1
Uzbek-Jewish	1
Uigur-Kazakh	1
Ukrainian	2
Unknown	42
Total	158[14]

These figures reflect only the owners of the apartments and not all their inhabitants. A considerable number of migrant Kazakhs who were tenants are not reflected in these figures.

Up to 1992 the neighbourhood had preserved the shape it took in the 1970s. Since then it has changed with five new kiosks, a restaurant, a shashlyk bar, a furniture shop, a food shop and the illegal street market. As a result of this development, many different goods from different countries are available in the neighbourhood. Even the state shop offers foreign goods, although a considerable part of its goods are still local ones. Parallel with changes in physical appearance, the neighbourhood has undergone deep demographic and social change. The most dramatic demographic change is related to the emigration of non-Kazakhs and immigration of rural Kazakhs. As far as I could map it out, 28 families had left the neighbourhood since 1986. The following table shows the destinations and the numbers of the emigrant families.

Table 2.2: Approximate pattern of out-migration from the neighbourhood

Destination	Number of families
Australia	1
Canada	1
Germany	2
Greece	1
Israel	2
Russia	17
Ukraine	4
Total	28

The immigration of Kazakhs into the neighbourhood was a considerable phenomenon. Although it was impossible for me to determine the exact number, I could estimate around 100 individuals, most of whom were young couples or single young men.

The social change in the neighbourhood was signified by the emergence of free trade, the presence of foreigners and foreign goods, poverty, unemployment, prostitution, suicide, hooliganism, steel doors and the emergence of new religious sects. Free trade was regarded in an ambivalent way. While it had solved the endemic shortage problem, most people described it as an immoral and parasitic way of making a living, alien to their soviet scientific and industrial life. In spite of such derogatory attitudes, most families were involved with trade in one way or another. The presence of foreigners and foreign goods was considered a dramatic change and was the object of identity politics (see chapter 6). Although there were foreign students and foreign visitors in the Soviet era, they were kept in the student hostels or tourist hotels isolated from the local population. Now there were many foreigners who lived in or visited the neighbourhood. In addition to myself, five Iranians and two Indians were living in the neighbourhood. Moreover, the neighbourhood was frequently visited by South Korean and American missionaries. Every Sunday afternoon they hired the neighbourhood's culture house and held services there. Poverty, unemployment, prostitution and a surge in suicide, according to the locals, almost unknown in the Soviet era, were all of considerable concern to the neighbourhood during my stay there. Another dramatic social change had been the emergence of hooliganism and the disintegration of the neighbourhood as a moral community. According to most people, most houses celebrated collectively occasions such as New Year's Eve, the Eighth of March, and May Day. Moreover, their doors were often open for each other and they invited each other frequently. Such celebrations and close relations had ceased to exist.

Because of poverty, people could not afford to provide food and drinks for such parties now, and they did not trust each other as before. Indeed, each person I met warned me of the dangers the others might pose me. The fact that almost half of the front doors in the neighbourhood were changed from wooden to metal ones shows people's fear of each other. Such fears were intensified by the presence of hooligans in the neighbourhood. Some hooligans lived in the neighbourhood, others visited the neighbourhood cafe and a third group made raids into the neighbourhood. There were often fights in the neighbourhood, or late, noisy comings and goings by hooligans. These were, according to locals, post-Soviet phenomena as well.

These changes had brought the following new social categories into neighbourhood life: illegal street traders (*torgashi*), suitcase traders (*chelnoki*), private kiosk and shop owners, foreigners (*inostrantsy*), prostitutes, migrants, hooligans and the dispossessed. Illegal street traders traded along the main street. They were local women and Kazakh migrants (both men and women). They sold similar goods: vegetables, fruits, cigarettes, wine, matches, pasta, beer and so forth. The interesting thing about these traders was that competition was not between individuals but between groups. First, urban inhabitants and migrant Kazakhs were jealous of each other. Second, within this larger framework smaller groups competed with each other. Usually two to four women, who were friends or neighbours, or a group of rural Kazakh men and women, who were relatives or came from the same village, sold things beside each other. Not only was there no sense of competition between individuals within these smaller groups but they tried to sell things for each other. This was important because each trader had a particular number of customers who bought goods exclusively from her/him and to whom s/he sometimes gave goods on credit. For example, if a man asked a trader for vodka and s/he did not have it, she would not let him go. Instead s/he would refer him to a friend beside her/him who had vodka. On the other hand, if a trader ran out of a particular item, her friends would sell her some items at the purchase price.

The new social relations formed around the street trade brought about radical structural change in the neighbourhood. First, it created tension between old inhabitants and migrant Kazakhs, the main body of the street traders, a continuous tension the main dimensions of which will be explored in chapter 7. Second, the illegal street trade provoked a new form of surveillance by the police. As the trade was illegal, the police took bribes from traders and frequently made raids on the market. In addition, the trade established new relations between the urban inhabitants of the neighbourhood as sellers and buyers. The five kiosks in the neighbourhood were run by a combination of family workforces and wage labourers. The two largest were owned by Kazakhs. A very small one was owned by a Russian/Tatar, a medium one by a Russian and a bread kiosk by an Azerbaijani. The employees in three of the kiosks came from the same ethnic group as the employers. The other two had a core of employees from their own ethnic group but sometimes employed others. However, they knew the employees personally or recruited them through friends and relatives.

   As with the street trade, a new set of social relations within and outside the neighbourhood was formed around the kiosks, shops, the restaurant and the cafe-bar. Within the neighbourhood, networks of relations had been created between the owners of the kiosks and the neighbourhood inhabitants. For example, the owner of a kiosk with whom I had established a good relationship showed me a list of 14 people to whom he gave goods on credit. He had learned the tastes of many customers and kept their favourite alcoholic drinks cold in the fridge, and because of that they bought exclusively from him. Moreover, a group of men, a drinking circle, had formed around his kiosk. The establishment of interpersonal relations between sellers and buyers, and the provision of goods on credit, were important elements of commerce in the neighbourhood. I personally bought on credit from three kiosks and the shashlyk bar. In addition to creating new relations within the neighbourhood, the kiosks linked the neighbourhood to wholesale shops on the one hand and different authorities (mentioned in chapter 3) on the other. The restaurant and the shashlyk bar created new places for meeting between local men, but they were also places where hooligans met, fought each other and terrorised others.

ALMATY

Tinshan mountains stretching towards China tower over the city and its suburbs. The city is divided into rectangular areas by two ranges of long parallel streets stretching from east to west and from the foothills and mountains in the south to the north. The rectangular blocks consist of buildings; the majority are five-, nine- or twelve-storey cement houses. Stores and government offices are usually located on the streets. The residential areas inside the blocks include houses and large yards, often with playgrounds and trees. While the apartments are small and usually crowded, the city offers you enough green space. It has many parks and most of its streets are like boulevards. In addition to this, there are large open spaces between neighbouring residential areas and between each area and its surrounding streets, all filled with trees. In appearance the city is homogeneous. Everywhere, except the newly emerged villa area in the southeast, is covered by similar buildings. However, socially the city is divided between the centre and the rest. The centre, where the elite and most foreigners live, has more green space, is cleaner and has some sophisticated and pompous buildings. Most of the recently created business centres, night clubs and shops are located there. Moreover, it is protected from hooliganism. The centre is part of the east and Southeast of the city where the Hotel Kazakhstan, once the presidential palace, and most of the departments of state are located.

Almaty was founded in the middle of the nineteenth century by Russians in the southeast of the Kazakh steppe. Then it was called Verny ('faithful' or 'loyal'). In the 1920s the Bolsheviks changed its name to Alma-ta, a Kazakh word which means 'the mother of apple'. Then it was a poor and slummy little town (Trotsky, 1930). In 1929 the capital was transferred from Gyzlarda to Almaty and in the 1930s the city was connected to Moscow by railway. The city expanded rapidly due to the modernisation launched by the Soviet government (Dombrovsky, 1991). During the Second World War the Almatians provided the fronts with manpower, weapons and food. They also hosted thousands of refugees from the German-occupied territories. The refugees from the European parts of the Soviet Union contributed significantly to the modernisation of the city. Indeed, some of the most prestigious cultural and scientific institutions of the republic including the Academy of Science (*Akademiia Naok*) were founded during the 1940s.

After the war the city developed further on such a scale that in the early 1950s the city had changed completely in comparison with the 1920s. Now, it housed a population of half a million educated people who could impress an American, Marshall MacDuffie, who visited Almaty in 1953, by their knowledge of foreign languages and passionate involvement in international politics (MacDuffie, 1955). After 1950 the importance of Almaty increased, due to the increased importance of Kazakhstan in the Soviet Union.[15] From the late 1960s until the commencement of *perestroika* the city experienced the most expansive urbanisation and modernisation in its history. Most of the city's existing buildings and infrastructure were built in this time. Most people got new apartments, and new hospitals, nurseries, schools, colleges, universities, sport centres, parks, theatres, music halls and state shops were created. The streets were asphalted and the living standards and the general level of education increased. The introduction of *perestroika* injected a spirit of euphoria and optimism into city life and stimulated cultural and intellectual growth. But this spirit was overshadowed and very rapidly replaced with one of fear and insecurity with the arrival of economic crisis and ethnic tensions. The economic crisis expressed itself in the shortage of consumer goods which hit very hard in 1988–92. Since 1992 the shortage has been solved by the import of foreign goods, which has been encouraged by the lifting of the state monopoly over foreign trade. 1992 also marked the beginning of a qualitatively new era in the history of the city.

After the lifting of the state monopoly over foreign trade there emerged thousands of illegal street traders, thousands of kiosks, tens of medium-sized shops, and the large supermarket Sum which sold local and foreign goods. Many bazaars have been created and expanded rapidly, the largest of which is Chinese Bazaar (*Kitaiskii Bazaar, Barakholka*). This bazaar, located on the outskirts of the city, consists of hundreds of different chambers in which traders sells goods imported from China, the Middle East, Southeast Asia and Central and Eastern Europe. Such goods are sold in tens of other minor bazaars inside the city as well. Consumer goods with famous marks from Europe, the US, Japan and Korea were sold in special medium-size shops or in the Sum supermarket. Volvo, Mercedes, Philips, Nike, Adidas, Sony and some other famous multinationals had opened their own outlets in the city. Another remarkable change in the city was the presence of multinational companies, like Chevron, Traktebel and Shell, all involved in exploring or exploiting the vast mineral resources in the republic. An important part of the new commerce are numerous places of entertainment (hotels, bars, sex clubs, restaurants, night clubs, fashion salons) which have been created since 1992 and supply services for rich locals and foreigners.

The life blood of all this new commerce is the US dollar. Commodities are priced in the US dollar and money is saved in dollars. In Almaty there are tens of places where one can change dollars. The dollar as a symbol alongside the word US and the US flag, evokes contradictory feelings among different parts of the population. Some wear them on their tee shirts as symbols of power, freedom and success. Others, particularly the dispossessed, hate them as the symbol of evil, degrading forces. To supply the demands of the new rich and their foreign counterparts, pompous new buildings like Hotel Ankara, Hotel Marcopolo and Hotel Astana have been built.[16]

KAZAKHSTAN

Kazakhstan is a vast country, the second largest post-Soviet republic after the Russian federation. It is located in Central Asia and has an area of 2,724,900 sq km and borders Russia on the west, northwest, northeast and east, China on the southeast, Kirkhizia on the south, Uzbekistan on the south and southwest, Turkmenistan and the Caspian Sea on the west. Its landscape includes mountains, vast deserts and steppes. It has a population of 16.5 million and more than 100 different ethnic groups, but the largest ones are Kazakhs, Russians, Ukrainians, Germans, Uigurs and Koreans.

The original inhabitants of Kazakhstan were Kazakhs who trace their origin to Turkic tribes of ancient times. However, according to Olcott (1987) the name Kazakh appeared in history in the fifteenth century with the formation of the Kazakh Khanate. The khanate expanded and consolidated in the sixteenth and seventeenth centuries, and finally disintegrated into three *Zhuz* (tribal alliances) in the eighteenth century. The smallest unit of Kazakh society was *aul*: a group of nomadic families who were related to each other through kinship and moved together. Their nomadic life-style entered a process of decline as a result of the expansion of the Russian Empire eastward from the middle of the eighteenth century. Agriculture became an important part of the Kazakh economy, and alongside it a considerable sedentarised rural and urban population emerged among Kazakhs. The emergence of the modern schools, a written language, books, a Kazakh press, the rise of literacy and the formation of a modern Kazakh intelligentsia and national consciousness were other landmarks of change (Batunsky, 1994; Kreindler, 1983; Oraltay, 1994). Another major change was the emergence of a settler community. In 1916 Russians constituted one third of the total population in Kazakhstan, and the majority lived in the northern parts (Demko, 1969: p. 169).

Kazakhs resisted the colonial power in various forms including the Kenisary revolt (1837–46) and the rebellion of 1916 (Olcott, 1987). After the fall of Tsarism in Russia, Kazakh nationalists founded the Alash Orda government (1917–22). The Bolsheviks abolished it, but assimilated its members into the Soviet government in Kazakhstan.

The Soviet authorities, launching a project of modernisation, expanded modern education and brought women into the public sphere (Massell, 1975; Akiner, 1997). The Kazakh language was standardised, and became the language of instruction in Kazakh schools. The 1930s were a decade of stormy changes. Politically, not only the intellectuals affiliated to Alash Orda, but also most of the Kazakhs who had joined the Bolsheviks during the civil war were eliminated. Economically, a policy of forced sedentarisation of nomadic Kazakh and forced collectivisation of livestock was implemented. After the outbreak of the war with Germany millions of refugees from the German-occupied territories were moved to Kazakhstan. Among the refugees were highly skilled workers, high-ranking scientists and academics who lifted the cultural and academic level of the republic. The exile of people such as Chechens, Crimean Tatars and Volga Germans into Kazakhstan further influenced the ethnic combination of the republic.

By the time of Stalin's death in 1953, in spite of all the tragic events of the two previous decades, Kazakhstan had been transformed into a modern republic with a formidable native elite who were in charge in many key posts in the republic. Although Stalin eliminated the old Kazakh elite, he was careful to create a new one and assert his hegemony over Kazakhs through this new elite. The most dramatic undertaking in the post-Stalin era was the implementation of the Virgin Land Project by Khrushchev in Kazakhstan. As a result of this project, a vast area of the Kazakh steppe was ploughed and cultivated (1955–63). This project brought about major ecological and demographic changes. As millions of Russians, Belorussians and Ukrainians moved in connection with the programme, Kazakhs became a minority in the republic (Matley, 1969).

Despite this, the period from 1960 until 1986 was marked by the expansion and consolidation of the Kazakh elite in the key institutions of the republic. Indeed, in this period Kazakhstan experienced rapid urbanisation and expansion of the bureaucratic apparatus and higher education. Dean Mukhmed Kunaev, a Kazakh, was the secretary of the communist party for almost the whole period. He was a close friend of Leonid Brezhnev and a member of the politburo. He used his influence to promote Kazakh interests in general and those of his clients in particular. Kazakhs, like other so-called 'titular nationalities', enjoyed preferential access to higher education and higher administrative posts. Indeed, Kazakh patronage networks dominated higher education and administration at the end of his rule (Masanov, 1996a).

Since the commencement of *glasnost* and *perestroika* Kazakhstan has undergone major political, demographic, economic, cultural and ideological changes. The major political changes were the intensification of ethnic conflicts, Kazakhification of the state, the abolition of the communist party and independence. From the mid 1970s ethnic tensions between Kazakhs and non-Kazakhs began to develop due to the combined effects of two factors. On the one hand, the percentage of Kazakhs in the population increased because of a higher birth rate. On the other hand, more Kazakhs graduated from universities and demanded better jobs. This created dissatisfaction among Russians, reversing their migration direction. During 1976–80, 414,000 Russians left Kazakhstan, and between 1979 and 1988, 784,000 left (Dunlop, 1993: p. 47). Ethnic tensions entered a new chapter in Almaty on 17 December 1986. Gorbachev had sacked Kunaev as the first secretary of the communist party and appointed Kolbin, a Russian from outside Kazakhstan, in his place. A big crowd of Kazakh students demonstrated in Brezhnev Square and the protest was repressed by the Soviet Army. The event was related to the Kazakhification of the state. Ousting Kunaev was part of Gorbachev's anti-corruption campaign. Kunaev, like all other leaders of titular nationalities, had established his own network of patronage and used state resources for private ends.[17] Kolbin held office until 1989 and removed Kazakhs from some key posts, without being able to achieve Gorbachev's anti-corruption goals. Nazarbaev, who replaced Kolbin, followed the Kazakhification policy on a greater scale. Kazakhification took a new turn with the independence of Kazakhstan on 15 December 1991. Indeed, independence was imposed on Kazakhstan. Although Kazakhs demanded greater autonomy for Kazakhstan within the USSR and a greater role for Kazakhs within it they were not by any means separatist. In a referendum in March 1991 more than 80 per cent of the population of Kazakhstan voted for remaining in the Soviet Union. When the USSR was dissolved, Kazakhstan hesitated for a while before declaring independence.

Independence led to further Kazakhification of the state by declaring Kazakh as the state language and purging non-Kazakhs from the state institutions (see chapter 7). Russians reacted to these policies by demanding an equal constitutional status for the Russian language and the right to double citizenship. Another result of the dissolution of the USSR was that the communist party and other Soviet organs were abolished. However, such abolition did not question the position of the old Kazakh communist elite. The same elite, with greater power than before, continued to rule under a new guise. The best illustration of this is the fact that N. Nazarbaev, the first secretary of the communist party, was elected as the first president. But the country did undergo considerable political change. A new constitution was ratified, the parliament was established and a wide range of NGOs emerged.

Another important political change has been the openness towards the outside world. The old strict regulations on travel abroad by citizens of the republic have been replaced by milder ones, but not completely removed. To travel or live abroad one still needs permission and must pay a fee. Foreigners travelling to or living in Kazakhstan are required to register and always carry their passports. But unlike the Soviet era, they can rent apartments in any neighbourhood and communicate freely with locals.

The most remarkable demographic changes have been migration and increased mortality. We can distinguish between three different trends in migration: emigration of non-Kazakhs, immigration of Kazakhs and refugees and internal migration. In 1994 alone about 480,839 people left Kazakhstan, around 70,000 migrated into the country and 330,000 migrated inside the country (Masanov, 1996b: p. 2). 283,000 Russians, 92,000 Germans, 37,000 Ukrainian and others left. Around 310,000 (93.7 per cent) of migrants inside the country were Kazakhs who moved mainly from *auls* to cities.

Migration on this massive scale was the direct result of the post-Soviet change. The Kazakhification of the state, the growth of ethnic tensions, the economic decline and sinking living standards are among the main reasons for the migration of Russians, Germans and Ukrainians out of the country. Among these Kazakhification was mentioned by the Russians as the strongest motive for emigration. The collapse of the rural economy is the main reason behind the migrations of Kazakhs to the cities.

Kazakhstan experienced rapid economic change, the main elements of which were the privatisation of the state property, the emergence of private business and the abolition of the welfare state, resulting in a dramatic social polarisation. Another radical economic change was the lifting of the state monopoly over foreign trade and investment in Kazakhstan. The political openness toward the outside world has been accompanied by a cultural openness. While different cultural streams have found their way into Kazakhstan, the dominant trend is the American style of consumerist

culture. This type of culture has penetrated different spheres of life, particularly those of the media, entertainment and consumer goods. Although
consumerism has become a kind of symbolic capital for particular groups
in society, it is restricted to a relatively limited proportion of the population.
This is so because commodities which represent this consumerist culture,
films shown on TV excepted, are very expensive for the majority of the
population. Yet cultural Americanism has provoked a cultural resistance
among the dispossessed which is expressed in a strong nostalgia for 'the
Soviet Culture'.

3 *BARDAK*: ELEMENTS OF CHAOS

In this chapter I will present a general overview of the post-Soviet conditions through the eyes of those who have become dispossessed. As mentioned in chapter 1, most people described the situation as chaos (*bardak*). The following were described as the most important aspects of such chaos: first, the rapid accumulation of wealth in a few hands through supposedly immoral methods such as privatisation, manipulation of credits, bribery and extraction of tributes; second, the disintegration of society as a moral community, the emergence of lawlessness and widespread violence; third, the destabilisation of families as a result of new sexual practices. In response to this chaos, people have developed strong nostalgia for the Soviet era and a conspiracy theory. In this chapter I will discuss wealth differentiation, lawlessness, loss and the conspiracy theory. Sexuality will be touched upon briefly here and discussed thoroughly in chapters 5 and 6.

ACCUMULATION OF WEALTH IN A FEW HANDS

The post-Soviet change is characterised by the rapid accumulation of wealth on one hand and poverty on the other. The new rich (*novye bogatye*) are accused of collecting their wealth through the following methods: dissolution of the welfare state, stealing and selling public property through privatisation, manipulation of the credit system, creation of monopolies, taking bribes and extracting tributes, drug trafficking and the creation of a transnational prostitution business. I was told the new rich come from three sources: the old partycrats (*partikraty*) (high echelons of the communist party and Komsomol), old black marketeers and new Mafioso. They dominate the rest of the population by the combined use of political power and violence exerted through the intertwined networks of state officials and the mafia.[18]

These have, accordingly, resulted in mass poverty, mass sexual labour,[19] child sexual labour, child labour, a dramatic expansion of alcoholism, divorce, despair and suicide[20] for the majority of people. In this sense, the dispossessed consider their interests diametrically and antagonistically opposed to those of the new rich. As a result they make a clear dichotomy between themselves, labelled interchangeably as we (*my*), us (*nam*), people (*narod*), labouring people (*rabotiashchie liudi*), below (*vniz*) and the new rich, labelled interchangeably as they (*oni*), the bosses (*nachal'niki*), the leadership (*nachal'stvo, rukovodstvo*) and the new rich (*novye bogatye*). The interesting fact is that when the dispossessed counter-pose the *narod* to the new rich, these concepts are not merely applied to the population in the post-Soviet Kazakh territory but to the population of the former Soviet territory as a whole. In this sense the dispossessed and elite in Kazakhstan are considered respectively as sections of the dispossessed and elite in the whole former Soviet territory. This kind of the dichotomising consciousness has its root in the fact that both the emergence of the new rich and the impoverishment of the majority of people have happened almost overnight, and through extra-economic methods used by the state officials and mafia. In the following I will look at some of these methods, often mentioned by the dispossessed.

Privatisation as theft
Up to the end of 1996, 15,101 enterprises were privatised in the three following ways or a combination of them: the management and workers bought the enterprise, or there was a direct sale to buyers, or sale through auction (*Kazakhstan Economic Trends*, fourth quarter 1996: p. 156). However, in January of the same year the preferential treatment of workers in relation to privatisation was abolished. Now two methods of privatisation remained: direct sale to investors, and auctions. Moreover, the social guarantees for the employees of the private enterprises was abolished in the same month (*Economic Trends*, p. 61). From the point of view of the dispossessed, privatisation is the stealing of public property. Such opinion is well represented by the following statement made to me by a Russian woman worker on the shop floor, where I did fieldwork: 'Privatisation is stealing people's property (*Privatizatsiia eto vorovstvo sobstvennosti naroda*).' First, the dispossessed, still attached to the Soviet values, thought the privatisation of the state property was in itself a theft. Second, they argued that the ways in which privatisation was carried out were corrupt.

They usually associated privatisation with plunder, abolishing the welfare state, tightening discipline in the workplace, restricting workers' rights to use products and the means of production for private ends, redundancy of workers on a massive scale, postponing the payments of wages and liberalisation of prices.

As a result of crisis and reforms a universal welfare-state has been completely demolished overnight. The needs which were covered by the Soviet welfare system exceeded those of the most advanced welfare-state in the West, namely Sweden. Lifetime employment was granted in the Soviet Union but not in Sweden. Food, rent, transport, telephones, sport, art and other forms of entertainment constituted a smaller portion of salaries in Almaty than in Stockholm. Health-care, education and child-care were almost free of charge. As Humphrey (1983) and Clarke (1992) suggest, the welfare-state provisions were delivered primarily through workplaces, which provided labourers with various services: housing, nursery, resting facilities, clinics, pensions and travel. Both on the factory shop floor and in the neighbourhood, workers told me that their bosses (*nachal'niki*) were not committed to them anymore and spent the income of the enterprises on purchasing luxurious cars, building villas for themselves and putting the money in the banks abroad. Most enterprises not only stopped delivering any service to their workers, but did not even pay the salaries on time. While managers justify this by claiming it is the result of external factors such as lack of money and the economic crisis, workers consider it a deceit (*obman*).

Workers also thought that the privatisation had undermined their control over the labour process and also the opportunity to use means of production and products for private ends. Ticktin (1992) argues that Soviet workers exerted considerable control over the labour process. In the post-Soviet era privatised factories enforced discipline. The sharpening discipline is related to and enforced by mass redundancies. Now fewer workers must do the work previously done by more. The cause of the tragic suicide of Aleksaner Petreovich Terletskii, described in chapter 1, highlights this shift in discipline. A Russian unemployed electrician, who gave me the news first, said that in the Soviet era absence for sickness or even drinking at a workplace would not cause somebody to lose his job. The huge army of unemployed have made workers docile in relation to management. Aleksander (see chapter 4), told me that they could not protest against the managers, because they would reply, 'thousands like you are waiting outside the factory door'.

The methods of privatisation were also considered by the dispossessed to be corrupt. As Humphrey (1991) and Clarke and Kabalina (1995) have argued in the case of Russia, the local managers and other local authorities had become *de facto* owners of enterprises during the collapse of the Soviet state (1988–91).

These new authorities used their new powerful positions, in the absence of any central control, to collect wealth by illegal methods. They sold raw materials and other products illegally abroad and imported consumer goods illegally and sold them for very high prices on the black market. Another effective method was hoarding. According to most of the people I talked with, during this period people in Kazakhstan experienced almost famine conditions. While the state shops were empty, one could purchase everything on the black market for prices much higher than official ones. Such illegalities were not practised individually, but by the networks of managers, black marketeers and top bosses of the communist party. The formal privatisation, initiated in 1991, not only legalised the stolen property, but also distributed the remaining state property between the members of elite. In the companies, owned by cooperatives of the staff, I was told, managers had begun to buy workers' shares or to tell workers that they must make sacrifices and accept the postponement of their wages and payment in kind. In relation to the other two types of privatisation, there was a widely shared opinion that the enterprises were either sold to friends and relatives for nominal prices, or sold underpriced for high bribes. Among different ethnic elites Kazakhs were the main beneficiaries of privatisation. They used their monopoly over political power to monopolise the economy of the republic (Olcott, 1997: p. 117). They managed this through manipulation of the voucher system. People were given vouchers which they could deposit in holding companies. These companies could buy up to 20 per cent of large state enterprises which would be privatised. From 170 such companies which were registered, 20 companies accumulated 60 per cent of vouchers, another 19 got 20 per cent. The largest single holding, Butia-Kapital, which accumulated 10 per cent of vouchers belongs to a Kazakh, named Buta (Olcott, 1997: pp. 117–18). People believed that Buta was a relative of Nazarbaev. Although, as Olcott (p. 118) suggests, it is difficult to verify whether such a claim is true or not, it alludes to a widespread nepotism through which the Kazakh oligarchy appropriated state property.

People were particularly sensitive about the foreign buyers. When it became known, in spring 1996, that the Belgian multinational Traktebel had bought Almaty Energy, people became both furious and afraid. A Kazakh woman, cursing both foreigners and the government, said: 'People say that the Belgians will cut off the gas if the bills are not paid on time. But how can people pay bills on time while the payment of salaries is postponed for months?' Then she added: 'Our leaders sell our enterprises to foreigners for bribes. They sold the Almaty Tobacco to Americans, the Karagandy Steel to English people and now they sell the gas to Belgians. This is shameful (*stydno*).' As this example illustrates, not only those who worked in enterprises, but people in general, opposed privatisation. They were particularly afraid for the privatisation of electricity, water, transport and health-care, which they thought in combination with the liberalisation of prices would increase the level of their poverty.

The dispossessed seemed to have benefited from the privatisation of apartments. In the neighbourhood where I lived most of the people owned their apartments in 1992. The state had given people coupons in proportion to the numbers of working years (*trudovoi stazh*) of each individual. People could either sell the coupons or buy their own apartments. Most people in the neighbourhood had chosen to buy. However, although people liked the idea of owning the apartments, all of the families, with the exception of four well-off families, thought privatisation had brought trouble rather than comfort. First, as a result of privatisation the costs of rent, electricity, gas and telephone had increased. In the Soviet era all these costs amounted to some five to ten per cent of official family income, while in September

1996 they swallowed half of the salaries. Second, they now had to repair the apartments themselves. In my house, water was leaking from a third-floor apartment into the apartment below. The third-floor neighbours repaired the bathroom temporarily but water leaked again and again. Although the two parties quarrelled several times, they held the state responsible for this. The third-floor neighbour told me that in the Soviet era he could manage to repair the apartment by giving someone a bottle of vodka, but now he needed at least $200 to repair the bathroom, money he didn't have.

Manipulation of credits

The dispossessed presented the manipulation of credit as one of the main forms of plunder. A Russian man commented on the bankruptcy of the Kazkomerts Bank as follows:

> To open a new bank I need credit from the central Bank. But those in power lend money only to their own friends and relatives for opening a new bank. When the bank is opened, credit is divided between people who have established the bank together. Bank managers give credit to people who they know will not pay back the money. Say I am a bank manager, then some high official in the central bank will call me and ask me to lend $1,000,000 to a nephew of his to establish a business, I have no choice but to do it, because my bank is dependent on the central bank. Then a powerful minister calls and asks for a loan for his nephew, and I lend the money. As I constantly lend money to the cousins and nephews of ministers and managers, I know that my bank will become bankrupt very soon. Then I lend money to my own cousins and nephews as well. Of course, I will not forget my own interests. I open my own secret bank account in Switzerland and transfer millions of dollars there and then declare the bank bankrupt. In these ways while the manager and the members of the state racket (*reket*) have increased their wealth, the ordinary clients are the losers, they will never get back their money.

The scenario might be exaggerated, but during my stay local newspapers reported several cases of huge sums of money disappearing without trace. Charles Clover reported: 'Huge sums have disappeared from government coffers over the past few years, such as $500 m payment by US oil company Mobil, for a share of Tengiz oil field in west Kazakhstan' (*Financial Times*, Wednesday 17 June 1998).

Financial speculation was also described as a way through which the elite steal public money. Such speculation results in the fluctuation of the exchange rates of the national currency (tenge), which makes it untrustworthy. People made their transactions in US dollars and those who could afford to save also saved in US dollars. The fact that people had lost all of their savings as a result of a dramatic depreciation of the currency from 1992 to 1993 was instrumental in this mistrust.

Bribery
A rule of thumb in Almaty was that nothing could be done without contacts or bribes. A well-known Kazakh professor and opponent of government policies, put it to me as follows:

> The system is corrupt from top to bottom. Each ministry is leased out according to its potential for taking bribes. For example, if the minister of education must pay $100,000 a year, the minister of justice or those in charge of customs must pay twice this. Then the minister of education appoints his own clients as directors of different universities for different sums of money depending on the status of each university. Then the directors appoint the deans of each faculty, and the deans appoint their friends and relatives as chairs of different departments, professors, lecturers and so forth, who take bribes from students. They then take a part for themselves and pass the rest above.

The professor's statement might be simplified and exaggerated. But most of the people I spoke to shared the idea that bribery was a main source of income for the elite and for state officials in general. Bribe (*vziatka*) is officially defined as money or other valuables given to a state official as payment for illegal services (Ozhegov and Shvedova, 1996: p. 78).

Education and corruption
Saken and Amira are Kazahk students, married to each other and they come from the south. Their four-year-old son lives with Amira's family in the *aul*. They are poor. Each of them receives a small grant. In addition their families contribute meat, but to survive they work at nights for another Kazakh, a former classmate of Saken, in his kiosk, receiving 5 per cent of sales each night. Saken and the owner of the kiosk both completed their first degree two years before. While Saken continued to study, because he could not find a proper job, his classmate, Norlan, found a job as a customs officer through his brother who was the dean of the faculty in which Saken was a student. Saken told me that the brother knew a boss in the customs service and bribed him with $2,000. I asked him where the dean had got the money from. (I asked the question, because with the official salary of a dean one would not be able to save the money.) Smiling, Saken told me that their dean had a lot of income. First, many students fail the entry exam but are admitted because they come from rich families and pay high bribes. Second, many students pay to pass their exams. The rate for a *zachet*[21] is 500 tenge and for an exam up to $100. In addition there are students from

wealthy families who do not study well, but who want to have red diplomas (*Krasnyi diplom*). The rate for a red diploma is up to $500. The job as customs officer had paid off very quickly. While Norlan's official salary was 2000 tenge ($34), according to Saken he had bought two cars, two apartments, one for his family and one to rent, and had bought two kiosks. I met him, his wife and his children when they came there to count the night's sales and bring goods to replace the ones that had been sold. They all were well-dressed in foreign designer clothes. Saken estimated Norlan's total income from bribes, customs, kiosks and the rent of the apartment at around $6,000 a month.

This figure, compared with Saken and Amira's total income per month ($148) or the minimum wage 1,700 tenge ($24) in the third quarter of 1996 (Scheremet, 1996: p. 36) is huge. Norlan's assumed income was 40 times greater than Saken and Amira's total income and 250 times greater than the minimum wage. Although, according to Saken, he was not at all a rich man by Almatian standards, the ways he was amassing his fortune is a good illustration of the methods the new rich use in order to accumulate wealth.

One cannot get a lucrative job only by offering bribes. S/he must have the right contacts as well. There is great competition for such jobs, and the job is given to a friend or acquaintance who can be trusted in the illegal deals in the workplace. Saken said: 'Many were prepared to pay more than twice the money his classmate paid for his job, but they won't get it. They give the jobs to their relatives (*rodstvenniki*) and acquaintances (*znakomyi*). They do not trust strangers (*ne znakomyi*).' Then he added that a boss in customs was a friend of the dean, and because of that his brother got the job. He admits the relatives of the customs boss to the university and takes care that they get good marks and red diplomas and the boss gives a job to his brother.

I heard similar stories frequently from different sources. Zhulduz and Dana the sex workers we will meet in chapter 5 paid money to pass their exams. A university student told me that all eight persons in his group, including himself, had been admitted through bribes and contacts and they often joked about it. He himself had been admitted through a cousin of his mother, who worked at the university. He said that they paid money, gave expensive drinks and a leather jacket to the cousin, which he passed to someone on the admissions committee. The taking of bribes is an open practice. A story told by a young Kazakh girl about her former class tutor (*Klassnaia rukovoditel'nitsa*) is typical. She had told the whole class openly and collectively, that if they wanted to get good marks they should buy her a TV, a crystal chandelier and a video. They collected the money and bought these things. Then she forced them to help with the repair of her apartment. The girl said that they were surprised to see her expensive furniture, dishes, carpets and curtains.

Students told me that even allocations of grants abroad were taking place through contacts and bribes. A young Russian woman told the following story:

> There are scholarships for language courses in Germany, for three or six months. The applicants send their documents through the ministry of education to Germany. The people in Germany choose some students. I and some others of my class mates applied for the scholarships but never received an answer from Germany. Those who were sent were not the best students. In Germany they will not discriminate against us, because they do not know us. Those in the ministry of education have not sent our documents to Germany at all, otherwise we should have received replies that we had failed in the competition. We went to the German House here in Almaty and asked them about why we had not received replies. They avoided giving us an answer. It is possible that the German house is cooperating with the Ministry of Education.

She added that they had learned from one of her teachers that those who want to go to Germany must pay $300 to $500. To whom the money should be paid was a secret, but those who wanted to pay would know to whom and how to pay the money.

Although the people who told me the stories above suggested corruption was universal, there were teachers who were strongly against bribery. Among my acquaintances there were six who taught in different universities and resented bribery very strongly. A Kazakh colleague of mine told me that he would not accept bribes even if his family starved. Another young Kazakh historian who taught at Kazgu (the Kazakh State University) was risking his job for protesting against the corrupt methods of admission of students. In addition there were students who were admitted without paying bribes, because they had scored high marks in the entry exams and passed their exams without paying bribes.

Corruption in trade

This section is mainly based on talks with Roslan, a Kazakh man who owned a kiosk in the neighbourhood and had been involved in trade since 1992, and street traders. A main element of the post-Soviet change was the emergence of the private trade: illegal street trade, suitcase trade, kiosks, middle-size shops and wholesale trade. According to locals, all these are sources of illegal income for state officials and the mafia. Let us look at each from the bottom to the top. In my neighbourhood, each illegal trader paid the police officers 30 tenge, except the butchers who paid 300 tenge a day. The kiosk owners did not like the illegal traders who sold the same goods they sold legally. The police, aware of this tension, had offered the kiosk owners a deal: if each of them paid 1,000 tenge a day, the police would prevent the street traders from selling goods around the kiosks. But the kiosk owners found the fee too expensive.

Kiosks started to mushroom in Almaty in 1992. At the time of my fieldwork thousands existed in Almaty. My neighbourhood had five kiosks. According to one of the owners, they usually had to pay bribes to: hygiene officers (*sanepidemstantsia*), fire inspectors (*pozharnaia inspektsiia*), tax inspectors (*nalogovaia inspektsiia*), the organisation of struggle against economic crimes (*OBEP*), the local police (*uchastkovyi militsioner*) and the mafia.

Although the first five offices are legal institutions, they share, according to Roslan, two attributes with the mafia: their representatives act in arbitrary ways (they resort to law and Mafioso to violence); they constituted nodal points in wider overlapping networks of influence. An owner of a kiosk must pay them the sum of the money asked for, unless he is well-connected with influential individuals within such networks, regardless of whether he runs his kiosk in accordance with legal requirements or not. As they interpret the law arbitrarily, they can always find something wrong and either close the kiosk or fine it huge sums. There is no point in an owner taking a state official to court, because the official in question does not act individually but as a member of a network, well-connected to networks within the judiciary system. The sum of money paid to each of these organisations, Roslan said, is negotiated individually, depending on the owner's connections. To show me how it worked, Roslan took me to the tax department in our district. There, on a wall of a long corridor in front of the rooms of the inspectors, hung long lists, each containing hundreds of names. People were standing around each list, searching it. He told me that the lists consisted of the names of the private businesses in our district and their respective inspectors. And the people who were searching the lists were owners of such businesses, trying to find out their own tax inspectors and negotiate the amounts of tax and bribe money they must pay. The negotiation process and the sums in question depend on the owner's contacts. If he has influential contacts, he mentions them to the inspector, and then the inspector will contact the mentioned person(s). If he finds them powerful enough and they confirm that the owner is their person, then the owner, depending on the influence of his patron, may avoid paying at all or pay a much smaller sum. Roslan said that inspectors take part of the money for themselves and pass the rest above. Each inspector has to pass a minimum amount of money to his bosses each month or he will be sacked. If an inspector avoids taking part in the system, he will be sacked and then disappear. According to Roslan, the relations with the other authorities mentioned above are negotiated in the same way. He himself did not pay either the police or the mafia but paid the tax inspectors and OBEP 3,000

tenge ($50) each month, the hygiene officer 700 tenge ($11) and the fire
inspector 300 tenge ($5). Concerning the mafia he said:

> When I bought the kiosk a young Kazakh man came to me and asked
> whether I needed a roof (*krysha*, protection). I told him no thanks I have
> got one, and mentioned the name of a relative of mine who is a boxer. He
> said I will speak with him and went away, and they never bothered me
> again. It is the way it works. They all know each other and cooperate,
> the police and racketeers respect each other. If somebody says he is my
> person, don't bother him, the others say let us negotiate. They usually
> solve conflicts peacefully. But if anyone has not got a roof and still
> avoids paying the mafia, then they will either burn his kiosk or beat him.

Pointing towards the local police station, he said:

> I had a problem with them for a while, they took from me each day beer,
> vodka, juice and other things for around 1,000 tenge. I couldn't do
> anything until I found a contact through my brother in GSK.[22] The GSK
> man went to the police station and told them he is my person, don't
> harass him (*ne trogaite ego*). Since then they have stopped coming here
> for a year. But recently, they have begun again to tell me that I should go
> to the police station. But I will not do it. They can't do anything, I have
> got my contact.

The suitcase traders, in addition to those mentioned above, pay customs
officers. As result of the post-Soviet change thousands of people, mainly
women, are involved in suitcase trade abroad. They can pass up to 20kg of
luggage through customs without paying tariffs, for each extra kilogramme
they must pay tariffs, but instead of paying tariffs they bribe the custom
officers. Bribery in customs was a hot topic of discussion for both
newspapers and the public for a while. However, the big fish for the
customs officers and others mentioned above are the wholesale importers.
Roslan sold 45 items of goods, imported from 21 different countries. He
argued that in Almaty there were thousands of kiosks which mainly sold
imported goods, most of which were provided by around 25 to 30 wholesale
import companies, which he called *green-khouse* (greenhouses). He was of
the opinion that such greenhouses pay bribes not only to the institutions
mentioned above but even to the high state officials.

I knew a Russian who imported food from Germany, France and
Denmark. He always complained that the state racket (*gosudarstvenyi-
reket*) was plundering him and other businessmen. First he had established
a production factory, which did well, but then went bankrupt because the
state took 90 per cent of the profit for tax and other fees. Then he started to

import food. But now, he claimed, he was about to become bankrupt again. The reason for this was the discrimination of the Kazakh state officials against non-Kazakhs. He said:

> If you have no contacts at the top, you will become bankrupt like me. I imported a huge amount of drinks for which I should have paid $100,000 tariff tax. But I bribed the customs for $20,000 and took the goods out of customs. But I found suddenly that the retail prices for drinks are less than my finished cost. This means that there is a fellow, who has an influential uncle, who takes care of him. This fellow passes free of charge his goods from the customs, uses the buildings and transport free of charge, does not pay to the mafia and different state officials (*chenovniki*). Otherwise how could the prices of the drinks be so cheap in the market? If you have no contacts you cannot succeed in business here. I pay 70 per cent of my profit to the state mafia. Before, the state had the monopoly over foreign trade, now the friends and relatives of the ministers have such a monopoly. It is the same with credit, they divide it between their own clans.

Although it was impossible for me to verify the true value of the stories told above, they represent truly the opinion of the ordinary people on how things were working. In Almaty there is a wide consensus that, as these stories also suggest, the state officials and networks of influence called *mafiia* own and distribute the main resources between themselves and their relatives. As the stories suggest, different networks compete for the same resources. The tensions between them are resolved through contacts, payment of bribes and tributes, or violence. People who are in a powerful position extract bribes and tributes from less powerful people. People who have the necessary contacts with particular power centres are not only free from payment of any tribute and bribe but may use the public services free of charge. Others may pay less owing to such contacts. However, such privileges are unstable because of the continuous shifts of the balance of power between rival networks, owing to the chaotic mode of domination. The state officials play a key role in such networks. The appointment of a new individual to a high state office makes the renegotiation of the relation of the networks, both formal and informal, related to this office inevitable, because he wants to promote his own kin and friends. The members of the weakened networks not only lose free access to some resources but must pay new bribes and tributes. Violence is an important factor in the processes of renegotiation.

VIOLENCE

Violence was a great source of fear. People described it as a major element of chaos (*bardak*). According to most people, widespread violence surged from 1988 to 1989 as a result of the collapse of the Soviet state, peaked from 1990 to 1993, and had subsided after 1994, when the state organs, which had been restored to a limited degree, checked and disciplined the mafia and eliminated many hooligan gangs.

   The sources of violence were considered to be the mafia and hooligans. People distinguished very clearly between these two groups. Accordingly, the two groups differed in their origins, manners and methods. The mafia members were considered to come from the ranks of Komsomol, KGB, MVD, the police, army officers, sportsmen, managers of enterprises and black marketeers. According to a Russian academic, these people were politically well informed and had well-established contact networks with each other. As early as 1988, he said, they felt that the Soviet state was perishing and reorganised themselves into mafia groups with the deliberate purpose of filling the power vacuum which resulted from the death of the Soviet state. The Mafioso were considered to be part of the new rich and to have well-established contacts with the state officials. They were described as educated (*obrazovanie*) and cultured (*Kulturnye*). Their use of violence was described as rational. According to most people, the Mafioso resort to violence as the last solution and usually try to settle conflicts through peaceful means. On the other hand, the emergence of the mafia was related to two elements of the post-Soviet economic change: the privatisation of enterprises and the emergence of new private businesses.

   The formation of violent networks was primarily a corollary of the appropriation of state property during the period, when the Soviet state was disintegrating (1988–92). The disintegration of the coercive and legal apparatus of the state, resulted in a general surge of violence and the mushrooming of networks of criminals and violent individuals. The networks of the managerial and political elite needed the support of elite violent groups to protect their wealth and expand their spheres of influence. On the other hand police officers, sportsmen, army officers, Afghan war veterans and criminals provided such services for the first group in return for a share of the plundered wealth. The fact that most of the managerial and political elite and leaders of mafia had high positions in both the communist party and Komsomol, facilitated the formation of the new networks of influence.

   Beside privatisation, the emergence of the new private commerce underpinned the emergence and consolidation of the mafia. The mafia had a twofold relation with such commerce. First, they provided protection (*krysha*, roof) for protection fees. Second, they were among the shareholders and part of the new businesses.

   At the time of my fieldwork (July 1995 to October 1996) actual violence by the mafia was not high. However, there was a deep fear of them, and their invisible presence was felt everywhere. The two following sentences which were used by different people on a daily basis illustrate this:

'Racketeers are the master in the street (*Reket khoziain na ulitse*)' and 'racketeers are the master in the city (*reket khoziain gorada*).' I was told that the mafia played the role of courts and police. If somebody did not pay back borrowed money, or did not fulfil his business commitment, his partner would report him not to the police but to the mafia, because the mafia managed the thing much more quickly and efficiently.

It might be that fears of an over-powerful and omnipresent invisible mafia, as Verdery (1996a: p. 219) has argued, symbolise the fears of the newly invisible market forces. However, in Almaty, such fears are related to a history of actual violence committed by mafia in the years 1988 to 1994. Since 1994, as the police had acquired the upper hand, the relations between different mafia groupings had been settled and the violence had diminished, although it still existed. Everybody I spoke with told stories about how Mafioso burned kiosks and shops, or beat their owners or fought with each other, and about how they kidnapped and raped women. A young Kazakh female student of mine said that up to 1994, rich men forced young women into cars and then raped them. The victims could do nothing, because these men had contacts with the authorities. If a woman reported the offender to the police, the courts found her guilty instead. According to her, this had become so prevalent that some influential people called on the government to intervene. As a result of such intervention, the phenomenon had subsided, but without disappearing. Without exaggeration every young woman I spoke with told me a dramatic story of violence, to herself, a relative, a friend, a friend of a friend, a neighbour, or a classmate. Less dramatic physical and verbal harassment was part of the daily experience of most young women.[23]

Gulzhan, a young Kazakh woman historian, who sold goods in the illegal market, told the following story:

It was 1990. After exams I and two of my girl friends went to a disco called Iris to relax and have a happy time. At eleven o'clock we decided to go home. But a group of young Kazakh men surrounded us and said that they wanted to take us with them. They said they wanted to take us because we were the most beautiful girls in the disco. We told them, you are Kazakhs and we are also Kazakhs, take Russian girls, please take them. They answered we take those to whom we are attracted. We cried, implored, we resorted to their ethnic sense (*na ikh natsional'nye chuvstva davili*), told them we are Kazakhs. What are you doing? Why don't you respect us? It didn't help... They forced each of us into a separate car and took us to the great market (*Barakholku*). They stopped the cars there, left us in the cars and went away for ten minutes. We three jumped out of the cars and hid ourselves in the sewer. They looked around for us, but then thinking that we had run away alongside the road they started the

cars and drove towards the main road. We came out from the sewer, ran
towards the road and stopped a car and asked for help. The man took us
into the car. It was already two o'clock in the morning. The man brought
us to our home.

Although young women were the main victims of violence, the
population in general was targeted. Everybody I talked to expressed feelings
of fear and insecurity. For example, a male colleague of mine said: 'I am
longing for the day when I can walk the streets free without worrying that
somebody will knock me down.' In 22 of 45 apartments in my block the
wooden entry doors had been replaced with steel doors. My landlord, who
had replaced his own single door with a double one, commented on this as
follows: 'In the Soviet time our doors were almost open, but today when
somebody knocks we do not open the door before recognising the person.'
'Never open your door to strangers (*ne znakomyi*),' he advised me.

So far I have argued that the disintegration of the Soviet state, privatisation and the emergence of private business have been the main causes of the
dramatic growth of violence. The disintegration of the Soviet moral system
and the so-called ethnic revival (*Vozrozhhdenie*) have also underpinned this
process. Although the last decades of Soviet society witnessed a general
moral crisis, in Kazakhstan the moral disintegration which contributed to
widespread violence is a post-Soviet phenomenon. Gulzhan, mentioned
above, related the surge of the violence to the post-Soviet moral decline in
the following way:

> Before, in the Soviet time, there were moral limits. ... You understand,
> there existed a moral code (*moral'nyi kodeks*), which was observed well.
> People were truthful. They were brought up in a good way. But today
> people have become like savage animals. They behave according to the
> law of the jungle. Everybody who is stronger, hits, rapes, murders and
> robs everybody else who is weaker.

The communist party, in spite of its corruption and ideological contradictions (Ticktin, 1992), played a significant role in the production of moral
values. Thus, the disintegration of the party resulted in both political and
moral chaos. The result was the mushrooming of hooligan (*khuligan*)
networks. Hooligans are said to come mainly from Kazakh migrants from
the south and rural areas, although Chechens, Russians and others
supposedly exist among them. Culturally, they were described as uneducated
(*neobrazovannye*), uncultured (*beskul'turnye*) and stupid/ provincial
(*menbeti*). They were described also as sportsmen (*fizkulturniki*): those who
engage in boxing and wrestling and body building, wear training clothes and
gymnastic shoes in public, cut their hair short and move in groups. They

were assumed to be involved in small and middle range crimes and to have contacts with middle and low rank officers. Jambyl and his friends, described in chapter 7, provide an example of such hooligan networks.

The dispossessed feared more the violence of the hooligans than that of the mafia. However, the distinction between these two groups is not clear cut. According to Roslan, the kiosk owner, the leaders of the most prominent hooligan groups are related to the mafia. Moreover, they are recruited as guards in business which supposedly have mafia connections. Fear of hooligans was not only caused by the widespread and random aspects of their violence but by the way it was ethnicised and gendered in relation to the ethnic revival (*vozrozhdenie*). An element of the Kazakh ethnic revival is an emphasis on Kazakhs' primordial claims over the territory of Kazakhstan. Resorting to such claims, the hooligans use violence to subjugate people from other ethnic origins in public places. However, the violence does not stop once dominance over non-Kazakhs is achieved, but continues to be the main way different Kazakh gangs fight among themselves for dominance over the places. As I will discuss the ethnic dimension of violence in chapter 7, let us consider here the gender aspect.

According to the women, whose voices will be heard in more detail in chapter 5, Mafioso have changed their tactics in relation to women. They do not use violence any more, but act as 'gentlemen' (*dzhentl'men*). If they want a woman, they try to seduce her by sending flowers and expensive gifts, and they invite her to a restaurant or to travel abroad. Hooligans, who were identified as the main source of violence, were considered also to be predominantly Kazakhs. The gang violence against women was galvanised and legitimised by two interrelated gendered discourses of identity politics: namely the revival of a Soviet identity and the ethnic revival. Women's bodies and sexualities were considered the bearers of both the Soviet and ethnic identities, and so they were expected not to break the rule of sexual modesty. If they did they were exposed to violence and stigma. As I will explore the ways in which the discourse of the Soviet morality legitimises the use of violence against women in chapters 5 and 6, let me describe here the ways the ethnic revival has contributed to the surge of violence against women. This was related to two elements of such revival: linguistic revival and the gendering of ethnic revival. While the first element only pertained to Kazakhs, the second was a common feature of all 'ethnic groups', however, with different levels of intensity. Let us start with the first reason.

The years 1988–93 witnessed a surge of Kazakh ethnic nationalism, with a strong linguistic element. The loss of the Kazakh language had become a main theme for the media and popular discussions. Moreover, the state adopted a policy of replacing the Russian language with Kazakh at a stroke, by setting up Kazakh language courses and threatening to sack those who were not willing to learn Kazakh. This instigated a conflict between

Kazakhs and non-Kazakhs on the one hand, and between Russian-speaking
Kazakhs and Kazakh-speaking Kazakhs on the other. The Russian-speaking
Kazakhs were not only stigmatised as impure Kazakhs (*chala Kazakakhi*),
but were exposed to the violence of hooligan gangs who had a claim on an
authentic Kazakh identity. This kind of violence was particularly targeted
against women. Almost all young Kazakh women I spoke to complained
that they were harassed by Kazakh men from the south (*Iuzhanini*), when
they were heard speaking Russian. They were reminded that they should
speak Kazakh, not Russian. Such harassment was at its peak in the high
days of linguistic nationalism from 1988 to 1993. According to a Kazakh
woman student, in those years the hooligans from the South stopped the
young Kazakh women in the streets and started to talk to them in Kazakh.
Those women who failed to answer in Kazakh were insulted, beaten or even
raped. According to her, this kind of violence was practised on such a
massive scale that many young Kazakh women did not dare to walk the
streets without male company. Gulzhan, mentioned above, described these
years as the worst time of trouble (*samye smutnye vremena*).

According to the women mentioned above, the hooligans' violence in its
linguistic guise was mainly targeted against young Kazakh women. They
did not bother Kazakh men or people from other ethnic backgrounds. They
had not, I was told, the courage to stop the Kazakh men because the latter
could fight back. And they did not care whether people from other ethnic
backgrounds could or could not speak Kazakh. The hooligans also harass
non-Kazakhs widely, claiming that Kazakhstan is their homeland. Such
harassment is particularly imposed on non-Kazakh women, because,
according to women, hooligans claim that the Kazakhs' primordial rights
on the territory of Kazakhstan entitle Kazakh men to an undisputed right
over the bodies of women who live in Kazakhstan. And they frequently
resort to violence to enforce such claims.

It is important to note that the ethnically motivated violence against
women is not limited to Kazakhs from the South but prevails among all
ethnic groups. Considering women's bodies as both the bearers and repro-
ducers of ethnic identities has contributed significantly to the surge of
violence against them. This is so because the ethnic revivalism includes a
rise in a masculinism, the main goal of which is to push women back to
their assumed 'traditional' roles prior to the changes brought about by the
Soviet state. They are ordered to obey their husbands, devote themselves
mainly to their domestic duties, and observe carefully codes of modesty.
Although such demands in Kazakhstan are common among all ethnic
groups, they are more evident among the Muslims than Slavic people. A
strong emphasis on virginity, the revival of taking bride wealth (*kalym*) and
the widespread stealing of brides (*alebghasheh*) are part of the ethnic
revival. On the other hand, young women from urban backgrounds,

regardless of their ethnic affiliations, are more inclined to the images of femininity propagated by late capitalist consumerist culture and in demand in the current sexual market. Moreover, as I discuss in chapter 5, a considerable number of them practise sexualised economic strategies which challenge both the perceived Soviet and pre-Soviet sexual moralities. As these women are considered deviant from the norm they are not only stigmatised but exposed to violence on a daily basis. As I will return to the violence against women in chapter 5 let us consider in the following sections another element of chaos, namely feelings of loss.

FEELINGS OF LOSS

Perceived losses are considered a dimension of chaos in the sphere of personal life. The crisis and reforms have made the conditions of life extremely unpredictable. The post-Soviet change is conceived like a natural disaster or an epidemic which has descended suddenly from nowhere and is not culturally understandable. A Kazakh woman described this as follows: 'Our feelings about the disintegration of the Soviet Union are like the feelings of a family whose house has been destroyed suddenly by an earthquake or burned down by a fire.' Phenomena like mass unemployment, mass sex-work, child sex-work, child labour, begging and looking in the garbage for food, are alien to the Soviet 'habitus'. So people lacked any skills or predisposition to deal with them, either individually or socially. To be sure, some people remember the wartime hardships and the famine after the war. But the difference, Aleksander (chapter 4) said, is that in that time they dealt with problems collectively and with solidarity and were sure of the future. Today, nobody cares about anybody else and they have no future. The Soviet era is compared with the present situation and remembered with strong feelings as the time of prosperity, happiness, stability, security and trust.

Loss of prosperity
The material poverty which resulted from the combined effects of unemployment,[24] cutting wages and delays in payment and inflation is felt as the greatest loss. Indeed, Brezhnev's era was remembered nostalgically as one of mass consumption. For illustrating this Ivan, a Russian unemployed electrician, who worked for himself, told me that in 1975 he and his family moved to a newly built apartment, which they received from his factory. Since that time they had purchased the following items: a car, a three-seat sofa, a Hungarian wardrobe, a wooden Hungarian bed, four carpets which still hang on the walls, a vacuum cleaner, a fridge, a TV set, a gramophone, a washing machine, a kitchen table with four chairs, and fishing and skiing equipment. He added that each year they bought new clothes and that his family not only had enough meat and fruit but could afford even to buy ice

cream and sweets for children. He, in the local manner, put a hand on his throat and said 'the salary was enough up to here' (*zarplata tak khvatalo*). In addition to this they had saved a considerable amount of money, like many other families in the neighbourhood. At the time of my fieldwork his family, and most of the families in the neighbourhood, could hardly provide for food and rent. As a sign of his poverty, he showed me his worn out shirt and said, 'I have worn this for two years and have not got money to buy a new one'. Most people could not afford to buy meat, vegetables or fruit. According to Ivan, his family purchasing power has reduced to a quarter of what it was in the Soviet time. The loss of material prosperity was considered to be a result of the loss of work and the devaluation of industrial work.

Loss of work and the devaluation of industrial work
Unemployment was experienced as a great disaster. Ivan, mentioned above, argued that in the Soviet era, finding a job was not an issue and they had a greater opportunity to choose a job they desired:

> In the Soviet time, after finishing high school, if you wanted to go to university you could do so, or you could choose a profession and learn it in a college or a technical college in one or two years. When you were ready with your education, you could easily find a job. But today only those who have rich parents can enter universities. Even if you get a place for your children in a college by bribing someone, it is useless. There are no jobs available, they are closing the factories.

Now finding any job without connections or bribes was an almost insurmountable problem, because the rate of unemployment was much higher than that of new job opportunities. Unemployment, which virtually did not exist in 1991, reached the figure of 391,747 in 1996 (Istileulova, 1996: p. 45). While this figure might be much less than the real figure, it shows the sudden growth of unemployment. According to the same source unemployment doubled in the course of the year 1996. The official unemployment benefit was 2,151 tenge in 1996 (Istileulova, p. 42), but the unemployed in the neighbourhood with whom I talked denied that they received any money. Unemployment is higher among the male Slavic men who traditionally worked in the industrial sector, which the economic crisis has hit more harshly. Factory closures and unemployment have caused poverty, suicide, domestic violence and divorce. Let us begin a short discussion of alcoholism with the following example.

Mariam was a Kazakh widow and worked as an accountant in a state store. As her salary was not enough for survival, she traded illegally in the early morning (6–9am) before going to her job, and on Sundays. I joined her each morning from 7.30 to talk with her and observe what was going on. Apart from her, only two other women started their trade so early, a Russian *Babushka* and another old married Dungan woman. The main articles the customers bought so early were local vodka, beer and cigarettes. In one morning Mariam sold seven bottles of vodka, the Dungan woman five and the Russian Babushka six. Indeed, most of the men who bought seemed to have had a very heavy drinking night. Some of the men who bought vodka were on the way to their jobs, and others were unemployed and came early to buy vodka.

I asked Mariam: 'Why are these people buying vodka so early in morning, when they are already drunk?' She answered: 'They want to get rid of their hangover by drinking new vodka (*opokhmelit'sia*).' Mariam knew some of these men, and some of them received vodka on credit from her. She explained to me:

All these have social reasons. Our men were the breadwinners (*zara-batyvali na khleb*), they have lost their jobs, they cannot trade like us women, it is shameful (*stydno*) for them to trade. They have lost face, so they drink to forget.

Although in the Soviet era both husbands and wives worked, as Mariam said, the former were considered the main breadwinners because they usually earned more than their women. Moreover, culturally men have always been considered the head of the family (*glava sem'i*) and are expected to provide their families with decent lives. Being the main bread-winners gave men hegemonic positions in the family. To be a breadwinner has been one of the main ways masculinity has been constructed among the working class. This gave different meanings to work in relation to the formation of gender notions. Although work is important for women not only for survival but for being persons (Ashwin, 1999), it is considered as one of the main parameters of manhood. A working class man becomes a man through doing socially valued work. Those men who possess good working skills are called not by other men but by women, 'men with golden hands (*zolotye ruki*)'. In contrast men who did not work were called parasites (*tuneiadtsy*). Thus, a man who contributes less than his wife, or fails to contribute at all to the economy of the family, is in danger of losing his manhood in the eyes of his family, relatives, neighbours, friends and even himself.

This has created a sensitive new problem in the relations between spouses. I knew several women at the university and the factory and in the neighbourhood, whose husbands were unemployed or earned less than them. Although most of these women did not blame the men for the situation, they recognised a major problem in their family lives which they dealt with in different ways. I knew several cases, but in only three was the relationship between spouses undamaged, because the women were careful not to undermine their husbands' injured self-esteem. One of these three women was 50, a Russian working in the factory. As she had kept her job, she earned 7,000 tenge a month. But her husband had lost his job in another factory and was working in a swimming pool as a guard for 3,000 a month. While she considered this a great loss for her husband, she said that she would never mention it to him, but instead would be supportive during these hard times.

In the rest of the cases women blamed their husbands for being lazy (*lenivye*), or alcoholic, or intended to divorce them. Indeed, many women had divorced for such reasons and the husbands of two such women had committed suicide. These women complained particularly about two things. That their husbands avoided getting involved in the street trade, the only economic choice available to them, and that such men drank heavily and became abusive.

Indeed, although street traders earned more than average salaries, urban men refused to get involved. Urban men, particularly those from working class backgrounds, still considered trading in terms of Soviet values. They found it immoral (*ne moralnye*) and labelled traders as parasites (*parazity*) and profiteers (*spekulianty*). Kazakh urban men justified their refusal with an additional reason. They considered trading alien to the Kazakh honest nomadic 'national character' (*natsional'naia cherta kharaktera*) and associated it with Uzbeks and Uigurs, whom they considered cunning (*khitrye*) and profiteers (*spekulianty*).

Urban women shared these derogatory attitudes towards trade. Trade, from street trade to large scale importing, is one of the main ways of making money in post-Soviet Almaty. Together with the economic crisis and unemployment, this has led to a process of deindustrialisation and strongly devalued people's professional skills. This was experienced as a great personal and social loss. People felt their society was transforming from one of workers and scientists to one of parasites and cheaters.

Many women with higher education who were involved in street trading or suitcase trade felt that they had been forced to choose such jobs with negative status and low quality to survive. Pensioners excepted, around half the women in my neighbourhood illegal market had higher education.

A considerable number of suitcase traders are professional women whose status has been tarnished by the occupation in three ways. First, they are accused of sleeping with their trade partner abroad for getting better deals. Second, they feel that they have been forced into this kind of occupation, which is still considered a parasitic way of making a living. Third, they feel that they are losing their cultural and professional competence by leaving their professions. Examples of such women were the mother of a student of mine, a 40-year-old Russian and her Uigur companion. After working eleven years as a doctor, the Russian woman had left her job and was now involved in the suitcase trade between the Arab Emirates and Kazakhstan. She was successful, and had two chambers in two different bazaars, one of which she shared with an Uigur woman, younger than her, and a well-qualified laboratory specialist. Indeed, the material living standards of both women had improved in comparison with the past but both of them found the job humiliating and felt that they were dispossessed from their knowledge and expertise.

In spite of their negative attitudes, women got involved in trade out of concern for their children. They probably do so because in the local ideologies womanhood is mainly defined in relation to motherhood and nurturing. The loss of self-esteem and blame from their wives drove unemployed men to alcoholism and suicide. Puzzled at how these men got money to buy alcohol, I asked one Russian street trader who often complained about her husband's drinking habits. She answered: 'The pig finds the dirt' (*svin'ia griaz' naidet*). As men usually drink with friends, usually someone gets the money from somewhere, or those who have a salary or pension buy the drinks. Some of them took the vodka their wives were selling. Another Russian woman had left a husband and later a lover, because both of them drank the vodka she had for sale. A Kazakh woman, a university lecturer who traded in the evenings, told me:

> My husband is unemployed. He doesn't look for a job. He sits at home, invites his friends there and drinks my vodka with his friends. When I tell him, 'don't drink this, it is for sale', he, answers, 'I will drink. Here is my home, take your vodka and go wherever you want.' The apartment belongs to him, I have not got my own apartment. If I find a man with an apartment who is not an alcoholic (*alkash*) I will leave my husband.

Loss of leisure

Leisure is a privilege people think they have lost completely. In Soviet times it included travel, relaxation in particular places, sport, theatre, cinemas, music halls and celebrations. It is now theoretically possible to travel abroad, but most people are too poor to travel to other cities in Kazakhstan, let alone abroad. In my neighbourhood people had close relatives in the neighbouring republics of Russia, Kirgizia and Uzbekistan whom they had not been able to visit in recent years. They had not even been able to call them or write to them. People complained that train and aeroplane fares, telephone calls[25] and stamps had become very expensive. A Russian woman worker told me: 'I am a simple worker (*prostaia rabotnitsa*). In the Soviet time I travelled to Moscow, Leningrad, Kiev, Tashkent, and Riga. But now I cannot visit my daughter here in nearby

Bishkek.' Another young woman, half Russian and half Ukrainian, had divorced her husband. Her mother had returned to Ukraine two years before. She had been waiting to leave Kazakhstan and join her mother for almost two years because neither she nor her mother had $200 for the ticket. Travel to other parts of the former Soviet Union and the former Eastern block, which was quite usual, has been restricted by the new political geography. They were particularly unhappy with the post-Soviet borders between CIS countries, which they dismissed as having divided their country, the former USSR, into artificially different political entities. People complained that the police in other republics, particularly in Russia, made a lot of problems for the citizens of Kazakhstan. A young Russian single mother, a suitcase trader whose parents lived in our neighbourhood, had lived illegally with her son in Moscow for two years. She told me that to buy a *propiska* (a permission to stay) in Moscow is very expensive and those who have no permission are continuously harassed by the police. And furthermore Central Asians and Caucasians are subjected to racism, which people think is caused by the division of the Soviet Union.

   In the Soviet era people also had one month's holiday from work (*otpusk*) each year. They used it to travel to other places to visit relatives or they spent it in nearby beaches on Kapchagai (a lake 70 miles from Almaty) or Iccyk-kul' a lake in Kirgizia. In addition, there were health resorts and rest homes, access to which was possible with a pass (*putevka*) provided by the workplace and the union (*profsoiuz*) paid a considerable part of the cost. Although these passes were distributed through connections, many people had access to them through giving a gift or a bribe, or demonstrating good work performance. Summer camps were available for children. Although most of them, particularly pioneer camps (*pionerskie lageria*), were used for ideological indoctrination, young people retrospectively evaluate positively the entertainments provided by such camps. Swimming, skiing and ice skating were cheap and popular sports. Visiting theatres, cinemas and music halls was a part of people's cultural habits, because it was cheap.

   An important form of leisure were celebrations (*prazdniki*), both private and public. People told me that in the Soviet era celebrations were one of the most important forms of leisure. People not only celebrated life-cycle events, but even celebrated privately the official days like the Eighth of March, May Day, New Year's Eve, the day of the Soviet Army and the day of the October revolution. The celebrations were encouraged by the particular relationship of the Soviet state to rituals (Lane, 1981) and by the fact that the Soviet type of economic relations and power structures promoted ritualistic consumption of food and drink (Humphrey, 1983). The shared consumption of food and drink and the exchange of gifts in private celebrations were among the main ways of creating and sustaining networks and also provided people with an autonomous sphere *vis-à-vis* the state. In the relaxed milieu of friends and relatives around kitchen tables, people endlessly mocked the Soviet authorities by telling jokes.

Because of post-Soviet poverty most ordinary people can no longer afford any of these forms of leisure. A Kazakh teacher said: 'I have not got the right to rest. I have holidays, but of what rest can I speak when my salary is only enough to buy me and my wife tickets to Iccyk-kul'.' The dispossessed still try to travel to Kapchagai, but they have no access to the rest places mentioned above. The average price for such places was 700 tenge ($11) per person per day in the summer of 1996, while the average monthly wages were 5,000 tenge ($80). In addition to low wages the giving of *putevka* had been effectively cancelled. Most of the workplaces did not pay wages on time let alone provide *putevka*.

For sport, the cheapest monthly ticket for swimming cost 900 ($12) tenge in the autumn of 1996. Ice-skating cost 100 tenge a time. Those who did not own boots had to pay an extra 100 tenge to hire them. Art consumption had collapsed. The most tragic change in leisure has been the cancellation of celebrations and parties. People in Almaty are hedonists, they love to eat and drink for a long time, give toasts and play games.

People saw the the collapse of the Soviet cultural apparatus as a regrettable process which had brought them cultural poverty. Moreover they were very nostalgic for what they considered to be the authentic Soviet culture.

Loss of security
People identified the Soviet era with security in two senses: economic security and social security in general. Economically, the collapse of the welfare state was described as the main source of insecurity. People said the life was secure, because the state guaranteed the provision of jobs, health-care, higher education and other services for everybody. 'But today,' an Uigur electrician told me, 'if you have a job today, you are not sure you have it tomorrow. If I become seriously sick I will die, because I do not have enough money to pay for medication.' The fall of the standards of public health resulting from psychological stress and the lack of necessary nutrition, in the context of the collapse of the heath-care system and the re-emergence of epidemics, is a source of great agony. The increased nepotism and commercialisation of higher education have made it almost impossible for ordinary people to send their children to universities. Because of this they feel the future of their children will be one of poverty and misery. The erosion of job security and stability of prices, postponement of payment of salaries and pensions and fluctuations of the exchange rate (*vis-à-vis* the US dollar) and financial speculations are other reasons for economic insecurity.

The social dimension of this loss of security was related by people to the disintegration of the state and the destabilisation of their networks. The breakdown of the Soviet legal, administrative and moral system has led to the crime and violence of the Mafioso and hooligans; now an inseparable part of daily life. The general fear of violence described above and the arbitrariness of state officials contributed to the feelings of insecurity. 'In the Soviet time', an Uzbek woman from the neighbourhood said, 'they did not bother ordinary people, but today they can expropriate even your apartment or take anything they want from you.'

The ethnic wars in Chechnia and Tadjikistan were another source of insecurity, because people felt they were happening in their own homeland (Soviet territory) and among their own people (*Sovetskii narod*). Moreover, the widespread presence of the war refugees reminded people of the possibility of ethnic war in Kazakhstan. Another post-Soviet social change which undermines security is the break up of trust under the pressure of the cynicism which is the moral dimension of wild capitalism.

Despair
Because of all of these factors, people feel they have lost happiness in life. A Kazakh teacher said:

> Before we had our general secretary ... We complained openly that we had nothing while we had everything. But now we have got everything, we have got Snickers, Finlandia [a Finnish vodka], Smirnov, Absolut [a Swedish vodka], skirts and shorts [he mentions these with disgust] but we have nothing. We had everything but we complained that we hadn't. Now we have all goods in the market but cannot buy them. We have everything in the shops but we have lost our way of life. In the Soviet time we had our money, our strength, our aspirations. But now we have nothing, we are corpses. We are moving corpses, and this is awful and regretful.

An indicator of despair was widespread suicide. Indeed, among people I knew, six of their relatives or neighbours had committed suicide since 1993. All of these people were men, five Russians and one Kazakh. Five Russians killed themselves because of alcoholism, family disputes and divorce, and the Kazakh because of heroin addiction. As Buckley (1997) argues, suicide is more common among men in Kazakhstan because their public recognition has been more damaged by post-Soviet change. By implication suicide might be highest among the Russian male industrial workers because post-Soviet change has damaged their position more than any other group. This speculation is supported by the fact that five out of six men who had committed suicide in my neighbourhood were Russian workers.

Loss of an egalitarian society
As well as the lack of security, people felt that they had lost an egalitarian society. People saw the Soviet system as a more egalitarian or less socially

polarised system in comparison with the present system of *dikii kapitalism* (wild capitalism). People blame the new system for destroying the foundations of solidarity and egalitarianism. Egalitarianism has been destroyed in two directions: the increasing gap between the elite and the people; and the stratification between ordinary people.

In the understanding of the local people, the old society was divided into two groups: *oni* (they, elite) and *narod* (ordinary people). The elite consisted of the partycrats (*partikraty*), the high echelons of the communist party and the leaders of Komsomol. They occupied the highest positions everywhere. They lived secluded and segregated lives, and had access to exclusive services and goods. In spite of all of these, the social gaps in the Soviet era, from the point of view of those below, are by no means comparable with those of the present situation. To illustrate this difference people usually compared the house of the ex-secretary Kunaev with the present newly built presidential palace. Actually Kunaev's house was very modest compared with the villas of new rich class which are mushrooming alongside Lenin street towards Medeo, let alone the new presidential palace.

Although the old elite enjoyed a privileged position, people say the rest of the people were in egalitarian positions in relation to each other. The patterns of marriage and housing illustrate such relations. The majority of houses in my neighbourhood were five-storey cement houses built in the late 1960s and early 1970s, called Khrushchev houses. These Khrushchev houses dominate not only the neighbourhood but all Almaty. In the neighbourhood, people in these houses came from different positions in the division of labour, mainly workers, but also teachers, directors, university professors, police officers, engineers, doctors and so forth, and from many ethnicities. So there were no significant differences in people's housing patterns. The same was true of marriage patterns. Both on the level of the neighbourhood and university, workers married doctors, engineers, teachers and others from the intelligentsia. This was because some Soviet workers[26] usually earned more than some categories of the intelligentsia, and the cultural gap between workers and the technocratic intelligentsia was much less than in the rest of the world. It was not so because of the 'low' level of culture of the intelligentsia but the 'high' level of the Soviet workers' culture. Workers (especially women) from both the neighbourhood and the factory told me that they often (twice a month) visited theatres, watched ballet or attended concerts of classical music. This can be explained partly by the Soviet 'habitus', and partly by the quality of this art and its low price. This is not to suggest that cultural differences between workers and all strata of intelligentsia were levelled. The intelligentsia trained in humanities have particularly negative attitudes towards workers and depict them as *kalkhozniki* (from *Kalhoz*, collective farm), meaning uncultured, provincial and backward. But the technical and scientific intelligentsia have mixed

with workers through marriage and their cultures are practically indistin-
guishable. But today this picture has changed. In addition to the formation
of a new lumpen bourgeoisie with its roots in the old elite, a stratification
is taking place below. Some individuals are better positioned than others,
through trade, contacts, working for foreigners, bribes, or involvement in
middle rank mafia activities. They have improved their material conditions
while the absolute majority have become poorer. This has destabilised the
relations of former neighbours, friends and relatives because the new
material asymmetries have changed the previous reciprocal balances in
exchanges of gifts and foods. Now to be rich is something distinctive,
proudly shown through clothes, cars, or by sending children to exclusive
schools, giving them good pocket money and buying them chocolate. Those
who cannot afford these feel excluded, humiliated, and express anger and
bitterness.

The egalitarian character of the Soviet system might be a myth. That the
myth is so appealing to the dispossessed today depends less on the merits
of the past than the misdeeds of the present.

CONSPIRACY THEORY

The elite try to justify the situation by two related rhetorics of capitalism
and independence. According to the first rhetoric, capitalism is the natural
order of society and in the long run it will bring prosperity and democracy
for everybody. The Soviet past is depicted as a deviation from this order
and is blamed for all of the present evils. To put the train back on the right
rails, it is claimed, a surgical transitional period (*perekhodnyi period*) is
necessary to establish capitalist order. In spite of the short term sufferings,
it is argued, this transition is necessary to bring about the capitalist Eden.
During the last ten years, while the elite have been promising this Eden, the
living standards of the majority have sunk below the poverty line. So they
have become disillusioned. They believe there will be no improvement for
the foreseeable future and expect worse to come.

Gulzhan, the historian and street trader mentioned earlier, mocked the
whole concept of the transitional period in the following way:

> We Soviet people[27] (*Sovetskii narod*) are a lucky people (*schastlivyi
> narod*). We are sitting always in the trans-Siberian express. We are
> always in transition. For 70 years we were in transition from socialism
> to communism, and now I don't know for how long we will be in
> transition from socialism to capitalism. But the drivers of the train are
> the same people. Before, they promised us the paradise of communism
> but they failed to take us there. Now they promise us the paradise of
> capitalism. But nobody believes them any more.

The rhetoric of independence is used to counteract this disillusionment. It highlights the sovereignty (*suverinitet*) of the state as the only guarantee of the freedom and sovereignty of the people (*narod*) and individual. Moreover, it is related, if not to the material welfare of the present, to the welfare of the generations to come. The protection of sovereignty, it is claimed, is not only the most important moral agenda but an absolute pre-condition for the creation of a prosperous future. In relation to these three concepts of future (*budushchee*), country (*strana*) and people (*narod*), the rhetoric of independence (*nezavisimost'*) is deployed to create a moral community identified with the new state and its territory. Then the rhetoric goes on to say that the protection of sovereignty demands a high degree of economic self-sacrifice and this self-sacrifice is again praised as a contri-bution to the future.

From the point of view of those who suffer from the situation, this is obviously a phoney rhetoric for two reasons. On the abstract level the new capitalist ideology of the elite puts self-interest at the heart of economic activity but the elite demand that ordinary people sacrifice their own present interests for the future of an imagined moral community. On a practical level, while the members of the elite use all available means to get rich and spend enormous amounts of money on conspicuous and lavish consump-tion, they demand that ordinary people endure the present hell of hunger and poverty for the sake of the future of such a community.

In contrast to the elite's propaganda and rhetoric and quasi-theories of right-wing Western analysts, the people do not see the crisis as a necessary outcome of the contradictions of the old system either. Nor do they see market reforms as a necessary and adequate remedy for the contradictions. It is assumed that both the crisis and the reforms are results of a deliberate conspiracy jointly prepared by the corrupt former Soviet elite, who are still in power, and the West. Accordingly, the old elite with the new mask of democracy on its face, is the main beneficiary of the reforms. 'They have changed from partycrats to democrats to get rich' is a standard judgment on the elite in Almaty.

A central element of common evaluations of the past is sympathy for the Soviet distribution system and hatred for the Soviet elite. They do not identify the system with the elite. Accordingly, the old system was a com-promised one in which the elite dominated and exploited others, but the interests of the ordinary people were also considered to a great extent. Through the reforms the elite broke the social contract based on the compromise and took away the whole cake for itself. Thus *narod* (the people) lost the rights they had achieved during 70 years. A factory worker summarised the transformation from the Soviet past to the present in the following way: '*Ran'she oni vorovali, no nam khvatalo, seichas oni voruiut no nam ne khvataet.*' (In the past they stole but there was enough for us. Now they are still stealing but there is not enough for us.)

CONCLUSIONS

An important meaning of chaos, in the local description, is the extreme contingency of conditions of life: the total unpredictability of the future. Although contingency is a basic condition of becoming (in a Hegelian sense) generally, its probability, in the social field, increases with the growth of complexity. For this reason, the modern societies have invented various mechanisms such as social safety nets, insurance systems, regimes of health care, various social movements and so on to minimise the negative effects of contingency. Paradoxically, the same mechanisms which make the relative predictability of social life possible are also often the mechanisms of control and hegemony. We need to distinguish extreme contingency from balanced contingency of conditions of life. In the former, the basic conditions of life become unpredictable to a degree that erodes existential security and individual agency; and makes even minimal planning for the future almost impossible. On the other hand, balanced contingency is a prerequisite of agency and relative freedom. Because if contingency is completely erased, then everything will happen according to a predetermined plan, an iron cage (fate), which will make life a boring prison. While the extreme contingency is an untamable danger the balanced contingency could be a source of adventurous pleasure. In the post-Soviet context the extreme contingency is expressed in two main spheres: the sphere of political economy and that of existential security.

   In the first sphere, the extreme contingency results from the articulation of economic policies and processes (neo-liberal economic policies, flexible accumulation and financial speculation), to particular political processes (disintegration of state, formation of the shadow states and informal networks of power). Privatisation of state property is considered by the dispossessed as the root of chaos. First, it has created a moral chaos, because those who benefit from it are supposed to steal the public wealth massively and openly without a qualm. This has destroyed the foundations of social commitment and social trust, resulting in a universal immorality. Raskolnikov without a conscience, described vividly by a Kazakh man in the first lines of this book (chapter 1), personifies this situation. Second, the dissolution of the welfare state, financial speculation and the rise of networks of influence (agents of violence and corruption) are described as sequels to privatisation. The dissolution of the welfare state has dispossessed the majority from their means of security. The fact that people never expected this to happen has caused great mental trauma. Financial speculation, violence and corruption, which have made people's lives shaky, are ways through which the networks of influence exert their power and collect their wealth.

These are characteristics of a predatory rule enforced through the following strategies: the partial privatisation of the state administrative and coercive powers by the predatory networks of influence; making the accumulation of personal wealth by the members of these networks through plunder the prime goal of economic and social policies; and the carrying out of this plunder by the privatised state. The privatisation of the administrative and coercive powers of the state has occurred in two main forms: the governmental institutions have become the personal fiefdom of these networks; and the informal organisations (mafia) have partially taken over important functions of the state such as providing security for and taxing businesses, supervising business transactions and mediating in disputes among businessmen (see also Humphrey, 1999). Plunder, financial speculation, money laundering and conspicuous consumption (see chapter 6) characterise the economic 'habitus' of these networks. Making quick money through plunder has become the main goal of the new elite; and plunder itself has become the major function of the privatised state. The partial privatisation of the state administrative and coercive powers has important implications for the theory of state on which I will comment in the concluding chapter of this book.

The convertibility of money, contacts and violence is the main rule of various games of predation. By contact, here I mean a position in a particular network of influence. One can buy both contacts and violence. For example our customs officer got his position partly by paying money. One can also buy protection for one's own business or hire an organisation to intimidate or eliminate a rival. But contacts and violence also generate money. A member of a network of influence uses his position to earn money either by avoiding to pay the fees he should pay or by extracting bribes, tributes, credit, business licence and profitable contracts. Means of violence in the form of protection (*krisha*) is a very profitable commodity. The instrumental role of coercion and patronage in the extraction of economic rent, masculinise and ethnicise the wealth accumulation.

The decentralisation of the coercive powers, settling disputes in the public places by violence (see also chapter 7), and the importance of coercion and patronage in the extraction of economic rents give a quasi-feudal appearance to the power relations. However, they are different from the feudal type of power relations in two ways. First, in the feudal society contacts and violence were not commodities. The very convertibility of money with violence and contact gives a capitalist feature to the post-Soviet power mechanisms. While this type of political economy expresses the particularity of post-Soviet conditions, it also represents the emerging features of late capitalism in the periphery (see also Castells, 1998). Moreover, violence had a high ethical value in the feudal society (Elias, 1978). The post-Soviet violence of state officials, the mafia and hooligans are considered to be evil phenomena, though the use of violence in self-defence or the defence of others has a high ethical value.

With regard to the existential sphere, the extreme contingency of conditions of life results in an existential insecurity and disorientation. The very extreme randomness of social conditions of life minimise the possibility of reflexivity. People lose their ontological orientation of time, and death becomes a tangible and imminent threat. The future is cancelled. Nostalgia and the conspiracy theory are responses to such a situation. Nostalgia is a replacement for this cancelled future. However, the post-Soviet dispossessed is different from Walter Benjamin's angel. The later, although looking backward, has a sense of movement and direction, because the winds under its wings blow towards the future. The post-Soviet era is rather a whirlwind, which implodes under the pressure of its own violent disoriented forces. (For more on this nostalgia, see chapter 6.)

The dispossessed share the opinion that the mafia and the political and managerial elite, supposedly instructed by the Americans, intentionally created chaos and lawlessness and want to make it a permanent state of affairs. This was because when nobody is held responsible according to law, a limited network of bureaucrats, Mafioso and businessmen, agents of American influence, can control the main material resources and check the whole population through spreading a general feeling of fear, the exact source of which is not clear. This theory has a grain of truth, because the economic reforms which led to the chaos were the instructions of the IMF and the World Bank and serve the interests of the elite and the US. However, this theory also represents the feelings of disorientation and weakness among the dispossessed. We know that no political actor can engineer fully the course of events according to a predetermined plan. Indeed, this is particularly true of the elite and the IMF policies in Kazakhstan. These policies were confused and did not bear the expected fruits. The dispossessed's notion of the elite and their supposedly American masters as overpowerful conspirators expresses rather the feelings of their own disorientation and helplessness. In such a fearful and hopeless situation networking is the main possible way through which people try to survive and still keep a minimal level of a sense of agency. I will deal with this in the next chapter.

4 NETWORKING AS A RESPONSE TO THE CHAOS

The main focus of this chapter is reciprocity and its related form of social organisation, namely networks, and their implications in the post-Soviet Kazakhstan. Under the post-Soviet condition people have deployed a variety of strategies for surviving such as taking things from work places, engaging in the street or suitcase trade, working intensively on their dacha lots, taking small bribes and conserving vegetables and fruit in summer. Each of these strategies is very important for the economy of each household and thus deserves a detailed analysis. However, I am not primarily concerned with separate kinds of economic activities here, but rather I want to explore how the resources of individual households are linked to each other, and thereby constitute a larger aggregate potential resource through reciprocal exchange within networks.

DEFINITIONS

Following Sahlins (1972: p. 188), I treat 'redistribution' as the collection and redivision of wealth by a central authority and 'reciprocity' as an exchange between two parties. Reciprocity does not necessarily imply a symmetry of positions between partners, but is a form of exchange based on interpersonal relations as opposed to the casual and alienated market-orientated exchange (Lomnitz, 1977: p. 133). From this it follows that: the partners have at least a minimal knowledge of each other; the relation is sustained over time (Lomnitz, 1977), although the objects of exchange may change; the relation may be described by participants in terms of commitment, obligation and trust, which are different from those which are applied to market exchange; the economic exchange is always accompanied by a minimal level of rites and ceremonies associated with interpersonal relations, such as greetings and expressions of concern for each other's lives and families. Further, people may exchange goods and services for gratitude, love, respect, blessing, reputation, prestige, status, authority and power. As Bourdieu has demonstrated in the case of both less and more complex societies (1977, 1984), cultural assets such as prestige and status and material wealth such as money, goods and services are mutually convertible. Thus, the criteria which determine the reciprocal character of a relation is neither the nature of the exchanged objects (tangible or intangible), nor the symmetry of the relation, but the degree to which the partners conceive of the exchange as a component of a wider, multidimensional interpersonal relationship.

Here I treat networks as a set of such relations which are linked to each other. Although this definition of a network is a very limited one, in the sense that it does not exhaust all meanings and functions which are associated with the term in the era of multimedia communication (see Hannerz, 1992a: p. 41), it suffices for the present purpose. As a set of face to face relations, networks are the social organisation of reciprocity. I have no intention of reviewing the anthropological literature on networks here[28] but I will mention three basic network-related concepts, originally developed by Mitchell (1987), which are of particular interest for this chapter. These concepts are: 'reachability; multiplexity and intensity' (Rogers and Vertovec, 1995: p. 16). Reachability measures whether a given network line, which consists of at least two links, is circular or open ended. Multiplexity indicates the different types of social bonds which relate two persons to each other (kinship, friendship, sharing of work, marriage). And intensity is related to the degree of commitment or instrumentalism which partners may display in a relation (Rogers and Vertovec 1995: p. 17). With reference to my field experience I would add that a network which includes many intersecting circular lines, with a high degree of multiplexity, and as a result with a high degree of commitment by its members to each other, is considered by the members as a 'moral community' (Cohen, 1966: p. 25). In such a community, those included are treated differently and with different expectations than outsiders. Individuals are expected to be generous and committed to fellow community members, while instrumentalism is legitimate with respect to outsiders (Caplan, 1981: p. 64). Networks, which are often based on workplaces or kinship or marriage and include ties of neighbourhood, are examples of such moral communities in Almaty.

RECIPROCITY AND NETWORKING AS STRATEGIES OF SURVIVAL

From the point of view of the welfare of ordinary people one of the most important economic changes in post-Soviet Kazakhstan is the change in the balance of redistribution and reciprocity, as respective functions of the state and networks. The Soviet system organised one of the most comprehensive welfare systems in the world. The interesting fact about the Soviet redistribution system was that the very nature of the economic system and the ways in which redistribution was organised actually encouraged reciprocity. As Humphrey (1983) demonstrates, in the Soviet system power was a matter of status rather than wealth. The fact that the accumulation and transformation of wealth was limited by the law encouraged people to reciprocate their material resources for status or for access to influential individuals, who could offer privileged access to resources (Humphrey, 1983).

Another base for reciprocal exchange was the shortage (both real and artificial) of some goods. It is a well-known fact that shortage was an endemic aspect of the command economy.[29] In Almaty shortages were not universal, but were restricted to particular goods, like cars, refrigerators, TV sets and apartments. The shortage was both partly a result of the dynamics[30] of the system and partly an artificial one, as those at the top (*verkh*) sold goods on the black market for much higher prices. Although such goods were rationed mainly through work places, privileged access to them was possible either through the black market or by reciprocity.

In order to understand the change brought about by the post-Soviet reforms in the spheres of redistribution and reciprocity, let us consider the following equation:

$$A = B+C+D+E+F$$

Where:

A = the total resources of a family.
B = the sum of the family members' salaries and pensions.
C = the sum of contributions of welfare institutions.
D = the sum of the products from domestic production (from dacha allotments and domestic animals, conserving fruits and vegetables, fishing, gathering and hunting).
E = the sum of resources acquired through reciprocity.
F = the sum of resources created through trading (*torgovat'*) in the market.

The amount of E depends on the social positions of a given family's members and their networking skills.

In the Soviet time, B+C constituted the main bulk of household resources and D+E played an auxiliary, but important, role. F=0, for most of the ordinary families. Although D+E was very important for enhancing the household economy and E included goods which were in short supply, they were not necessary preconditions for survival; a family's basic needs could be satisfied by B+C.

The economic reforms which followed *perestroika* and independence resulted in basic changes in the above equation. First, because of the dismantling of the welfare state much of the redistribution related to family welfare collapsed. As a result, C practically ceased to exist. Second, B either does not exist as a result of unemployment, or has been reduced threefold as a result of the combined effects of inflation and wage cuts. And the payment of B is usually postponed for several months, making it less effective in the household economy. This means that the aggregate contribution of B+C to the family economy has declined dramatically. As this constituted the main bulk of the family income, its decline has meant that the majority of families have found themselves below the poverty line and survival has become the main issue of their life. This has given a new importance to D+E, which have become the main resources for survival. To these two resources F has been added through suitcase and street trading. In order to illustrate this abstract, but simple model, let us look at the different ways one worker's family manages to survive.

Aleksander is a man in his late forties. He is of Moldavian background but calls himself Russian (*Russkii*). He is married to Ludmila, a half-Russian and half-Ukrainian woman who calls herself Russian (*Russkaia*) as well. They have four children, two sons and two daughters; an unusually large number for a Russian family. Three years ago Kostia, the oldest son, left with his wife's family for Russia. The rest all live together with *Babushka*, Marina Aleksander's mother-in-law and Sharik a black dog in a three-bedroomed apartment in a *khrushchevskii dom*.[31] Aleksander is a skilled carpenter in a factory, where he has been working for 24 years. The factory has been privatised through division of the shares between the personnel. At the beginning the factory director got 25 per cent of the shares. Later he bought most of the workers' shares very cheaply, under the pretext that the banks would only give credit if the majority of shares were concentrated in one hand. While the production volume, Aleksander says, has increased, the director has reduced the number of workers from 1,400 to 600. In Aleksander's team (*brigada*) three workers have been sacked and their duties transferred to him.

Aleksander works six days a week and his salary is 5,000 tenge. This was $83 in October 1995, and fell to $71 by October 1996 as a result of inflation.[32] The family's official income consists of the sum of his salary and his wife's mother's pension (1,400 tenge, $20).' My salary,' Aleksander says, 'is one third of what it was in the Soviet time.' Usually the payment of his salary is postponed by at least four months; fortunately his mother-in-law receives her pension regularly. He eats his lunch in the factory canteen on credit, which is then deducted from his salary. Those in charge in the factory insist that workers should accept part or all of their salaries in kind. But workers, Aleksander says, resist this, because the prices in the factory shop are much higher than those outside and the quality of the goods on offer is bad. The manager barters windows, doors and furniture with other factories and big food shops for food, wine, sugar and other goods. He later tries to persuade the workers to accept these bartered goods instead of money. Aleksander claims:

The Director tries to kill two birds with one stone, to sell his goods and make extra profit at the same time. The manager says that there is no money for paying our salaries. But he lies, because he is building an expensive house for himself and has recently bought a Mercedes.

The expenditure of the family is at least 25,000 tenge a month. This consists mainly of food, rent, fuel for the car and vodka and beer. Every evening he drinks two bottles of *zhiguli* (a local beer) and two *stakans* (small cups) of vodka, which together cost 70 tenge. Their clothes are not new, and they cannot afford to buy new ones in the New Year as they did in the Soviet era. However, when winter was imminent both daughters, Natasha (21) and Nastia (19) argued with their mother about buying *sapogi* (boots) and *pol'to* (an overcoat). Their mother, Ludmila Mikhailovna, opposed their demands, showing them her own worn-out shoes and saying, 'Look at me. If I had money I'd buy a new pair of shoes for myself.' But Aleksander was of a different opinion. 'It is time', he said, 'for them to marry and nobody will look at a girl with worn-out clothes.' Some days later, he told me he had bought the boots and overcoats. I asked him how much they had cost. He answered *becplatno* (free of charge). How?!, I wondered. He said he had got them from his niece who runs a shop with her husband in the Nikol'skii bazaar, they are *chelnoki* (suitcase traders). 'What generous relatives you have!' I exclaimed. 'Yes, but', he answered proudly, 'I help them as well; at the beginning of the summer I changed their windows and doors free of charge. I took the material out of the factory without the Director knowing. You see, that was a very risky business.'

Aleksander's family survive through the involvement of all the family members in economic activities. Aleksander himself, as his wife and neighbours would say, is a man with golden hands (*zolotye ruki*), a man who is master of several skills. He is a good carpenter; he knows how to weld and build; he is a good farmer, fisher and hunter. In addition to all these, he is an excellent networker. Through combining his professional and networking skills, he earns money for the family's needs. First of all, he manages to work for himself as well as in the factory. He finds customers through relatives and friends and then he 'steals' some of his director's customers by charging them less than his boss does. This is possible because the manager sends them to him to order the work. He also manages to take out some material and instruments from the factory and sell them through friends and relatives, usually for cheaper prices, but sometimes he gives them away free of charge. He usually helps a number of different people by providing them with material, installing doors and windows and repairing them, and receiving help from them when he is in need.

From all these activities Aleksander earns between 12,000 and 20,000 tenge a month, which constitutes the main bulk of the family income, much of it more or less being illegal. To manage it he bribes the guard (*akhrana*) and has the consent of his colleagues on the shop floor. Aleksander does not consider what he does to be theft, because, according to him, the main thief is the director himself, who has cheated the workers by buying their shares very cheaply and now does not pay them decent wages on time.

Aleksander's mother lives in a village 60 miles from Almaty. She worked the whole of her life for the neighbouring Kolkhoz as a *doiarka* (milkmaid). Her husband, who was a tractor driver, is dead. Now she has retired, but has her own *ogorod* (garden) where she grows fruit and vegetables and keeps domestic birds and animals. In addition to this she has received a piece of land where they plant potatoes. All the members of the family except Natasha (the older daughter), who considers farming degrading, contribute to the work. Part of their meat and milk and the whole vegetable and fruit consumption is provided through the land. Women together conserve vegetables and produce jam in summer for the coming winter (around 60 three-litre bottles of tomato chutney, and around 40 half-litre bottles of jam). In the summer (1996) they had a potato harvest of 2,000kg. They sold some of the potatoes and bartered some for a small pig. They gave one sack to a Russian man named Valerii who provides them with fishing nets, and two sacks to Aleksander's sister whose husband has committed suicide. They also kept some for the summer and autumn consumption, and stored the rest in the *pogreb* (cellar), for the rest of the year until the next harvest.

In addition to their own land the whole rural area is used as a resource for survival. The lake, six miles from Aleksander's mother's village, is the most important resource after the garden. Each time he goes to the lake, Aleksander catches up to 20kg of fish. He gives some of the fish (the best part) to a local Turk, Memet, who is in charge of the lake, and some to the Russian Valerii. The rest of the fish is divided between his mother, her sisters, his nieces and his own family. Occasionally he gives fish to some friends on the factory shop floor or to the guard there. Over the years Valerii and Aleksander have become friends, sometimes spending a whole night on the lake, in Aleksander's small boat, drinking vodka and fishing together. In addition to giving fish to Turkish Memet, he gives him fruit and cuts wood for him with his electric saw which he has brought free of charge from the factory. Aleksander has developed a good relationship with Memet. On all of the occasions when I went with Aleksander to the lake, we would first visit Memet in his home, a few hundred yards from the lake. He usually received us with vodka, tea or watermelon. Before fishing we stayed there for some hours and talked. Aleksander also hunts birds, but not as often as he fishes. He has an old rifle which is repaired by a Russian friend, who receives a share of birds and a bottle of vodka each time he repairs it.

The neighbouring *Kolkhoz* is another economic resource. Aleksander barters things from the factory with villagers (*kolkhozniki*) for milk, fruit and meat. In addition to this, he receives hay for his animals free of charge from the *kolkhoz* and picks maize from the collective farm for family consumption. In the summer, family members eat a lot of maize and also give it to friends and relatives. The first time I saw Aleksander picking a big sack of maize from the collective farm, I asked whether it was illegal. He burst into laughter, and cited a local proverb: '*vse vokrug kolkhoznoe vse vokrug moe* (everything around *kolkhoz* belongs to me).' Later, at home when Aleksander's wife, Ludmila, brought the cooked maize to the table, he told the story to the family. They all laughed loudly, amused by my ignorance. In the summer, Aleksander usually receives free watermelon from the local Koreans for whom he may provide casual services.

Each Friday evening he buys cheap vodka and cigarettes from the *optovyi bazar* (wholesale market) in Almaty and brings them to his mother. The old woman then sells them for cash or barters them during the week. Before selling the vodka she adds some water to it to increase the volume.

Ludmila, who is 46 years old, worked in a factory until she developed a problem with her spine. She was operated on twice before becoming completely unable to work. She left the job without a *Kopeika* (a penny) as insurance, nor does she receive a pension. She contributes to the family economy by selling cosmetics with the help of her younger daughter, Nastia. Her older son Kostia, who is involved in suitcase trade between Russia and Kazakhstan, brings them these cosmetics. He receives in exchange fruits, eggs and vegetables, all of which are more expensive in Russia. Mother and daughter sell the cosmetics mainly through friends and relatives. But they also advertise them through *Karavan*, the most popular local newspaper.

Natasha, before marrying a Turk-Bulgar and leaving for Istanbul, was involved in illegal street-trading. First, she received some goods from her cousin's shop and cosmetics from her mother, sold them in the streets and received 5 per cent of the sales from the cousin. However, she complained that her cousin and cousin's husband were cheating her, that other girls worked on more favourable contracts, that in winter it was very hard to stand in the cold, and that men harassed her almost every day by offering her money or jobs for sex. In late summer she sold textbooks in the street, which she received from a Kazakh woman by the name of Gulia. Gulia was her friend's sister and was working in a school library. The books actually should have been sold through the library at school, but instead they were sold for higher prices on the black market. Neither Gulia nor any other member of her family dared to sell the books, because of the fear of being identified by somebody from the school. The illegal sale of the school books was not limited to Natasha, at the beginning of August they were sold everywhere in this way.

Natasha was more satisfied with the terms of her contract with the Kazakh woman than those with her own cousin. For each book they paid a certain amount to the school and the surplus was to be divided equally between them. Natasha, who is exceptionally honest for a young woman from Almaty, cheats Gulia a little. She does so because she feels that Gulia in her turn is cheating her. She suspects that Gulia pays less to the school for each book than she tells Natasha. Thus, if Natasha sells a book for 150 tenge she tells Gulia 120. Natasha was generally ashamed to trade (*torgovat'*), but she tried to ease the burden by joking: 'It is better to sell stockings and books than sell your body.'

After finishing high school at the age of 17 she wanted to enter university, but the family had neither the connections nor the money to obtain her a place through bribing, so she failed to be admitted to any university. Later her father bribed a manager of a technical college for $200. As a result she received one year of training and became an electrician. Then her father found a job for her in the army through his cousin, a retired army colonel. In exchange he had to provide the colonel with doors and windows for his new apartment. The family also had to play host to the colonel and ten of his friends and former colleagues for dinner: a dinner which would cost the family at least $100.

Natasha did not like the job, because the army people had a reputation for being both drunkards (*alkashi*) and womanisers (*babniki*). She was really afraid of being sexually harassed, but she had to take the job anyway because street-trading was so unstable. She did not like to be involved in the suitcase trade with other countries, mainly a female profession, either. This was because, according to a widely shared local opinion, women who are involved in this kind of activity sleep with their trade partners abroad to get the goods for lower prices. Natasha would usually say: 'I will not fuck (*trakhat' sia*) with Arabs and Turks for *khleb* (bread).' Fortunately, she met the Turk-Bulgar and married him. As a result she was freed from taking the job, and her family were freed from their obligation to the colonel. To find a good husband is not only a matter of prestige and survival for a young woman but for her family too, because the groom and his family constitute a link to new networks. Later the colonel asked Aleksander to bring the doors and windows free of charge for him. Aleksander avoided doing so and instead asked for one hundred 'boxes' (his word). Aleksander told me that it was just to charge the colonel in spite of the fact that he was a relative because according to Aleksander, the colonel was tricky (*khitryi*) and rich, and that it was dangerous for Aleksander to take the things out of the factory. 'They cost two hundred dollars in the market, I charge him just half that,' Aleksander said.

Baba Marina, the mother-in-law, in addition to her pension, contributes to the family economy by illegally selling cigarettes, vodka, chewing gum, wine, beer, Turkish and Chinese pasta on the pavement in the evenings in summertime. In spite of all of these activities, the family save very little money, they just survive. We must also keep in mind that much of the trade in which Aleksander's family is involved is illegal.

As the above example illustrates reciprocal exchange constitutes one of the main strategies of survival for ordinary people. The exchanges take a variety of forms including: sharing of alcoholic drinks; sharing of food and drinks; giving gifts (*podarok*); exchange of words (*khvalit'*, *govorit' khoroshie slova*), giving help (*pomoshch'*) and some others.

From the point of view of survival in Almaty, we may classify reciprocal exchanges into two types:[33] the reproductive ones, which are related to the reproduction and maintaining of those social relations vital for survival; the urgent ones, which contribute directly to survival. The sharing of food and drink, exchanges of gifts and words are prime examples of the first type, and help with immediate needs is the most important example of the second one. The first type occur routinely and recurrently. Exchanged goods and services are expected, but not demanded, by the receiver and the giver decides on the nature of the objects offered. Moreover, the exchange is an element of the rituals of daily life, the life-cycle of a person or an institution or cultural events. Although the recent poverty resulting from the recent 'Thatcherite' onslaught on people's living standards has made the continuity of this type of exchange problematic, it is still expected to take place. The second type occurs when the objects of exchange are demanded by the receiver, who needs them desperately, and is not personally able to provide them. This type of exchange which covers a vast number of needs from repairing a toilet seat to finding a job or a place in university, is understood by locals as help (*pomoshch'*).

Analytically these two types of reciprocity are distinguishable from each other. In reality their functions overlap. Some forms of reproductive reciprocity like gift exchange (see below) are intended to contribute to the receiver's household economy while on the other hand any form of exchange bolsters the existing relations between partners. Moreover, both types of reciprocity are usually elements in multiple exchanges between the same partners. For example, Aleksander and his relatives, including the family of his nieces and less frequently that of the colonel, visited each other and in celebrations exchanged gifts and words of honour and affection. On the other hand Aleksander drank vodka and beer with most of the men with whom he exchanged goods and services. The two types of exchange presuppose each other.

Sharing food and drink

Home has a higher symbolic value than a bar or other similar places where people gather casually. It is the place where people receive relatives and friends and share food, drinks, words and affection. One can distinguish between two types of sharing food: the ordinary sharing of food between family members on a daily basis and the ceremonial sharing of food. The latter occurs either as public celebrations, ceremonies of life-cycle of individuals and institutions, or when a person or a family or a group of persons are invited as an acknowledgement for some help they have provided or are expected to provide for a member of the family, or when the person(s) invited are 'prestigious'. In the latter case the guests' prestige is meant to enhance the self-esteem and reputation of the hosts, so they invite some of their relatives and friends as well to show off their 'honourable' guests. The meal usually takes place at home, but it can take place in a restaurant, or some official place like a workplace. The length of the ceremony, the type and the total amount of food and drinks served depend on the occasion, the place, and the wealth and social importance of guests and hosts. However, the amount of food and drink, in contrast to the poverty of most people at present, is usually impressive.

Consumption is controlled from the beginning to the end. A person who is called *Tamada* (usually in weddings or other official big parties), or the most senior person, opens the ceremony by mentioning the relevant event and persons, and giving a toast (*tost*). After the toast everyone drinks together. Then follows the consumption of the cold food (*kholodnoe*) or first food (*pervoe*). While eating, at approximately equal intervals, the *tamada* gives each person a turn to offer a toast. And of course people raise their glasses and drink together again, and then eating resumes. Between toasts, people chat and tell jokes and anecdotes. After a while the warm food (*goriachee*) or second food (*vtoroe*) is served, and after that the dessert. When the eating is finished and the last person has given his/her toast, the same person who opened the ceremony closes it by once more addressing the hosts, the guests and the event.

Actually, toast giving, particularly among Kazakhs, is an art of oratory, and the toast is more like an elaborate speech. While the form of each speech changes according to the respective teller's skills and taste, the content of all includes some invariable elements. First, all of them thank the host, as the head of the family (*glava semi*), for his generosity in providing the impressive food table (*stol*). Second, they admire the hostess' cooking skills and hospitality (when the celebration takes place at home). Third, they highlight the event and address those persons who are particularly related to it. Fourth, they link the individual to the group by emphasising the collective bonds between people who are present. With regard to this, people usually hold with the rhetoric on the virtues of collective bonds like kinship and friendship and so forth.

The order of the toast giving is determined from the top down, according to seniority. On official occasions and in religious communities seniority is defined by rank, and in private parties by age and gender. In the latter case the priority is given to men and those who are older. While in pure Muslim gatherings the gender aspect is usually observed more strictly, in Russian or mixed gatherings it is negotiated more flexibly. Toast giving is a significant way through which power relations are legitimised discursively. This occurs through the order and the content of the toast, its length and the body language of the teller. The ways in which people address each other depends on the symmetry or asymmetry of relations. This is signified in the ways the name of the addressee is mentioned. A person of higher status usually calls the person with a lower status, if younger, by a nickname (Medinka instead for Medina, and Alesha instead for Aleksei). A person from a lower status always calls a person of higher status by his/her name plus the patronymic (*Otchestvo*), like Sergei Mikhalovich, or Medina Hosenovna. When they use related pronouns a person with higher or equal rank/status calls the one with lower/equal status '*ty*' (you, subject), *tebe* (you, object) or *tvoe* (yours), while the latter use the pronouns, *Vi* (you, subject), *Vam* (you, object) and *vashe* (yours). The first group of pronouns are used for the expression of intimacy or for patronising someone, and the second signify distance and respect. The body language and the content of the toasts are in tune with this logic of hegemony. As the senior person feels (or gives the appearance of feeling) confident, his/her voice is didactic and the body is relaxed. While s/he chooses her/his words more freely and mixes them with anecdotes and jokes, s/he usually mentions the achievements of his/her junior addressees in an evaluative but approving manner, and usually gives him/her the highest mark; then reminds him/her of the appropriate moral conduct in life, gives him/her instructions and mentions what is expected from him/her in the future.

A person from a lower status, with a modest voice and a humble face flatters and praises the higher person, depicts him/her as exemplary in character, highlights her/his moral and academic, but rarely economic, achievements. S/he uses more formal and standard words of praise and flattery. Moreover, people in higher positions usually speak longer and address a larger number of persons than those in lower positions. Toast giving is gendered, in addition to the gendered order of the giving, by the way a woman is addressed. A woman, regardless of her social position and professional achievements, is praised at first hand for her moral achievements in relation to her family life. She is depicted as an exemplary wife and mother and is wished the love of her husband and children. In the case

of a woman who is unmarried, she is wished a good husband and is advised
how to behave as a good wife and mother.

Gifts (podarok)

Gifts are a very ambiguous category, and are mixed up with bribes and
tributes. They are usually given in a celebration, and are accompanied by
toasts from the givers to the receivers. The manner in which the toast is given
depends on the symmetry/asymmetry of the relation as described above.

The gift is usually given collectively, by a family, a group of friends or
colleagues, or those who share the same religious faith. The recipient is one
person, or two in the case of marriage. In special cases a gift is given individually as well. The most usual case is when it is given by a man to his
mistress or fiance. Another case is when the gift is a cover up for a bribe
or tribute. So a gift often symbolises the belonging of an individual to a
group and such a link is explicitly highlighted by the toasts which
accompany the gift. The ways in which a counter-gift is usually dealt with
have to do with the symmetry/asymmetry of relations between the people
involved. In the case of symmetrical relations the counter-gift is always
given and its monetary value usually matches that of the gift. The exception
is when the gift or counter-gift is given partly as a compensation for
something the recipient has already done or expected to do for the giver in
the near future. In such a case the gift and counter-gift, depending on the
social distance, are not necessarily of equal value. In the case of asymmet-
rical relations the giving of a counter-gift is treated differently depending
on the occasion and the type of hierarchical relation between the parties
involved. In this context we may distinguish occasions related to the
individual life-cycle from the rest.

The hierarchical orders which may influence the counter-gift are social
rank and gender. With regard to life-cycle ceremonies a counter-gift is
always given but its amount and type might be influenced by the social hierarchies mentioned above. For example, while the birthdays of all staff in a
particular work unit (a department in a university (*kafedra*) or a team
(*brigada*) in a factory) might be celebrated and each member of the staff
might receive a collective present from the rest, the presents received by
those in higher ranks (head of the department (*zaveduiushchii kafedroi*), or
the leader of the team (*brigadir*)) are distinguished by their higher values.

On occasions which are not related to an individual life-cycle, a counter-
gift is treated differently depending on the type of hierarchy in question. In
social hierarchies gifts are given by those below to those above but counter-
gifts are not given. At the Eighth of March celebration at the university
three women who worked as secretaries at the dean's office gave her
expensive flowers and two bottles of expensive (expensive in the local
context) shampoo as a gift without receiving anything in return, except

probably her protection. On the same day most of my female students brought flowers for their teachers but did not receive anything from them. During exam time at of the end of the year, students in each class collect money and buy gifts for teachers without receiving anything from them, but winning their kindness in giving marks. Actually this kind of gift, which is very close to a tribute, is a well-established practice in Almaty. Those who want to be on good terms with their bosses provide them with gifts. With regard to gender, men usually give gifts to women, and in turn receive their hospitality and affection. In post-Soviet Almaty, giving presents to women by men has become a strong symbol of masculinity, not only for the rich but even for the poor. For the Eighth of March celebrations, a young worker spent the whole of his salary to buy earrings for his girlfriend.

The gift usually consists of money or objects with direct utilitarian characteristics unless the receiver is a foreigner. In the latter case people usually give artifacts which symbolise the local 'traditional cultures'. I was involved with a group of friends who believed in a quasi-religious cult, the cult of Ivanov. They celebrated the birthday of each member. I was the only person who received a Kazakh traditional hat, the rest received money. On another occasion, in a modest working class wedding in the neighbourhood where I lived, all who were present gave gifts in the form of money with the exception of the groom's mother and the uncle of the bride. While the former gave the bride gold earrings, the latter gave them travel tickets to St Petersburg. The most impressive gift came from the mother of the bride. She had taped together dollar notes and had made a long band from the notes. When she gave her gift all who were present cheered. Other people had put the money in envelopes.

As the gift is oriented towards utilitarian ends, the amount is quite important. It varies depending, on the one hand, on the wealth and status of the receiver and givers and, on the other, the social distance between them and the occasion. In the cult group, each member contributed 300 tenge and the sum of collected money amounted to around 3,000 tenge ($50) each time. However, when the gifts were exchanged between relatives or close friends it could be more.

Help
Celebrations (*prazdniki*), the sharing of food and drink and exchanges of words and gifts are ways of sustaining relationships over time and creating new relationships in which a wider range of goods and services are exchanged. The latter includes a variety of forms, the most important example of which is help (*pomoshch'*).

Giving help (*pomoshch'*) is the most prevalent form of reciprocity between relatives and friends. It acquires a quasi-barter form of exchange. As with barter, it is given in exchange for some help which the giver has received in the past or is expecting to receive in the future. But locals clearly distinguish between help (*pomoshch'*) and barter (*barter*). In the former 'the focus is on'[34] the relation between people and in the latter, on the relation between things (Humphrey and Hugh-Jones, 1992: p. 1). To clarify this, let us consider the following example. As the reader might remember, Aleksander's mother bartered vodka with some of the other villagers. She often donated vodka to her nephew who was living in the same village and who usually helped her with any emergency in the absence of Aleksander. I asked Aleksander whether his mother bartered the vodka with her nephew. He answered: 'No, she just gives it to him and he helps her, this is a relation between relatives (*rodstvennye otnosheniia*).' Then, I asked him what is barter? He answered: 'exchange of goods' (*obmen tovarov*). As this example illustrates, in barter the economic aspect of the exchange is recognised explicitly by the partners, while in the case of help this aspect is disguised by ideologies, discourses and feelings which are associated with marriage, kinship and friendship.

Moreover, while in barter the delivery and the receiving of the bartered goods by each of the partners occur either simultaneously or separately (Humphrey and Hugh-Jones, 1992: p. 1), the giving and receiving of help do not take place simultaneously. And the kind of help which will be received by the giver in future is unspecified beforehand. Although the receiver may compensate the giver partially by providing him with some money, gifts and food, this is not considered by any of the partners as full compensation. For example, the colonel mentioned earlier who found a job for Natasha would impose an expense of $300 on Natasha's family, $100 for food and drink, and $200 for doors and windows. In spite of this, the colonel would claim that he had helped Natasha's family and that they should be grateful and indebted to him, because, they would have had to pay much more if the colonel had not been a relative.

Return is delayed until the giver has an urgent need which can be satisfied by the receiver. However, the delayed return is not the end of the process but the beginning of a new cycle within it, which leads to a new giving. This cyclical characteristic means that the present act of giving is associated with acts of receiving in the past and future. In this way the relationship between two parties is sustained and renewed over time and thus requires a different morality than barter. As the continuity of relationship provides a protection against the contingencies which emerge as part of the passage of time, the sharing of food and drink and exchange of gifts and words are meant to keep the relationship strong. However, from this we should not conclude that the act of giving will be followed unproblematically with an act in return. The way the former recipient may react to the request of the former giver depends on how their relationship has evolved meanwhile. If the receiver finds the giver no longer reliable or thinks that the value of goods or services s/he demands are too high with regard to the current state of affairs between them, the receiver may either avoid providing him/her with goods or services or demand higher immediate compensation than usual. The same is valid for the case in which the receiver finds the giver less important owing to the promotion of his/her own social position or access to other people who may replace the giver more efficiently.

And finally it differs from barter in the sense that in barter the values of exchanged objects, although estimated subjectively and with reference to different 'regimes of value' (Appadurai, 1986, quoted in Humphrey and Hugh-Jones, 1992: p. 1), are assumed to be equal; with regard to help, people do not necessarily compare the values of exchanged 'objects'. For example, Aleksander and Memet did not match the value of fish and the cost of cutting wood. The fish Aleksander catches from the lake should have cost him 100 tenge each time, because Memet charged others who were fishing there this amount of money. If Aleksander had purchased the same amount of fish in the market in Almaty he would have paid 2,000 tenge. But neither the Turk nor Aleksander were aware of such a value. Aleksander never sold the fish and the surplus of the family consumption was given to friends and relatives. On the other hand, cutting wood with the electrical saw had no fixed value, Aleksander instead did it as a favour.

The second major characteristic of help is that it is often obtained through the illicit use of personal influence: *blat*. Resources which are reciprocated through *blat* are appropriated resources: resources to which the appropriator is not legally entitled. '*Poluchit' po blatu*' (to get on the quiet, come by through influence (The Oxford Russian Dictionary: p. 26)) has been a way of life in the late Soviet and post-Soviet social systems. As Berliner (1957: p. 182) suggests, the word *blat* is an old one, but under the Soviet system has acquired new meanings. *Blat* literally means crime, pull, influence, wangling, protection (Oxford Russian Dictionary: p. 26). But in daily usage the intensity of its negative connotations changes depending on the context. People from lower down the social scale usually condemn *blat* at the top of society as theft and crime while approving *blat* among themselves as a strategy of survival. Another context in which *blat* is invested rhetorically with negative meaning is ethnicity. Most of the non-Kazakh ethnic groups, particularly Russians, relate *blat* rhetorically, in a strong negative sense, to Kazakhs. They may tell you that Kazakhs monopolise the jobs and places in universities for their own relatives, or some may even tell you that Kazakhs are *blatniki* (corrupted, fixers, wanglers). On the other hand they justify their own use of *blat* as a way of getting on with life.

The illegal use of resources has been a universal phenomenon in the Soviet and post-Soviet eras (Dallin, 1951: pp. 181–96; Berliner, 1957: pp. 182–206; Grossman, 1985; Humphrey, 1983: pp. 221, 222–3, 324; Humphrey, 1991: pp. 9, 11, 12; Handelman, 1995: especially chapters 4,

5; Ashwin, 1996: pp. 28–9). Dallin and Berliner, on the basis of information gathered from Soviet émigrés, demonstrate that *blat* was already a
considerable phenomenon in Soviet society during the 1950s. But many
people told me *blat* was considered a serious crime before Khrushchev's
reforms, and so only people in higher positions were involved in it and
ordinary people could only do it marginally. During the rule of Khrushchev
blat began to expand because people feared the state less, but its expansion
was limited owing to people's commitment to socialist morality. The
blatniki were judged more severely than a decade later under Brezhnev's
rule when *blat* really began to thrive due to growing shortages (*defitsit*) and
general disillusionment with socialism and the subsequent moral decay.
Humphrey (1983), who deals with social relations in two *Kolkhozes* under
this latter period among the Soviet *Buryats*, observes that illegal methods
were used for access to goods which were in short supply or for the
allocation of educational places, and goods were also sold on the black
market. Grossman claims that while everybody was stealing from public
organisations this was morally legitimised by the public (1985: p. 256).

In Kazakhstan, in the same period under Kunaev's rule, *blat* became a
way of life. Everybody from top to bottom illegally appropriated 'public
property'. While the portion of a person's share from appropriated resources
was determined by his/her status and networking skills, most people had
their share of it. The saying '*vse vokrug kolkhoznoe vse vokrug moe*'
(everything in the Kolkhoz belongs to me) expressed by Aleksander earlier
illustrates this. Actually *blat* had become a very strong institution in any
workplace in Almaty. Whilst many scarce goods like cars and apartments
were distributed through the workplaces according to a queue, those who
had good connections or paid bribes received the goods sooner. Aleksander
and his wife mentioned, with anger, how the director of the factory gave
the car, which according to their position in the queue should have had been
sold to them, to somebody else.

On the other hand, while the directors of the enterprises sold considerable parts of the products on the black market or reciprocated them in their
own networks, ordinary workers were involved in the illicit use of resources
as well. On the state and collective farms they used tractors and other instruments illegally and they slaughtered animals, used crops, hay, fodder and
other things free of charge. Workers took instruments and products out of
the factories as well. Aleksander told me that while the director of their
factory forced the workers to work on Sundays to produce for the black
market, the workers took small things (*meloch'*) as well. He said:

I have brought the material for building the *bania* (sauna), the garage and
pogreb (cellar) from the factory. Everybody took things out. We workers

joked that Brezhnev had said, 'You can take anything out from the
factory as long as you keep it within the Soviet Union.'

Although in the early 1980s *blat* had become very widespread and almost
everybody was involved in it, the main body of resources were still distributed centrally through legal channels. Politicoeconomic changes during
perestroika and its aftermath in the late 1980s and early 1990s changed this
picture. During this period, *blat* became the main method of distributing
resources owing to two factors. First, as Humphrey (1991) demonstrates in
the case of 'provincial Russia', as a result of the collapse of central
economic and political institutions, the power of the local authorities
including those of the directors of different enterprises, increased dramatically. Now they decided how to distribute the resources. Second, there was
a dramatic increase in shortages. In Almaty goods such as milk, sausage,
butter, sugar, sweets, vodka, cigarettes and soap which were previously
available disappeared from the state shops. According to people, they were
'sold under the counter' (*torgovat' iz pod polu*) or on the black market for
several times more than the official prices. This shortage was partly a result
of the recession and the collapse of central planning, but hoarding was
instrumental as well.

This situation contributed to the further expansion of *blat* in several
directions. First, it became the main way through which different directors
and high officials of the party bartered goods and services with each other.
Second, the existing patronage system in workplaces expanded beyond
recognition (Humphrey, 1991: p. 9) as those below became more dependent
on those above to obtain goods. Third, the links between black-marketeers
(*spekulianty*) and leaders of different production units multiplied. And
finally, *blat* became a significant element in ordinary people's relationships
as well.

In spite of the fact that the shortages problem has been resolved as a
result of the lifting of the state monopoly over foreign trade, the *blat* system
continues to expand. This is primarily due to the shortage of money and
changes in the structures and functions of the state. Shortage of money in
the hands of ordinary people, in addition to the cutting of wages and unemployment, is caused first by the short supply of money in the country
(Scheremet, 1996: pp. 31–2). This has led in its turn to the enterprises either
postponing the payment of ordinary people's salaries or trying to pay them
in kind. According to Scheremet, enterprises' debts to private households
amounted to 50 billion tenge in November 1996.[35] For the same reason the
payment of pensions is regularly postponed as well. The state debt to
pensioners in September 1996 was 44 billion tenge (Verk, 1996: p. 2).
Another factor which contributed to the lack of money was that the value
of money which people kept in the *sberkassa* (savings bank) evaporated as

a result of the transformation from the rouble to the tenge (1992–93). For example Aleksander's family had saved 18,000 roubles during the 1980s, of which 6,000 was saved for Natasha's dowry (*pridannoe*) and the rest for buying a new car for the family. Aleksander's mother had saved 7,000 roubles as well. They lost all this money, which according to them was equal to the price of two cars, as a result of the reform. This was not an exceptional case. Most of the families in the neighbourhood where I lived had lost considerable sums of money as a result of the transition.[36]

This shortage of money encouraged further *blat* both among the elite and the ordinary people. At the top, different elite groups compete for the existing reserves of money through the manipulation of the credit system. At the bottom of society, the ordinary people cannot purchase a considerable part of needed goods and services from the market because of the lack of money, so they intensively exploit their dachas (land allotments) on the one hand and exchange goods and services with friends and relatives on the other. Illicit deals play a prominent role in the latter. Although the possibilities for people in a lower social position to appropriate resources illegally are very limited, they try their best to do this, as the example of Aleksander (earlier) illustrates. In addition to Aleksander, in our neighbourhood, I knew three electricians, two construction workers and one machinist who were doing the same kind of thing. The resources appropriated by each individual in the working classes might be very small, but the sum of such resources when pooled by the members of an extended family play a great part in their survival, depending on their ability to reciprocate them with other resources. Both the quantity of appropriated resources and the extent to which they are exchanged for other resources depends upon the scale of a given extended family's networks and their skills in exploiting these networks for reciprocity. I will deal with networks in the following sections, so let us consider the other key factors which enforced the use of *blat*.

First, the state ceased to fulfil its welfare duties and forced people to rely more than before on their networks, and thus on the illicit use of resources for survival. Second, what locals called 'privatisation of the state' (*privatizatsiia gosudarstva*), which means that each of the institutions of the state has become the 'fiefdom' of those in charge, has provided a new general ground for the use of *blat*. The leading bureaucrats on the one hand use these institutions for the collection of bribes and tributes and on the other reciprocate their resources. This has increased the grip of the bureaucrats on the social and economic life of the population in a more arbitrary way than before. They play a decisive role in selling the state's property, leasing land, issuing business licences, extracting taxes, using buildings and other facilities, giving credit, manipulating customs tariffs, distributing jobs, accessing higher education and giving protection through the control of the mafia's networks.

The privatisation of the state in combination with the prevailing mentality of '*dikii kapitalism*' (wild capitalism) has generated a widespread cynicism among people. They have lost any commitment to other people beyond their own relatives and friends. In such a situation, there are two main means for obtaining resources: through bribery and connection (*sviaz'*). Access to resources is much cheaper through illicit reciprocal exchange. Even if in many cases people have to bribe their friends or relatives in order to obtain resources, the amount of a bribe is much less than in the case in which the recipient is a stranger (*neznakomyi*). Owing to this situation networking has become the main way of obtaining resources in Almaty.

NETWORKING

An equivalent of the English word 'network' does not exist in the local language. The closest word to it is *sviaz'* (connection). Phrases like *cherez sviazi* (through contacts), *s pomoshch'iu, rodstvennikov, droozei, znakomykh* (with the help of relatives, friends, acquaintances) signify the basic strategies of exchange within networks. Networks include complex sets of links contingent upon time and place. But the most important and durable ones are those which link workplaces to kinship and marriage bonds. This 'network of networks' constitutes a framework for the exchange of different types of expropriated resources between people who occupy different niches in different branches of the division of labour.

A workplace is a strategically important social setting for networking for several reasons. First, due to the prevailing nepotism, many of the people who work in a workplace unit are related to each other directly or indirectly prior to starting the work.[37] This makes it much easier for them to establish close relations with each other.

Second, as in the case of the factory where I did part of my fieldwork, each work unit, such as a team (*brigada*) on a section (*sekh*), and the section itself, constitute some kind of strong community. Actually, not only are each of these units called a collective (*kollektiv*) but people have a strong sense of belonging to a collectivity. This is so because, as Humphrey (1983) has argued in another case, in the Soviet era those at the top and bottom of the hierarchy in a work unit were mutually dependent on each other. The bottom was dependent on the top for receiving different privileges and the top was dependent on the bottom's work for fulfilling the planners' demands. Moreover, the leadership of a given collectivity (*kollektiv*) represents and negotiates the interests of its members both horizontally and vertically beyond the work unit. Although the unity between managers and workers has begun to split as a result of privatisation, it has been enforced between the rank and file on the section and team levels. This has become so because in the privatised plants the managers have increased the control to stop the Soviet-type appropriation of resources by ordinary workers.

Third, as the welfare benefits have been cut and the payment of salaries has been delayed for several months, workers' and their families' survival are partly dependent on the appropriation of resources from a workplace. This involves multiple illegal deals between many individuals based on mutual trust.

The negotiation, achievement and maintenance of trust create an intimate milieu in the work unit. This intimacy is furthered by celebrations of each colleague's birthday, or official celebrations like the Eighth of March, shared consumption of drink and food and exchanges of gifts. In many cases, relations are extended outside the workplace. On both the factory shop floor and in the university several of the retired people had maintained contact with their colleagues who were still working. In both places their children had got jobs or educational places through their parents who had worked there or were currently working there.

Marriage and kinship networks are the most important forms of social organisation of reciprocity. However, their weight in this respect varies in relation to ethnicity. While marriage networks are equally important for all ethnic groups, kinship plays a lesser role in Russian networks than those of Kazakhs. This is expressed in two dimensions: differences in kinship obligations; and differences in the numbers of kinship links in a given family network. Kazakhs have much stronger kinship obligations than Russians. This results in Kazakh kinship networks transcending more successfully the distances in kinship relations on the one hand and the geographical distances between relatives on the other. While it is a common practice among the Kazakhs with whom I spoke to receive at home, feed and give accommodation to distant relatives (*dalnie rodstvenniki*) when they visit Almaty, Russians usually even lack contact with such relatives. Moreover, Kazakhs' strong commitment to kinfolk transcends the obstacle of geographical distance for networking. Kazakhs who live in distant areas from each other keep in contact and are engaged in reciprocity. On the other hand, geographical distance is a real problem for Russian kinship networking. Although Russians keep in contact with close relatives (siblings, parents, children) regardless of geographical distance, their reciprocal relations with relatives is affected strongly by geographical distance. The differences in the ways Kazakhs and Russians deal with kinship and geographical distances result in differences in the scale of their networks. Kazakh networks include a considerably greater number of people than those of Russians. The scale of ethnic networks, the significance of which will be considered later, is influenced as well by differences in the size of families owing to the higher birth rate among Kazakhs. A Kazakh person in his/her thirties has considerably more siblings, cousins, uncles and aunts, than a Russian person of the same age. The greater a network, the greater the possibilities of accessing the resources for its members, because its members can occupy a greater number of positions at the different levels of the total division of social labour.

Marriage creates a very strong alliance and commitments between the relatives of the spouses. Through marriage, the families of the couple create new channels for accessing resources and establishing new reciprocal relations between each other. Moreover, as the household is a place of celebrations and sharing of food and drink it is one of the most important places for networking. Due to the importance of marriage for relatives the choice of spouses is controlled, if not arranged, by parents. The control is usually imposed with regard to ethnicity, wealth and influence. Parents and relatives usually urge young people to find a socially suitable spouse within their own ethnicity. But while among the young people, particularly young women, the wealth of the spouse-to-be is very important, ethnicity has less importance for Russians than Kazakhs.

Both sides usually give the following reasons for the preference of an endogamous ethnic marriage: first, ethnic tensions make the communication between families of a couple difficult. Moreover, ethnic tensions may lead to ethnic wars which may cause a family based on a mixed marriage to split, and in order to avoid such a tragedy one has to avoid inter-ethnic marriage. Second, cultural differences, which are related to reciprocity, create difficulties and confusion. It is argued that Russians and Kazakhs have different traditions with regard to the consumption of food, religious ceremonies, relations with relatives, gender relations and relations to elders. Muslims may not eat pork, Russians eat more *borshch*[38] and vegetables, while Kazakhs eat more meat and *beshpermak*.[39] Russians celebrate Easter (*paskha*) while Kazakhs celebrate *korbanat* (feast of the sacrifice). Kazakhs usually depict Russian women as free (*svoboda*), which has a negative connotation. It can mean that the woman in question is sexually 'loose', but generally it means that Russian women are bold, do not obey their husbands and do not respect their husbands' parents and relatives. Russians consider Kazakh culture anti-woman. In relation to generation, while the Kazakhs say that Russians do not respect their elders and do not take care of them, Russians consider generational relations between Kazakhs as patriarchal. In relation to relatives Russians usually say Kazakhs have many guests and the women in a Kazakh family must work very hard feeding the guests and washing the dishes. On the other hand, Kazakhs consider Russians individualistic and greedy.[40]

Although ethnically endogamous marriage is the main pattern of marriage, especially among Kazakhs, it is far from being unproblematic. Against their parents' will, many young people choose to marry outside their own ethnicity. Moreover, while ethnicity is not usually an issue when both partners are of European origin, Tatars are famous for their flexibility with regard to mixed marriages.

The wider networks which result from the articulation of marriage and kinship networks to those based in workplaces, acquire an ethnic character for three reasons: the conceived relation between kinship and ethnicity, the dominance of endogamous ethnic marriage and the ethnic division of labour. In Almaty kinship is usually conceived as a subcategory of ethnicity and relatives in most cases belong to the same ethnic group. As I have already touched upon the role of ethnicity in marriage, let us here consider the ethnic division of labour. In the Soviet era different ethnic groups occupied different economic niches in Kazakhstan. Today this picture has begun to change because Kazakhs are purging others from their own zones and they are moving into niches which were traditionally occupied by other groups. But this has not yet gone so far as to change the previous pattern of the ethnic division of labour. Russians still dominate the middle and lower ranks in industry (the higher ranks have been partly replaced by Kazakhs) and Kazakhs dominate the political apparatus and higher education. For example, in the university where I taught 75 per cent of the staff were Kazakhs and all the higher positions were occupied by them. On the shop floor of the factory where I conducted fieldwork the situation was reversed. Out of 25 people who worked there, two were Uigur, three Kazakhs and the rest Russians. Both the Brigadier and the Master were Russian as well.

The prominence of ethnicity in networking has led to the current ethnic tensions. Kazakhs are usually accused by non-Kazakhs, including Muslims like Uigurs, Tatars, and Turks, of discriminating against others. The large scale of the Kazakhs' networks in combination with the Kazakhification of the state apparatus, given the determinant role of bureaucrats in the manipulation of resources, combined with the prevailing corruption, has given rise to a phenomenon which is called 'tribalism' by the local intelligentsia (Masanov, 1996a). Tribalism denotes the exclusion of non-Kazakhs from strategic resources, on the one hand, and the fierce contest between different Kazakh networks for such resources on the other. It is argued that the rival networks of the Kazakh elite compete for resources according to the old tribal alliances, called *Zhuz* (Masanov, 1996a: pp. 47–50, 55–9). The Kazakhification of the state which was carried out by purging non-Kazakhs during *perestroika* and after independence and the privatisation of the state, are the main factors which bolster 'tribalism'. But the monopolisation of strategic resources by Kazakh networks is a post-Soviet phenomenon. In addition to this, there are other aspects of social change which have negatively affected networking in general.

THE NEGATIVE EFFECTS OF CHANGE ON NETWORKS

The most important factors which have influenced the networks in this way, from the local point of view, are the following: wealth differentiation, the growth of the capitalist mentality, the growth of poverty, migration, the breakdown of trust and the problem of secrecy.

For students from urban origins, the most important criterion for choosing friends was class. After class, gender was important and ethnicity had no importance. They told me that one cannot mix with those who are richer or poorer than oneself, because those who come from families with different levels of wealth dress differently and spend different amounts of money. A teacher who told me that in the Soviet era they never chose their friends according to the criterion of class, but goodness (*dobrota*), complained that today their children are forced to do so.

> There are those who can afford to buy American jeans for their children, give them good pocket money and buy chocolate for them and those who can afford none of these. Children make remarks about this. Those who enjoy these privileges tell the poorer children, my parents are rich (*bogatye*) and yours are not. My own children hear these kinds of words every day.

It is not only among school children and university students that class matters, it has even influenced relationships between friends and relatives. As communication between families, then and now, is organised around the kitchen table and guests must be served impressively with food and drink, those who have become relegated to the lower classes cannot afford to offer food and drink at the required level or at the same level as those who have benefited from the current situation. Even if people with unequal access to wealth still keep their relations, the distances between them have widened and reciprocal exchanges, with the exception of those between close relatives, have practically ceased to occur. It must be underlined that from the local point of view it is not the unequal access to wealth in itself which has alienated people from each other but the new capitalistic greediness (*zhadnost'*) which accompanies it. People frequently complained that in the past (*ran'she*), people were generous (*shchedrye*) and kind (*dobrye*) but now they have become greedy (*zhadnye*) and evil (*zlye*).

What locals conceive of as greediness signifies a profound yet incomplete process of transformation in the Soviet 'habitus'. As Humphrey (1983) argued for the *Buryats*, such habitus was oriented towards shared consumption rather than accumulation of wealth. Although wealth was distributed unequally in Kazakhstan as well, the wealthier people, particularly those among Kazakhs, channelled the surplus of their wealth into redistribution through collective consumption in private parties and public ceremonies. But today because of investment opportunities on the one hand and the creation of new needs as a result of the emergence of a consumerist culture and availability of a wide range of new goods on the other, people tend either to transform wealth into capital or to use it to satisfy the new needs of the household rather than spending it on relatives and friends.

Although the significance of this new mentality in local experiences acquires a dramatic scale, because it represents a radical break with the past, it is still far from the prevalent individualistic materialist mentality in the West. It should be considered as a transitory phase between the old Soviet mentality and this materialistic mentality in the West. People still help their relatives on a scale which is unimaginable in the West. A Kazakh businessman had paid $5,000 to provide a place in a university for a distant relative. A Russian man who works as a doctor in Germany had provided for a cousin to study in Australia. In addition to this, the greed of the rich man in Almaty should not be confused with that of the Weberian ascetic capitalist. As the former acquires his wealth through parasitic ways, he is inclined towards a luxurious life-style. He spends a lot of money on himself, his family and his mistresses. If he has become greedy in the eyes of his neighbours, friends and relatives, it is because he has distanced himself from those friends and relatives who have not succeeded in catching up with him; and he does not respond to their expectations according to the perceived standards of generosity.

In the neighbourhood where I lived two families who were accused of being greedy by neighbours were both involved in middle range business. In both cases both husband and wife worked in the business. In the first case the wife was an Uzbek and the husband a Jew, and in the second case the wife was a Kazakh and the husband a Korean. When I asked both families whether they helped relatives, friends and neighbours, both told me that they helped close relatives (including parents and siblings) but they cannot afford to help neighbours, friends or distant relatives. Both wives complained that they must spend a lot of money on their own family. The Uzbek woman proudly showed to me the Italian furniture which she had bought for $19,000. She said: 'We have saved enough money for building our own house but we are afraid of this Kazakh racketeer state (*reket gosudarctva*). If you have a good house they may expropriate it from you at any time.' In addition she had a housemaid and a private teacher who taught English to her daughter for $10 per hour. The interior of the second family's apartment was less impressive but they had bought the neighbouring apartment and had extended their apartment from three to six rooms. In addition to this they send their daughter each summer to Cambridge.

It is not only the indifference of the wealthier towards the poor which has undermined networks; the impoverishment of the majority of people has also tended to undermine networks. For the majority of people net survival has become the main issue of life, and so they lack any surplus of resources for either inviting relatives and friends home or for helping those who are needy. Besides social stratification and poverty, the dramatic increase of physical distances between people as a result of ethnically based migration has had a negative influence on networking. The massive emigration of non-Kazakhs (500,000 persons per year) has led to people losing parts of their valuable contacts. Although some migrants from their new locations in Germany, Ukraine, Russia or Israel may send letters and money to their old friends and relatives or even invite them to their new homelands, they are not able to help them in the same way as they did when they were in Almaty. Even if this adds a transnational dimension to networks, on a practical level it has led to the weakening of networks. The negative effects of migration on networks are distributed unevenly with regard to age and ethnicity. Usually, old people of Slavic origin suffer from them most seriously because many of those middle-aged Russians and Ukrainians who leave Kazakhstan cannot afford to take their old parents with them and many Russians who are married to Germans and Jews migrate with their spouses to Germany or Israel, but because of emigration rules cannot take their parents with them.

Another factor which has affected networking negatively is the prevailing milieu of mistrust between people which has resulted from the general social chaos and its concomitant immorality. The dismantling of the welfare state and resultant poverty, alcoholism, break up of families and prostitution at the one extreme, and the prevailing mentality of the '*dikii kapitalism*', which is a combination of cynical individualism and propensity towards organised criminality at the other, are the main features of this chaos. The destruction of the welfare state is widely interpreted as the destruction of the larger society as a moral community, and this understanding has led to the individual ceasing to have any social commitment beyond his or her own networks. The result is that any person beyond someone's networks is not only excluded from the moral community, but is seen as a potential threat, on the one hand, and could be subjected to deception, chicanery, theft, blackmailing and even physical violence, on the other. The illicit nature of a considerable number of transactions within networks, with regard to the arbitrariness of state officials, makes trust an essential precondition for networking. If an official finds out about an illicit deal he must be bribed to keep quiet, or you are really in trouble. Owing to this people keep their deals secret from unrelated persons, because the latter may either blackmail them or report them to the officials. A Russian woman who herself had found her job through a relative, while refusing to tell me who had helped her, said: 'Here we know that everybody has got his or her job through contacts, but we do not reveal to each other who has helped us. You do not sit on a branch and saw it at the same time.'

This general atmosphere of fear and suspicion of strangers makes the establishing of new relations much more difficult than before. In addition to this, the social chaos, unemployment, poverty, divorce, addiction to alcohol and drugs undermine people's commitment to each other. Just as many former friends and neighbours, under the new pressure of change, have become 'estranged' from each other, so those who still keep their relations fear the risk of the same fate as well. This uncertainty and ambiguity of relations within networks, under conditions where relations are an absolute precondition for survival, create an existential paradox which is partly resolved through a moral rhetoric. A striking aspect of daily talk in Almaty was an overemphasised rhetoric of morality. Words like *verny* (faithful, loyal), *vernost'* (faithfulness), *doverie* (trust), *doveriat'* (to trust), *Poriadochnyi* (honest, decent, respectable), *ne poriadochnyi* (dishonourable), *obiazatel'stvo* (obligation), *reputatsiia* (reputation), *khitryi* (cunning), *prostoi* (uncomplicated) were frequently used to describe the assumed 'national personality' (*natsional'nyi kharakter*) of different ethnic groups or the attributes of a particular person. The main moral virtues which people highlight are honesty, obligation, trust, a good reputation and the ability to keep things confidential. One of the most usual words of praise with which people give credit to their friends and kin is *Poriadochnyi chelovek* (an honest, decent, respectable person). On the other hand the word *ne poriadochnyi chelovek* (dishonourable) is used to discredit a person. In toast-giving and on other occasions people praise in formal ways honesty (*poriadochnost'*), devotion (*predannost'*), loyalty (*vernost'*) and highlight the importance of having a good reputation (*reputatsiia*). Reputation as a part of 'symbolic capital' is gendered. From a woman's point of view a trustworthy man, among other things, should not be an *alkash* (alcoholic) and *babnik* (a womaniser). And from both men's and women's point of view a trustworthy woman should not be a *suka* (literally bitch, but used for stigmatising any woman with allegedly loose sexual behaviour).[41]

CONCLUSIONS

Reciprocal exchange through networks constitutes one of the main strategies of survival in post-independent Almaty. It consists of two types: reproductive and strategic. While the former contributes to the maintenance of social bonds between people, the latter is directly involved in survival. An important aspect of strategic exchange is that it is associated with the illicit use of resources.

The main pattern of social bonds which frame both types of exchange are friendship, acquaintance, kinship and marriage. The networks of each extended family's members are shaped around these bonds which acquire an ethnic character due to the close connections between marriage, kinship and the division of labour and ethnicity. This is not to claim that such networks do not include very important non-ethnic links, but that ethnic links overwhelm the former.

This, in combination with the large size of Kazakh networks and their dominance in the state apparatus, which still controls the main resources, gives rise to ethnic tensions. While Russians usually associate the current economic problems with the alleged corruption, nepotism and misman-agement of Kazakhs, the latter blame the former for their alleged colonial past. While this has given some currency to ethnicity, it has not yet led to other degrees of ethnic coherence or ethnic solidarity either among Russians or Kazakhs.

The main moral community for an individual is the family and the family's networks. Anybody outside the circles of relatives and friends, regardless of ethnicity, is feared, suspected and can be cheated and violated. Due to the vital importance of networks for survival, the individual is defined primarily by a role in the networks, rather than to any sort of 'imagined communities', including ethnic ones. Obligations, viewed as strategies of reciprocity, to partners within networks override all other types of loyalties.

In spite of their importance for survival, networks are in danger of dis-integrating under the pressures inflicted on them from the outside world. In order to counter such dangers people resort to a rhetoric of morality.

But good moral conduct is expected to be applied only in relation to friends and relatives, not to other fellow citizens in general. This type of morality, in combination with the fact that people from lower down the social scale feel alienated from the elite, due to the abolition of the welfare state and the arbitrariness and corruption of state officials, makes the 'imagining' of a nation-state or people-state from below problematic. The notion of a society at large does not exist for individuals unless as a crowd of strangers each of whom constitute a potential threat. It is a dark threat-ening wilderness of violence and crime from which the individual takes refuge in networks. This is an expression of what the dispossessed call chaos. In such a situation the concept of a civic society which consists of sovereign individuals who are related to each other through mutual rights and duties is alien to the networking habitus. Everybody knows the secret name is *sviaz'* (contact). Tragically and paradoxically networking as a response to the chaos perpetuates it.

5   WOMEN AND SEXUALISED STRATEGIES: VIOLENCE AND STIGMA

This chapter focuses on two inter-linked issues: the political economy of sex in Almaty from the point of view of the women involved in it, and the moral issues which have emerged among the wider population as a response to the new sex economy. As indicated in the first chapter, the process of wealth differentiation in post-Soviet Kazakhstan has been dominated by networks of small groups of men. Under such conditions, a considerable section of young and attractive women, who lack wealthy and influential relatives to provide economic security for themselves and their poor families, have no other choice than sexualised strategies. The most important of these are: finding a good job by responding to employers' sexual demands; finding a wealthy husband; finding a 'sponsor', a lover who will support her financially; and sex work.

In addition to the prevailing poverty, the desires created in young women by the consumerist culture are pivotal in tempting them to practice sexualised strategies. The availability of restaurants, bars, discos and fashionable clothes in Almaty creates a strong desire among the young people for the consumption of expensive goods and services. Such desires can be understood in the light of this kind of consumption becoming a part of youth culture and identity. For many young women without rich parents, the only way to access the pleasures offered by the 'free' market is to trade their own bodies. Although sexual strategies are seen by women who practice them as survival strategies the wider population consider them to be a significant element of chaos. Those who can afford to buy sexual services offered by such women are well-off men, both locals and foreigners. Women try to find such men either on the streets, through trying to get a lift in an expensive car or by attending places rich men usually visit, such as business centres, restaurants, night clubs and hotel lobbies.

FINDING A JOB

As mentioned in chapter 4, most jobs are distributed through connections. According to local people, many young and beautiful women without proper connections are forced or enticed to trade their sexuality for access to jobs with higher salaries than those paid by the state. These jobs are concentrated in the private sector. The expansion of commerce and entertainment have created new types of job for women as dancers, strippers, waitresses, sellers in private shops, secretaries and interpreters. However, people say, these jobs are distributed selectively, most of them are given only to young and beautiful women. According to widely shared local opinion, such women reciprocate sexual services to their employers for getting the jobs. This opinion is part of the local hegemonic patriarchal ideology for keeping women in their 'traditional roles', but the sexual exploitation experienced by women themselves is real. The following example illustrates women's worries and difficulties in this respect.

My landlord, a working class Russian family, had debts to relatives from borrowing money to pay compensation to the man with whom they had exchanged another apartment for the one I lived in. Their 21-year-old daughter and her husband lived with them. She was very fluent in English and taught it to some of the children of the neighbourhood and transcribed English translations of very complicated juridical texts, translated from Russian by a local Jew, very cheaply. I told her she could find a job as translator in a foreign company or translate for businessmen in exhibitions for a higher salary. She answered, 'my mother and husband will not allow me to do such a job, because women who work for businessmen must sleep with them.'

Zhana, a young unmarried Kazakh woman and friend of mine, displayed similar attitudes on another occasion. As the winter was getting colder I asked her to help me buy an electrical heater. She took me to Sum, the biggest supermarket in Almaty. The building is a large four-storey house. The interior of each storey is divided into several parts, separated by fences, with a store in each part. All types of goods, like carpets from Turkey, fashionable clothes from Calvin Klein, perfume from Christian Dior and TV sets from Japan are sold in these stores. While we were wandering in the supermarket I commented, 'so many beautiful women!'. 'Of course they are beautiful,' Zhana said, 'they are handpicked, they are mistresses (*liubovnitsy*).' Then she explained that the owners of the shops, who are men, usually give jobs to young beautiful women for sexual favours. Zhana's opinion was shared widely by the people in the neighbourhood and other places.

Three advertisements in *Karavan* (23 August 1996) under the rubric 'we are looking for work' (*ishchem rabotu*) illustrate people's general understanding:

- Woman (*zhenshchina*), 36 years old – work. Sex is not offered (*intim ne predlagat'*). Tel:..

- An intelligent woman (*intelligentaia zhenshchina*), high paid job (housekeeper, interpreter, and others). Sex is not offered (*intim ne predlagat*). Tel:..
- A girl (*devushka*) – work. Sex excluded (*intim iskliuchen*). Tel:..

The second advertisement is targeted at foreigners who usually employ housekeepers and interpreters. The interesting element in this advertisement is that the advertiser demands a high salary for cleaning.

Many young women had direct experience of situations in which men had tried to entice them into a sexual relationship by offering them jobs. The reader might remember young Natasha from chapter 4, who complained about sexual harassment imposed on her by men. Here is a story in her own words:

> When I was selling jewellery on the street, a Kazakh man approached me, and asked me: 'Do you need work?' I asked what kind of work? He answered, to sell in a cafe, located in some college. He gave me the address, I met him in this cafe and when we talked, he suggested I should become his lover (*liubovnitsa*). I did not accept this and rejected the job, but we exchanged phone numbers. After a while, he called me and told me that I could sell handbags, shampoo, and jackets for him and take 5 per cent for myself. I accepted this but went there with a Kazakh girl friend. After some days he called and asked whether I had sold anything. Then he asked me what about your friend, I want her to be my lover. I said no. He said why do you speak for her. I said because I know her. I sold one jacket but could not sell any of the handbags, so I returned his handbags. After a while he called and told me that he is going to establish a business in another city and asked me whether I wanted to follow him, I rejected him again.

A young Kazakh woman who taught English at university had a similar story to tell. She complained that the dean sent her own people to Europe to Tacis programmes,[42] and that she has applied twice but failed to receive the grant, although she was much more qualified than those who were sent there. Then she expressed her desire to visit Europe. I advised her to work for some international companies, suggesting that they might send her to Europe. She answered:

> They will not give you a job unless you sleep with them. Once I applied for a job in KLM. The Pakistani man who interviewed me told me you will get the job if you will be a good girl. I asked him what do you mean that I will be a good girl? He answered, behave in a way which pleases me. As the secretary in his room was laughing at me, I lost my patience,

took a piece of paper, and wrote 'sex' and handed it to him. When he read the word, he nodded positively. Then I got angry, told him, sorry, I can't be that good, find somebody else, and left the room.

In spite of the risks of sexual exploitation and stigma, many young women seek these jobs because in these sectors women usually earn two to four times more than in traditional occupations. For example, let me compare the salaries of Mira and her sister Gula who lived in my neighbourhood.

Their father is an Uigur and their mother is Russian. They divorced long ago and the children stayed with their mother. Mira is 28, has a son and is divorced from a Russian man. Gula is 21 and is married to a Russian. The older sister works as a waitress in a cafe which is a part of greater complex which includes a restaurant, bar and casino, and is owned by a local Tatar and a local Jew, who had become an Israeli citizen after *perestroika*. The second sister works in a bakery established recently by a Turk from Turkey. The first sister works 24 hours and has 24 hours off, the second works from 8am to 8pm seven days a week. Mira earns $200 a month, and Gula 3,000 tenge ($50). Mira got her job through her lover, a young Kazakh business-man who is a Mafioso and knows the owners of the complex. I asked Gula: 'Why don't you try to work in a cafe as well?' She answered: 'My husband will never let me do it. He is very jealous.'

Unlike the international business club, the male clients of the complex are locals or from other parts of the former Soviet union. Mira tells me that they are Mafioso and businessmen. Mira's attitudes towards having obtained the job through the Kazakh man are ambivalent. On the one hand, she thinks her salary is fine, and the manager and other customers respect her because of him. 'If somebody bothers me,' while pointing to the three young Kazakh men who work as guards, 'they will fix him. They are his acquaintances.' On the other hand she is in trouble because she does not like him any more but is afraid to leave him.

In the beginning I loved him, but once I discovered he was married and had a child, I felt cheated and lost my love for him. One day he brought his wife and son to the cafe-house and introduced them to me. I became friends with his wife, but can't tell her the truth. When he wants to spend a whole night with me, he tells her that he is going to do some business. As he realised that I do not like him any more, he told me that he loved me and if I disappear, he will burn our apartment and kill my sister and mother. He is a racketeer (*reket*); he will do that.

The notion of a mistress is a stigma in Almaty. A mistress is seen as an immoral and unworthy woman. However, Mira's mother, her sister and women friends know about the relationship and think it is all right. Mira herself says that she would not mind other people's judgments if she loved him. But she does not not like him any more. Yet it seemed to me that she tried morally to justify her own position, because once she commented on other young women who visited the complex, saying with a tone of disgust in her voice: 'a married woman will never come here, these girls are either prostitutes or mistresses (*liubovnitsy*).' The fact that she had accepted the position of a mistress was a matter of expediency rather than choice. In a way Mira felt hostage to her lover both because of his potential violence and her job.

Women who receive such jobs are very insecure, the employer may replace them with new women or simply become erotically fed up with them.

For example, Mira says, 'I have no future, the boss (*nachal'nik*) can sack me any time he wants, and if I get sick, nobody will take care of me and my son. I have no insurance (*strakhovka*).' I asked her whether she was a member of a union. She answered that capitalists (her word) do not like unions, they existed only in the Soviet era but do not exist any more.[43]

Although women who work in the bars, restaurants and casinos earn considerably more than those who work in most other sectors, their jobs are dangerous because a considerable number of the visitors to such places are Mafioso and hooligans. Several times I witnessed 'hooligans' eating in the cafe and trying to run away without paying, and Mira had to stop them. As they knew there were Kazakh guards they paid, but Mira felt insecure. She said they could hit her if they encountered her by chance alone somewhere. Viktoria who works as a dealer in the Casino Plaza, describes the unpleasant conditions of her job:

I am a dealer, I am not allowed to speak with clients, I can't speak a word. When you lose your money, you can say everything, ask your friend, you go mad. Our Casino is a new one; we have been working since September. In the beginning each month we had two or three fights between clients, then our boss asked the local police to protect us. When a client loses his money, he wants to kill you. You can be replaced by somebody else, but until this happens you must stand 20 minutes, and listen to every thing about your relatives, your family... Sometimes it is limited to insulting... In our casinos people shoot dealers...once they shot at a girl in another casino.

While the director of this casino is an Iranian man who has become a Turkish citizen, and all inspectors are young Turkish men, the dealers are young local women. The clients are men, both foreigners and locals. Among the foreigners German-speaking people predominate and among the locals, Kazakhs. Women who come to the casino, according to Viktoria, are prostitutes or mistresses accompanying men.

Zhana, who stigmatised women who were working in the Sum, and her friends worked for foreign businessmen in exhibitions (*vystovki*) as translators. The girls find out about the date an exhibition starts through media or friends. Then they try to be the first to attend the exhibition on the first day. When the gates are opened tens of girls rush towards businessmen in their exhibition shops. In each shop usually two or three businessmen do three-minute interviews with girls and choose those they find suitable. Zhana said:

> They choose girls, both according to their language skills and beauty, but beauty is obviously more important. I am not beautiful but I have learned to be charming. When you approach them you have got five minutes to entice one of the businessmen in the shop to fall in love with you.

Her friend Valentina, a tall beautiful Ukrainian, says that she uses her female attraction as a strategy for getting the job. She flirts with them and gets the job, but in the end if she likes someone she sleeps with him, otherwise she rejects him. While Valentina seems to master the situation with confidence, Zhana feels more vulnerable.

> I hate businessmen, they always try to buy me. They offer me, Valentina and Malena money in order to sleep with them. But so far we have rejected them. They usually start at $100, then they increase it to $200, $300. Once a Russian businessman offered me $500. But I refused him, he was so ugly and fat if I had slept with him I would have died. We say to each other how stupid we are, because if we had slept with them each of us would have had thousands of dollars by now.

Zhana and her friends have come into contact with foreigners through working as interpreters in exhibitions or visiting the international business club. Once when Zhana was working for two businessmen from Cyprus, I visited her twice during her work. At the university she had told me that she had charmed two businessmen. In the evening one of them, nearly 55 years old, invited her to dinner. I became upset, and as she realised my reaction she became slightly angry and told me: 'You have no right to be angry with me. It is my body, not yours, I can do with it what I want.' I agreed with her. Later she told me the following story:

> We dined in Marco Polo. When we ate he was always trying to touch me. Each time he wanted to tell me something he put his finger on my arm, my hands or somewhere else on my body. Each time he did this my

body reacted in a very bad way. Finally I moved away from him to such a distance that he was not able to reach me any more with his dirty hands.

At the end of her work, after three days, she had become really exhausted. She told me:

> Oh God! You cannot imagine how much energy I must spend in protecting myself. ... I and my friends discussed the possibility of sleeping for money for many months, finally we decided not to do this. ... Many times, the idea has tempted me. Yesterday I saw a leather skirt which costs $100, I loved it, but I do not have the money to buy it, if I sleep with somebody I can get the money and buy the skirt... I have no money to go to good places on my own. I get them to bring me to Marco Polo or the Italian restaurant, but finally I avoid them and quit.

While girls have room for manoeuvre with foreign men and can reject them, they have not the same power *vis-à-vis* the local men. They cannot play the same game with them. Once they are trapped in such a situation with a local businessman they have no choice but to respond positively to their sexual demands; otherwise they will be physically violated or raped for cheating the man. A young Kazakh female teacher told me: 'if our men give a you a box of chocolates they ask you to sleep with them. If you avoid it, they tell you I have bought this and that for you and you must sleep with me.'

FINDING A SPONSOR

Another way in which young women, mainly divorced ones, try to get access to material welfare is to find a sponsor. I actually encountered the phenomenon in the first month of my stay in Almaty. I mixed closely with a group of illegal street traders, a young single mother of Chechen, Kazakh and Russian mixture, a married couple (the husband Kazakh and the wife Uigur) and another unmarried couple who had recently begun an affair (the man a local Korean and the woman a Kazakh from Karagandy). As they were amused by my 'profession' (ethnographer) and were curious to hear about Europe, we met almost every evening and drank cheap beer or vodka. As Nina, the single mother, and I were the only single people in the group, an attraction developed between us which the married couple noticed. One day Talgar, the Kazakh man, asked me: 'Joma, do you want to be a sponsor of a woman?' 'What does it mean?' I asked. 'That you support her both financially and morally,' he answered. I found myself in a very embarrassing situation, partly because I usually do not like a third person to mediate in my relationship with a woman, and partly because I interpreted the word as protector. As I found this very insulting for both me and the woman, I explained to him in a very friendly way that I did not like the idea, and that I thought that a woman should be her own sponsor. After this Nina and I both found ourselves in an embarrassing situation, because they had interpreted my answer as a rejection, while I really liked her. I just denounced the sponsorship. Fortunately, another event came to our aid. My friend called me from Austria to say that I should return to sort out a problem which had emerged with my grant. When, after two weeks, I returned from Austria we both forgot about it. And I forgot the concept of sponsor for several months until it came up in the discussions I had with my female students. Through these discussions I discovered that sponsorship was a well-established institution in Almaty and that almost everybody between the ages of 15 and 50 of both sexes and of all ethnicities knew about it.

Sponsorship is a form of widely practised reciprocity between a man (the sponsor) and a woman in which sex is exchanged with money and other things. A young Tatar woman who was a university student, defined a sponsor as a man who provides materially for a woman (*muzhchina kotoryi obespechivaet zhenshchinu material'no*). To become a sponsor is the privilege of men who have benefited economically from the post-Soviet social change. This is expressed clearly from the following definition of a sponsor provided by Olga, 22 years old, half Russian/half Kazakh and a student of mine: 'He is a rich or a rich enough man who provides money, fashionable clothes and other presents for a woman and sleeps with her.'

A female colleague of mine told me this kind of reciprocity was practised even in the Soviet era to a limited extent. However, its wide practice, according to Olga, mentioned above, is undoubtedly a post-Soviet phenomenon. She said:

Living in the Soviet Union we hadn't such words... It is a new word. I will explain to you how the word appeared. When we began to have shows, big parties, and musical events it was necessary to find somebody to finance such events. These kind of people are called *metsenat,* it is just the same as sponsor. After that the girls started to call their lovers sponsors because of the money, because of the financial side.

While everybody knows about sponsorship, moral attitudes change according to generations among the women. Women over 40 are critical of young women who find sponsors and will not let their own daughters become *liubovnitsy.* In most cases they did not consider them to be proper women. The young women approve of it. Viktoria, the casino dealer, sees it as one of the strategies by which young women can have a share of the wealth collected by the men. Olga linked it to freedom:

A sponsor is a man who visits a woman two or three times a week, he gives just enough money to go and buy something fashionable and beautiful. Sometimes, if he is rich enough he gives gifts like a car or gold things like a gold ring. A husband is a man you see every day and sometimes he bothers you, or he begins to make you nervous... I have a lot of girl friends and neighbours who are divorced from their husbands. They don't want to marry, they want to have sponsors. Unmarried women prefer the sponsors to husbands as well. Women want the freedom but at the same time they want to have the money. You have no obligations, he is not your husband. You may get acquainted with another person whom you really love. You get the money from the sponsor and have the second man for your soul.

Another young woman, a Kazakh student, who told me boldly in front of her two female friends that she had five sponsors (actually her friends knew some of them) said that we girls call them among ourselves *koshelek* (wallet). She said that she had a boyfriend whom she really loved. Then she explained to me: 'Girls usually meet several men but one is for the heart and the rest for the money (*odin dlia dushchi octal' nye dlia deneg*).'

Olga and her friends speak openly about their sponsors to each other. 'To have a sponsor is not a secret. We usually discuss among friends who are married. Who are divorced. Who has a sponsor. What sum of money he gives her, and what does she buy for the money.' She added:

Women find sponsors in nightclubs, business centres and on the streets. It is very simple if you are on the street and see a man driving a very expensive car. You know that he is a businessman, that he is rich. You stop the car, pretending that you need a taxi. If he sees a beautiful woman he will never object to stopping the car and getting acquainted. Doesn't matter whether he has a wife, because he has the possibility to support another woman.

Although many women prefer sponsors to husbands, in addition to the risks involved in finding a sponsor, the instability of the relationship and the alienation involved in it make sponsorship problematic. This is expressed in Olga's nostalgia for types of relationships which supposedly existed in the Soviet era:

In Soviet times if you met a man you could prolong your relationship, your spiritual relationship, not a sexual one. You could meet for a month or two. But in these days if you meet a man, in the first encounter he asks you to go to bed with him. No one is looking for a soul mate, they just want sex. But in the Soviet time men wanted to find soul mates through getting acquainted with women. Now the times have changed.

I talked with tens of young women who had sponsors. I usually met them in a cafe in the Circus or in the cafe, mentioned above, where Mira worked.[44] Although most of them spoke comfortably about sponsorship (*sponsorstvo*) and their own sponsors they, like the young Kazakh girl above, clearly distinguished between a relationship based on feelings and sponsorship. The latter was considered a relationship based on money, but it was considered to be different from prostitution, because of the length of the relationship and the mutual friendship. Although many of them liked their sponsors, their prime motives for choosing them were material rather than emotional. They described sponsorship as alienating and dehumanising but necessary for survival. Most of them said that it was a common practice for a woman who had sponsors to have a true lover besides. They said that women gave their bodies to sponsors but they kept their hearts and souls for their lovers.

This understanding of personhood which divided a person between body on the one hand and soul and heart on the other was a way by which women tried to preserve a degree of self-esteem. The dispossessed usually thought that the growth of commodity relations was polluting their authentic Soviet humanistic values. People were particularly critical of the monetisation of sexual relationships. Women who had sponsors subscribed to such ideas but through dichotomising between body on the one hand and soul and heart on the other, tried to resist the alienation which the comodification of their bodies inflicted on them. They claimed that the essence of their personhood, soul and heart, was not for sale, it was exchanged only for love. The surface of the person, the body, could be transformed into a commodity without this being able to colonise the heart. Such dualism reflects the fact that most young women, while attracted to the consumerist culture and new sexual habits, find them enormously exploitative. Olga's nostalgia for the Soviet era's supposedly authentic relation between men and women illustrates this.

From the women's point of view a major problem with sponsorship is that although it is not considered to be prostitution it evokes disrespect and stigma. It is not a relationship which could be integrated into family relationships. Moreover it is unstable. So the ideal situation for a woman is to find a prosperous husband. And the young women are actively seeking such a husband. Indeed, according to all women I spoke with, a woman's only bait for catching a husband is her beauty and her feminine erotic skills.

FINDING A HUSBAND

I had discussions with three groups of my students on marriage, the first, third, and fourth year students.[45] The age of the participants varied between

17 and 22. While all these groups consisted of both sexes, the girls took the lead in discussions. They had much clearer ideas about marriage and the kind of spouses they wished to have than the boys did. One of the first year girls, half-Tatar and half-Russian, said in the group that they usually considered the boys of their own age as immature and communicated with those who were older than them. A half-Russian and half-gypsy 'boy' commented on her statement: 'They want oldies (*stariki*) because they have got money.' His statement created an agitated situation. Girls and boys argued loudly and in a disorderly way with each other, rejecting or supporting his statement. But when we returned to discuss the subject in an orderly manner all the girls admitted that money would be a main factor in their choice of a spouse. I will return to this later.

The girls' higher consciousness on this matter stemmed from the two following factors. First, all of them, with the exception of a girl with a Ukrainian father who had grown up with her single Uzbek mother, considered marriage and mothering the main goals of their lives. Second, they were at the age of marriage and were actively seeking husbands.

In all these discussion groups young girls said that they were actively looking for husbands, and that marriage was an economic matter in the first instance rather than a matter of love.

'To marry', one of my female students said, and the rest of them agreed with her, 'is the main career of a woman's life.' To be a good mother and a good wife is the most important status which a woman may acquire in her life. This is illustrated when women are addressed by a toast giver in a celebration. As mentioned in chapter 4, a woman is endorsed first for her domestic achievements in relation to her children and husband, rather than for her social and academic ones. Besides its cultural importance, marriage has acquired an important new economic role in post-Soviet Kazakhstan, owing to the gendered aspect of wealth differentiation. For many young women the access to wealth or well-being is provided through marriage with wealthy men. The age of marriage is between 17 and 22. When a girl reaches the age of 22 she is expected to have already found a suitable husband for herself. Otherwise she will be reminded by her mother to find a husband, be pressured by her friends' jokes and the gossip of neighbours. 'If she reaches the age of 25', said Natasha (from chapter 4), 'and is still unmarried, then neighbours begin to give her the nickname *staraia deva* (the old maid).' One of the most important events for a mother is to marry off her daughters (Natasha's example in chapter 6). Through marriage a girl (*devushka*) is transformed into a woman through the consummation of marriage and losing her virginity. People distinguish between a female child (*devochka*), virgin woman (maid) (*devushka*) and woman (*Zhenshchina*).

The dream prince for most young women is a man who has a good income and is physically strong. A poor man is considered by young girls to be morally weak. He obviously lacks the manly will, skills and determination necessary for earning money. A 'cowardly man' (*trus*), a man who lacks the courage and the skills to use physical violence to defend himself or his woman, is not desirable either. Usually, according to girls, men who have money are physically strong as well. They are Mafiosos themselves or have access to the mafia. The importance of a man's physical strength is partly a Soviet cultural inheritance. As a militarised society it highlighted the physical strength of men. They have a Day of Men (*muzhskoi den'*), 23 February, when women congratulate men. This day is also the Day of the Soviet army. In addition to this cultural-historical factor, the surge of violence against women in the post-Soviet era has forced women to seek protection from 'strong men'.

However, women have no taste for hooligans. The ideal type was called gentleman (*dzhentl'men*). The attributes of such a gentleman were described by many young women as follows: a man who has enough money, dresses elegantly and drives an expensive car; he takes his lover or wife to the place she works or studies and takes her back by car; he takes the hand of the lady to help her into or out of the car; helps her to put on her coat; defends her against aggressors; buys her flowers and expensive presents (*podarki*); invites her to restaurants and buys her fashionable clothes.

Below I describe the ways young women try to find such gentlemen, through the reconstruction of my talks with Gulmira, a student and friend of mine, a young Kazakh woman. What she told me had actually been said earlier and was said later by many other women as well and concurs with my own observations. (Although what follows is not a direct speech I have kept her as the narrator.)

Girls try to find a rich husband in bars, restaurants, parties and on streets. On the streets their main strategy is to stop expensive cars. But to stop an expensive car or attend an expensive nightclub is a risky business, because those who drive such cars or attend such places are part of M organisation.[46] Girls are not against having Mafioso either as their husbands or sponsors. However, they distinguish between two types of Mafioso: *Eristokratnye Mafioso* (aristocratic Mafioso) and *vulgarnye Mafioso* (vulgar Mafioso). An aristocratic Mafioso is of urban origin, has a good education, does not display violent behaviour in public places, and is involved in criminal activities in a rational, civilised (*tsivilizovannyi*) and sophisticated way. In a public place, when approaching a woman he behaves like a gentleman. They are mainly urban Kazakhs with some Russians among them.

Vulgar Mafioso consist of two groups: Kazakhs of rural origin and urban Caucasians. The first group are involved in sport, cut their hair very short around the neck and high in front and at the top, and wear jeans and gym shoes. They move in groups and go to bars, restaurants and discos. They have an organisation and force businessmen to pay them money, otherwise they burn their shops. In any market there are these kind of people. They have contacts with high authorities.

Caucasians dress like aristocratic Mafioso but their actual behaviour is vulgar. While the girls try to avoid the second type they desire the first type and have husbands and sponsors among them. But to avoid the second type of Mafioso is not an easy task, because if a girl, or a group of girls, attend a place without male company the Mafiosos think they are looking for men. Thus, usually, the second group of Mafioso approach girls, sit at their tables asking them for a dance and try to buy them drinks. When a girl is approached by a racketeer (*reketer*) she is already in great danger, because they move in groups and most of the groups know each other. But even if they do not know each other there is an unwritten law (*ne pisannyi zakon*) between men that they should never intervene on behalf of a woman. Women are plainly not worth a quarrel between men.

Girls tackle such situations in different ways. The most important rule is to keep quiet, and to avoid dancing. But you have to do this in a way which is not offensive; you have to play shy (*stesnitel' nyi*). If a girl starts to speak or smile, or accepts their offer of food, drink and dance, then she must follow them. Otherwise she will be beaten or taken away by force. Even if she will not speak with them, they may take her away anyway. It is very important to behave in the club like a modest girl (*skromnaia devushka*) not as a vulgar one (*vulgarnaia devushka*). The former keeps quiet, does not look around, is not dressed provocatively, does not smoke or drink alcoholic drinks, does not laugh loudly. The latter does all of these. If you behave like a vulgar girl you send signals to the Mafioso that you are available.

Another way to avoid a racketeer is to play stupid. Men usually think that women are stupid, and you can use this against them by pretending that you do not understand what they want from you. If the Mafioso are persistent a girl may accept their offers of a dance, but then try to run away, by saying she is going to the toilet. In such a case they act very quickly. Another way to get rid of this kind of man is to mention the names of well-known racketeers like Dolet Turlikhanov or Serik Kunakbaev. If a girl does this in a confident and decisive way the hooligans may believe her and go away.

But the dangers are not limited to those caused by the vulgar racketeers. The aristocrats can be very dangerous as well. Many men may play at being aristocratic in a public place, but once they bring a girl to an apartment they change. They may rape the girl, or beat her. Even worse is not to be raped by one man, but by several men, or to be beaten or killed, because when men get drunk they can do anything. They may rape you and then throw you out of the apartment without giving you money for a taxi. Then you are again in danger that other men may take you away and rape you again. You can never trust a man, even decent men who are fathers are involved in raping girls. They play different roles in different places. At home they are good fathers and husbands, but sometimes they need relaxation; they may pick up a girl from a disco and rape her.

The safest occasions for finding a husband are private parties like weddings and birthday parties. On such occasions you are more secure. A man whom you know may not rape you easily. But the problem is that it is difficult to find rich men in such parties.

Another problem for finding a husband is that men want to marry a virgin girl. Men want non-virgin girls for sex but once they decide to marry, they want innocent girls (*nevinnye devushki*). They think that if they marry women who have already slept with other men, then they may sleep with other men in future as well. But if the girl is beautiful and smart she can entice the man to fall in love with her, and even if she is not virgin the man will marry her anyway.

But once you find a good man who wants to marry you, you cannot trust him. Rich men have lovers as well as their wives. It is a fashion in Almaty. Both sides play with each other and cheat on each other, both sides often have sex with others (*otdykhaiut*)[47] but do not tell each other. Marriage does not last for a long time. I do not like womanising men, but if my husband is rich enough I will let him have relations with other women. Otherwise he doesn't deserve it.

The difficulties in finding husbands or sponsors drive many poor non-virgin women to prostitution.

SEX WORK

Sex work by women was a widespread phenomenon in Almaty. In my neighbourhood six women and a 14-year-old girl were involved in sexual labour. A young couple, who lived in one of the houses and were drug addicts, earned their livelihood through drug dealing, gambling and the husband being a pimp (*sutener*). In the last month of my stay in the neighbourhood a massage service was advertised in the neighbourhood, which happened to be a covert brothel. At least five other women from the neighbourhood had advertised sexual services in *Karavan*. The prevalence of sex work in Almaty is illustrated by the fact that it is widely advertised in the most popular local newspaper weekly, *Karavan*. In the issue of 23 August 1996, out of 136 advertisements under the rubric 'I am looking for work', 75 are concerned with sexual labour. Indeed, a prostitute is usually called a Karavan girl (*Karavan Devushka*). Only 50 of the total job searchers are men. Among women who are looking for 'ordinary' jobs few have declared '*intim iskliuchen*' (sex excluded). This is related to a prevailing praxis in Almaty, in which women are expected to respond to the sexual demands of their bosses.

In the following sections I will describe the life stories of three sex workers and the conditions of their lives and work and the stigma and violence imposed on women suspected of illicit sexual behaviour.

It was early evening of a nice day in May. As usual, I had been wandering along the pavement, in the street close to my residence and talking with people who sell goods illegally, or with those in the kiosks or those who gather in the cafe-house. I decided to buy a bottle of Coca Cola and go home. While I was greeting the shop keeper, a beautiful young Kazakh woman who had already bought cigarettes smiled at me and greeted me. I greeted her, and said: 'I have never seen you before. Do you live around here?' She answered: 'Yes, but we have moved here today.' Pointing to one of the block houses on the opposite side of the road, she said: 'We live there, on the first floor.' She waited for me to buy my Coca Cola. Since we had to go in the same direction, we walked together to the other side of the street. Close to my house I started to leave but she invited me to her apartment. I followed her.

The door was opened, and while we were entering the apartment another young woman with loud voice shouted: 'I want to smoke, why are you so late?' Then she stared a moment, with an unwelcome look at me, but turned to the woman I accompanied and with an angry voice asked: 'Who is he? Haven't I told that you are not allowed to bring clients here?' The first girl in an apologetic voice, said: 'He is not a client, he is a neighbour, he is a foreigner (*inostranets*).' When the angry woman heard the word foreigner she calmed down. With a changed mood she turned to me and said: 'Excuse me, I thought you were Caucasian. If they know where you live then it is difficult to get rid of them. They always come sit and drink and want to fuck for free (*besplatno*).' Then they invited me to tea. The first girl asked me what kind of business I was doing. I answered that I was not a businessman but an anthropologist. Then they asked me about anthropology and my work in Almaty. They were amused that I wanted to write about people's life in Almaty. After a while the first girl asked me whether I wanted to sleep with her for money, I thanked her, but said no and that I had a girlfriend (*podruga*). Then they asked me whether they could watch *Tropikanka* (a Brazilian serial) at my place. They did not have their own TV. I agreed. I met them for five months on a daily basis because they watched soap operas every day, first *Tropikanka*, later *Kassandra* and *Novaia Zhertva*. Later they were joined by two other women. They were called Zhulduz, Asel', Dana and Alma. The following is Asel''s biography.

I cannot include the biographies of the rest because of the lack of space, however, Asel''s biography is illustrative not only of sex work but offers an example of dispossessed migrant Kazakhs who are anti-Russians but Soviet patriots, with whom I will deal in chapter 7. Moreover, it illustrates the ambiguous and contradictory encounters of local women with the post-Soviet 'sexual revolution'.

Asel'

I was born in Taldykorgan in 1973. I have three sisters and one brother. The brother is older than me and my sisters are younger. My father and mother are both pensioners. My father was the head of the brigade (*Zav brigady*). My brother who lives separately with his own family is trading. He brings sugar from Taldykorgan to Almaty and sells it here. One sister is 22 and married, and the other two go to school. My parents are very poor (*bednye*), I and my brother support them economically.

At the age of 17 when I was still in Taldykorgan I began to go out (*druzhila*) with a Kazakh boy a few years older than me. After a while he wanted to fuck me (*trakhat'*). In the beginning I resisted, but he told me he loved me and we should marry. Finally I agreed. The first time I slept with him it was very painful, and I became unconscious. I had pain for a month, but later I got used to it and did not feel pain any more. We usually fucked in the streets at nights or in his brother's apartment when he was not at home.

For a while I was very ashamed of losing my virginity (*devstvennost'*) and I did not talked about it with anybody. After one year I talked with my sister (my brother's wife).[48] I told her, 'I sleep with Saken but he has promised to marry me.' She said, 'What can we do, Fate (*sud'ba*) has decided this.' I did not tell my mother about it, but I think she knew. I hid it very carefully from my father, as if he had known it he would have hit me. Our relationship continued until his family moved to another town. He never came back to visit me, I knew that he had cheated me and only wanted to fuck. I really loved him but he did not love me. I became very disappointed and depressed, and then I enrolled in the university in Almaty. Here I had two lovers (*liubovniki*) at the same time, before the accident, one Kazakh and one Korean, and I loved both of them.

It was 1993. I was living with my cousin (*dvoiurodnaia sestra*) in a dormitory (*obshchezhitie*). I was 19 years old and she was 17. One evening two young men, a Kazakh and a Chechen came to visit a girl who lived in the neighbouring room, but she was not at home. However, they stayed and ate food. At midnight, my cousin went to the common kitchen, and then these men followed her into our room. When she tried to stop them from coming into our room one of them punched her in the face. They had smoked *anasha* [a local equivalent of marijuana] and were very high. I began to cry very loudly, calling for help. One of the men put his hand around my throat and tried to strangle me. My cousin was a virgin (*devstvennitsa*). They wanted to do this [she makes a ring with one hand and by moving a finger in that ring demonstrates the act of penetration]. I resisted, and as he was drunk and high I managed to escape down to the second floor, to a girl who was living there. Then we went up together to the third floor to our room where the two men kept my sister; we succeeded in convincing them to let my sister go. We took her with us to the second floor to the girl's room and closed the door behind us. But as soon as we closed the door they banged on it. When we did not open the door they threatened to break the door down unless we opened it. The girl who was living in the room became afraid and opened the door. I jumped out from the window, wanting to call the two young men who were working in the kiosk around the corner for help. But I broke my back. The men in the kiosk who had heard my fall ran towards me and asked what was happening to me. I told them the story, and they ran to the second floor and helped my sister. Then they took me to the hospital in *Chapaeva/Zhandosova*. It was two in the morning, and there were no nurses and doctors and no facilities. I was crying the whole night because of the pain.

Next day the two men who had caused the event came to the hospital and told me they would kill me if I reported them to the police. The police came to the hospital, but I said that I fell by myself. After three months, when my parents came to visit me in the hospital, I told them what had happened to me. They reported it to the police, but the latter never found those two men. I laid six months at the hospital and six additional months at home. Then I walked for two months with the help of crutches (*kostyli*) before being able to walk normally. But I haven't recovered fully yet. I have pain in my back and legs in the winter when it becomes cold. And I have headaches continuously.

When this happened I was in my first year of university, studying a nursing course. Then I finished the course and began to work as a nurse in a hospital until six months ago. 25 women worked in our work-unit (*kollektiv*), nurses and doctors, seven of whom were young women. Most of the people with the exception of the older (*starukhi*) ones left the job. They were paid only 3,000 tenge ($50). It was very little money. Some of them began to trade, others to sell their bodies. From March I began to sell sex for money. I had friends who were already engaged in this job, and they took me with them to the hotel. I did not want to ask my parents or my brother for money. When I was studying they supported me, and now I am a grown up person (*vzroslye chelovek*). I support my parents with money. In addition to this I do not want to go back to Taldykorgan, as it is boring there. Almaty is more exciting. I like it, there are cafes, restaurants and dancing here.

The biographies of Zhulduz and Dana are in many respects similar to Asel''s, except that Zhulduz and Dana were students and this had played a role in their involvement in prostitution. Zhulduz puts this as follows:

> My teachers demanded money for letting me pass the exams with high marks. I had to pay $100 for an exam and $50 for a *zachet* [oral test]. As I did not know what to do I consulted girlfriends. They told me work. Then one of them took me to the hotel and introduced me to a pimp (*sutener*), a German man from Germany. He became my pimp and ever since has found clients for me. When he finds a client he gives me a ring and gives the address or telephone number of the client. Most of them stay at the hotel, but sometimes I go to their apartments. Most of my clients are Germans or German-speaking people. Sometimes I have English clients as well. Each night I spend with a client I receive $100 and my pimp receives $50. Ninety percent of the university students are working. In my class, six of my friends are working.

Dana gave the same story for her involvement.

Motives

As these biographies demonstrate, the women's main reasons for involvement in prostitution are economic. However, their tragic backgrounds have played a part in their choice of sex work.

The loss of virginity has been a great blow to the three girls' self-esteem. In fact Zhulduz regretted the loss of her virginity more than doing sex work. Although, all three chose to sleep with their lovers, afterwards they had developed strong feelings of guilt, and by the time I got to know them they had still not come to terms with their feelings of loss. They felt that they had lost a precious and essential part of themselves. This feeling of loss was felt more strongly by Asel' and Dana, who had loved the men who deflowered them and expected to marry them. Both felt betrayed. Then, as Dana's experience shows, because of the loss of virginity their chances of marriage have been made marginal. Although both women had enjoyed sex with several lovers, in their feelings extra-marital sex is structured as a type of perverted and deviant pleasure. As non-virgin and unmarried women who indulged in illicit sex, they had developed a negative image of themselves which contributed to their involvement in sex work. While Asel', Alma and Zhulduz distinguished between sex for pleasure and sex for money, Dana combined the two, but they all perceived their work to be morally illicit.

Although all the women share economic motives their economic goals differ. Dana wants to earn enough to survive, and pay her teachers. She has no particular economic plan for the future. In addition to money, she enjoys the company of other sex workers. As a result she is not actively involved in the work. She wants to finish her studies and become a doctor and live on her salary. Alma, Asel' and Zhulduz have clear economic goals. Zhulduz, in addition to paying her teachers, wants to save money. She says: 'I want to buy my own apartment in Shymkent, buy good furniture, a TV, video, buy myself a red diploma, travel to Spain and rest on the beaches. I want to be independent. I do not want to marry.'

Asel' has similar goals but she wants to marry. She says: 'If I have enough money and an apartment with good furniture I can buy a husband for myself.' Alma wants to collect $4,000 and start her own business. All the girls very clearly see their present work as temporary, a way of getting an independent financial start. They say when they get the money they need they will stop work. To collect the money the girls economise and work very hard. Although the girls are consumerists on the fantasy level (Turner, 1994), in practice, they live a harsh life, work hard and save money.

All four live in a one-bedroomed apartment with a small kitchen and a bath. The apartment's furniture when I visited it for the first time consisted only of a bed and an easy chair. At nights, Asel' slept in the bed and Zhulduz in the armchair. The blankets and sheets were old. When Dana joined them, she and Asel' shared the bed together. But when Alma was forced to move there, they asked their landlord to provide them with an extra bed, which he did. The apartment had a telephone, which was essential to their work. They loved to listen to music but could not until one of the Zhulduz's clients gave her a tape recorder as a present. They did not have their own TV either, so they watched soap operas at my place. They ate only twice a day. Their food was very simple, usually an omelette for brunch, and some simple food with meat, vegetables and pasta for dinner. They never bought wine, beer or other drinks. Their major costs were paying the rent, buying cigarettes and paying for taxis. They paid $130, $32.50 each, per month to a Kazakh man from whom they had hired the apartment. They spent money on buying cosmetics, dresses, dyes and wigs. But they said that although they enjoyed make-up and dressing well, they would not spend money on these things if it was not necessary for their job. They buy none of the popular journals, like *Kakado*, *Cosmopolitan* and *Speed*, which my female students bought and read. They borrowed some issues of *Speed* and *Kakado* from me and read them eagerly. When they go to the restaurant and the hamburger bar where they look for clients, they do not buy drinks and food. They usually try to get the male visitors to invite them to eat.

They usually charge their clients $100, but Asel' and Dana who are a little round, and thus have fewer clients, sometimes take clients who pay less. Although $100 is much higher than the average monthly salary of workers, the girls thought that it was not such great money, given the nature of their job. They argued that the work was difficult and dangerous, that they had no pensions and insurance, and that the length of the time a sex worker can work actively is relatively short. 'If a woman is over 30, she cannot work successfully as a prostitute, because there are many younger competitors,' Asel' said, and the other girls agreed with her.

The girls, with exception of Zhulduz, could not have more than three clients a week. The reason for this is that women who sell sex outnumber the men in their workplace. Another reason for the lack of sufficient demand for sex in the hotel is that, according to Asel', Almatian men prefer call girls to prostitutes who offer themselves in restaurants because they do not want to be seen with a prostitute publicly and call girls have the reputation of being first class prostitutes. Asel' said that although their work is much harder and more dangerous, the money is much less than the call girls receive. She said they may earn up to $500 per night. I asked her: 'How do you know that?' She said: 'Ring to a Karavan girl (*Karavan devushka*) and check yourself.' I asked: 'How can I find such a girl's phone number?' ' It is easy, I will show you, go and buy a weekly *Karavan*,' she answered. I went and bought the latest issue of the weekly *Karavan*. Under the rubric 'we are looking for work' (*ishchem rabotu*), she showed me announcements which were put within rectangles, and said: 'All these are call girls, call and ask.' I dialled one of the numbers and a young woman picked up the telephone. I said to her: 'I read in an announcement in *Karavan* that you need a job, what kind of job are you interested in?' 'Sexual service (*intimnye uslugi*),' she answered. When I asked the price she mentioned $250 a night. Then I called several other places, the prices varied from $50 an hour to $300 a night.

The girls' pimp finds some clients for them, but they themselves actively look for clients. They have two main ways of finding clients: using the telephone and visiting the hotel. They had got a lot of numbers which belonged to different rooms in the hotel. When a girl sleeps with a client in a room, she takes the number and dials it each day in search of new customers. But it seemed to me that they had somebody in the hotel who called them and gave the names and the numbers of the new guests in the hotel. Each of them called, in the afternoon, for at least 45 minutes. Around seven o'clock they went to their workplace. The place is a complex which consists of a well-known hotel in Almaty, but by Almaty standards a second or third rate one, a restaurant-casino attached to the hotel, owned by a well-known foreign businessman, and a hamburger bar owned by the same businessman. The guests of the hotel and the restaurant-casino are foreign and local businessmen, and local rich men. Girls walk the streets around the hotel, go to the cafe in the lobby, the restaurant and the hamburger bar. I walked there on several evenings. The striking aspect for me was that the girls outnumbered the men, and the girls confirmed that it is always the same, with the exception of the music festival, *Azia Dausy* (Voice of Asia), in the second half of July. Then, according to the girls, the hotel is full of guests and they work every night.

Dana said: 'We approach foreign men and ask "do you want sex for money?" but the *sovetskii* (the Soviets) approach us and ask "girls do you want to rest?" and we say yes.' The fact that the girls do not know any languages but Russian and Kazakh is a great disadvantage for them. They felt that they needed to learn English but had no time for that. However, they learned from me some elementary sentences in relation to their job.

The clients

The women have German, English, American, Czech, Lithuanian, Turkish, Iranian, Chinese, Russian and Kazakh clients. The women themselves classify their clients in stereotypes according to the clients' wealth, taste in women, their manners in relation to women and their sexual performance. First, they distinguish between two sorts of clients: our Soviets (*nashi sovetskie*) and foreigners (*inostrantsy*). The former, which consist of the people from the former Soviet Union (the three Baltic republics excepted) are divided into locals who live in Almaty (*mestnye*) and visitors (*priezzhie*) from other parts of the former Soviet territory. They say that the locals usually prefer call girls to them. Then they divide foreigners into Westerners (*zapadnye*) and Orientals (*vostochnye*). Among the Easterners they distinguish between Chinese and Muslims. Among the Soviets the majority of their customers are Kazakh businessmen from other cities who visit Almaty occasionally.

'The girls', says Asel', 'prefer foreigners to *Sovetskii*, because [putting her hand on her pocket] 'they have dollars. Local men may fuck you and not pay you.' Dana intervenes:

> Among the foreigners Europeans are better than Asians; they think that we are much more beautiful than *Russachki* but the Chinese think that *Russachki* are more beautiful than us. After sleeping with us, they ask us to find them *Russachki*. We ask them, 'aren't we good enough?' They answer, 'you are good but our girls look like you, we want to try blonde and white girls.' The Germans and English like us more than Russachki, because their own girls look like Russachki. Arabs, Turks and Iranians like *Russachki* more than us. When Arabs and Iranians prefer *Russachki*, we want to beat up *Russachki*, we want to beat up Arabs and Iranians as well.

Meanwhile, Zhulduz jumps up and kicks an imaginary Russian woman in her face in the air, and says: 'We have to beat up *Russachki* like this.'

Europeans, Asel' says, are more cultured. When they invite you to their apartments, they try to make it romantic. They turn off the light, light candles and invite you to drink wine.

Alma says: 'Russians are sex maniacs (*seksual'nye man'iaki*), first they touch your body everywhere and then have sex with you for a long time.' 'Chinese do sex like dogs,' Asel' says. She parts her legs and bows her knees forward, opens her mouth and shoots out her tongue, and begins to breath heavily and rhythmically to demonstrate the Chinese allegedly 'dog-like' way of doing sex. All the girls laugh for a good while, amused by Asel''s performance. Zhulduz says: 'I do not like Kazakhs, they watch pornographic films and ask us to suck them, but we avoid this, we are Muslims; then Kazakhs go to *Russachki*. Kazakh men like *Russachki*, they say *Russachki* are experienced and do everything.' Dana says proudly: '*Rossiani* like Kazakh girls. They travel here from Russia to fuck Kazakh girls.'

The women's views of their clients are related to the ways their clients objectify them and the ways they in their turn objectify their clients. In both cases the person is alienated and reduced to a stereotype.

The clients objectify the women by comparing their appearances and skin colour with Russians. This combined with the fact that supply of sex exceeds the demand has created a hatred towards Russian sex workers among them. Although migrants are generally against Russians these four sex workers expressed the strongest anti-Russian feeling explicitly. They were particularly against Russian women. The reason for such feeling was that they were compared with Russians on a daily basis and such comparison directly affected their incomes.

By creating stereotypes of their clients, the women make the clients the objects of their own knowledge, and thereby create a sense of agency and work out practical strategies for enticing and manipulating them. The most prominent of these strategies is the art of performance. To illustrate this, consider the following event.

One day when I was in the girls' apartment, Alma and Zhulduz began to perform (in a theatrical sense) a sexual act. They were moving their hips very fast backward and forward, as if they were making love, and were crying as if they were experiencing orgasm. While the other two girls were laughing at their performance, I became embarrassed. Asel' who had felt my embarrassment said: 'Don't worry Joma!, it's not to do with you, it is a rehearsal (*repetitsiia*).' I asked her: 'What do you mean?' She answered, any prostitute is an actress (*aktrisa*). Dana who was listening to her, intervened by saying why only prostitutes? Any woman is an actress. In our work, Asel' continued, we act like we enjoy sex and have orgasms. But we must do this very skilfully, like professional actresses, otherwise men will find it uninteresting, and will not hire us the second time, or recommend us to their friends.

The girls have learned the art of performance from other girls, through watching pornographic films, often with their clients, or reading magazines. The fact that through performing 'fictive sex' they get their clients involved in 'real sex', gives them the feeling that they master the situation. In Marxist terms, while girls sell their sex-labour power, they try to retain a partial control over the labour process itself. This bestows them with a sense of agency, which is amplified further by mocking their clients' sexual tastes and sexual behaviour among themselves.

In spite of this intensive acting of sex, three of the girls (Zhulduz, Alma, and Asel') said that they never feel sexual pleasure in sleeping with clients. They do it as a job, and their clients' bodies are part of the material conditions of their job, like condoms, the bed, mattress and pillows. Asel' obviously distinguishes between 'real sex' and what she does with her clients. She has a Kazakh lover she meets twice a week. She enjoys his company and sex with him. Dana, in contrast to the other three girls gets involved emotionally.

> The majority of them [with an ironic voice, and smiling] want to talk after sex. Please, they say, talk a little. But I am in no mood for talking. Of course it depends on the client, if I like him I will talk with him, and I will do intensive sex with him. But if I do not like him I just lie like a cow. In the latter case the client usually asks me why are you like this? I answer, I cannot help it. I really like sex. Once I had a client whom I liked, we had sex the whole night. In the morning, exhausted, we slept, when we woke up in the evening we had sex again and then separated.

All four women said that Dana was an exception, and most sex workers do not get emotionally involved with their clients.

They do not hate their clients but do not respect them either, because they think the clients also do not respect them. Asel' said: 'Each time I sleep with a client, I feel bad, because they do not respect you, they do not consider you to be a woman.'

In spite of this disillusionment they wished their clients would treat them more humanely. For them the ideal client is Richard Gere in *Pretty Woman*. All of them had seen the movie. Zhulduz carried a photograph of Gere and Julia Roberts in her wallet. When I saw the photo accidentally, I asked the women: 'What do you think of them?' Alma said he was a real man, he did not care that she was a prostitute, he loved her and married her.

Actually Zhulduz had her own Gere. She became emotionally attached to one client, a German (from Germany). From Zhulduz's point of view, the German was a good man because he wanted to help a poor Kazakh. The German, Zhulduz said, will donate his jeep to a poor Kazakh when he finishes his job here. The German had hired an apartment in Samal, one of

Almaty's best areas. Zhulduz visited him two or three times a week. For each time, she received $100. But the German bought her presents as well (a watch, a tape recorder, a dress and an electric piano). She always showed the presents to me and was proud of her relationship with the German, and mentioned him as 'my German' (*moi nemets*). The German taught her to play piano, and she taught him Russian. On her birthday, she told me the German had promised to call her. As the German did not call she became very sad. But next day when I met them she said with a happy face: 'The German came this morning and brought this piano as a birthday present. He could not call yesterday because he was in Tashkent.'

When the German was about to leave for Germany, Zhulduz became sad and quiet. She lay in bed and did not speak to anybody. Finally one afternoon she burst into tears, and cried and cried. Then she told me: 'The German will leave for Germany tomorrow. He will be away for six months. I love him, I will miss him. I said: 'Can't you travel to Germany?' She said: 'I have not got the money.' I asked her: 'Do you want to marry him?' She said: 'Yes.' I said: 'Then tell him you love him and want marry him.' She said: 'I am ashamed. I slept with him for money. I am a prostitute.'

Besides clients, the police and hooligans are the other important people in the girls' job, because of the dangers they impose.

The police

The place where the girls worked was safe, because it was protected from hooligans by the police. However, the police themselves occasionally harassed the girls. Asel' said:

> The police usually do not intervene, they usually negotiate the issue with our pimp. If they arrest one of our girls, the pimp will tell them, come and fuck our girls but do not disturb us. They fuck the girls and do not disturb us next time.

I asked her whether the police take money or not. Asel' answered: 'I do not know, but I think the sex is enough.' She told me that prostitution is illegal, a prostitute could be condemned to one year in prison and a pimp to three years. Dana is of a similar opinion:

> When we walk around the hotel we usually encounter the police (*minty*). Our relations with them are friendly. We greet each other. They usually ask whether we have clients or not. We sleep with them for free and they do not bother us.

In spite of this assertion, she said that the job was dangerous because of the police intervention.

It is a very interesting but dangerous job. It is interesting because you meet people from different parts of the world and talk with them about interesting subjects. It is dangerous because the police (*minty*) always control you. Once I was talking with an Arab, who showed me dollars and said that he wanted to fuck me. He did not know Russian and I don't know English. He just showed the sexual act with his hands. Five yards from us two GSK police in plain clothes were standing and watching us. One of them called me, 'Hey girl, come here.' When I went to him, he said, 'Aha, you are involved in prostitution.' I said, 'I am not such a person, I do not know what prostitution is.' He said, 'You say that you do not know what prostitution is.' I answered, 'Of course I don't know.' 'I will show you! I have seen you here before; another girl said that you are a prostitute,' he said. 'What girl? This man is my colleague, we work together in a company (*firma*).' 'What company?' he asked. I said a name. It was the Arab's fault. I told him 'Go into the hotel, I will follow you.' But he did not understand Russian, and continued to show me dollars and did not recognise the police. Then one of the police went to bring the girl, but suddenly a young Kazakh man saved me. He stopped his car and said to the police, 'She is my girlfriend and is waiting for me here.' The police had no choice but to let me go. I jumped into the car and he drove away. Then he said, 'Let's fuck.' I refused. Then he said, 'I saved you, otherwise you would now be fucking with more than one policeman. I said thank you and agreed to do it. We did it in his car.

Zhulduz had a similar experience of police harassment. Once when I was in their apartment an Italian man visited her. Next day I asked her how she knew this Italian man. She answered:

I met him yesterday when I was there in the hotel but the police stopped us and asked him for his passport. He showed his passport, and then they let him go, but they held me like this [she demonstrates the way the police gripped her by holding her hip very strongly by her right hand]. But the Italian paid $50 and the police let me go.

I asked her why the police had held her. 'Because I am a prostitute (*prostitutka*) and the police knew me.'

Hooligans
Girls are exposed to dangers from hooligans. They distinguish between them and Mafioso. Their description of hooligans coincides with 'the vulgar Mafioso' introduced earlier. As Asel' put it, Mafioso do not disturb a woman, they are gentlemen. If they want a woman, they invite her to a restaurant and buy flowers for her, but hooligans and *menbets* (*menbeti*)

bother women and foreigners. According to her these are mostly young Kazakh men of rural origin.

One evening when I came home late, around eleven o'clock, I saw a woman in the darkness smoking in front of the entrance to my house. I greeted her. When she answered my greeting I recognised her voice, she was Asel'. 'Why are you standing here?' I asked. She did not answer but instead said, 'Why are you so late? I knocked at your door at nine and you were not home. Since then, I have been waiting for you here.' 'What can I do for you?' I asked. She answered, 'Zhulduz has brought two Chechens to the apartment. They are her clients. She says they have promised to stay only one hour, but now they have stayed for several hours and drunk vodka. They want me free, but I don't like to do it. I came to your apartment to call Bakhyt, a young Kazakh man who is a boxer and a friend of Zhulduz. He knows that we work, but he has promised to help us against hooligans.' She called, but unfortunately Bakhyt was not at home.

Then Asel' asked me: 'Please come with me and call Zhulduz to the door. They may think that you are Bakhyt and leave.' As I did not want to confront the Chechens, I told her: 'Let's try another trick; I'll call Zhulduz and say I am Bakhyt.' I was afraid that the Chechens could tell from my accent that I was a foreigner, not Bakhyt but as most Caucasians in contrast to Kazakhs speak very bad Russian. I took the risk. I dialled their number but nobody answered. When I dialled a second time one of the Chechens answered. I said with an angry voice: 'May I speak with Zhulduz?' The Chechen answered 'You have dialled a wrong number,' and put down the telephone. I tried to dial the third time, but Zhulduz called and said they had left. I told Asel' they had left. As she was still afraid to go alone, she asked me to follow her. I took the knife from the kitchen and followed her. The Chechens were gone. I was irritated and asked Zhulduz: 'Why do you bring hooligans here?' She answered: 'What could I do? They have not their own place and I want to work. They promised to stay just an hour but stayed and drank vodka.' Asel' interrupted our conversation by kissing my face and saying 'Joma, you are very nice.' I calmed down a little, but still irritated told them: 'You know that I cannot fight with such madmen.'

Three weeks after this event, somebody woke me up at two in the morning by ringing at my door. When I asked who it was, Asel' said: 'It is Asel'. There are some bad men there [their apartment], could I come in for a while?' I opened the door. She was shivering not of cold, because it was middle of summer, but from fear and anger. I told her: 'If you want to sleep here, the mattress is over there.'

She accepted my offer with satisfaction and arranged the extra mattress for herself. After a while I slept but Asel' woke me again saying: 'Joma I am afraid, it is noisy at the yard, the men are calling me.' I heard the three men, who were making noises in the yard. Then they got angry and began to shout even more loudly in Kazakh. Then the car started, and they drove away, but after a while they came back.

I asked Asel': 'Why do you bring such idiots to your place?' She said: 'They are acquaintances (*znakomyi*) of Alma, they are from Karagandy.' Then I asked her: 'Why then did you flee here?' She answered: 'One of them wanted to sleep with me and I didn't like it.' A short time after this Alma was robbed in her apartment. A Korean acquaintance of hers, who was a drug addict, broke through the window into her apartment on the ground floor. By putting a knife to her throat he forced her to give him the $500 she had earned recently. The same man had forced her to pay him $200 earlier.

Such incidents were part of their daily life. They risk being beaten, raped or even killed someday by someone. However, they continued to work as sex workers, because they did not want to live in poverty.

Feelings about their job
The girls do not like the job. Three of them (Alma, Zhulduz, and Asel') consider it a humiliating way to earn good money. On one occasion Zhulduz told me: 'I feel I have lost my pride.'

Dana has more ambivalent attitudes. While she is not hunting clients as actively as the other three girls she tries to find some meaning in her job. First, she thought that their job had an altruistic dimension. Once she told me:

> I had two married directors from Shymkent last night. They were very satisfied with me [with a proud voice] and told me that they will call me next time they are in Almaty. You see we do a real job, we give people something their wives are not able to give.

Second, as she expressed it above, she enjoyed communication with clients. And third, she liked other sex workers.

> The girls who are involved in this job are very kind (*dobrye*) and honest (*prostye*). We have good relations with each other, we work in groups. Our group consists of four. When we meet the girls from other groups we greet each other and ask about their work. We work in the same place, we walk around the hotel. Sometimes we find clients for each other. For example once I and Asel' were walking, a girl from another group approached us and said we need two girls, the number of clients are more than our girls.

On the other hand she was the only one who said explicitly and repeatedly that she did not like the job. On one occasion she said, 'I don't want my daughter to be a prostitute. I do not want a daughter, I want a son.' Other girls expressed their derogatory attitudes towards their jobs indirectly. Because of her job Zhulduz did not find herself worthy enough to express her love for the German ('I am ashamed, I slept with him for money. I am a prostitute.') Soon after the German's departure Zhulduz, who was very sad, said: 'I don't want to live, but it is difficult to kill oneself.' Then she repeated again: 'I don't want to live.' I asked her: 'Why?' Crying she moved her finger forward and backward, pointing it towards between her legs, and said: 'I am tired of doing this, but I have nobody to take care of me in this world. I am alone.'

Asel' showed her negative attitudes about sex work when she said that a married Kazakh woman never gets involved in prostitution (see below). Another way they express negative feelings for their job is their strong nostalgia for the Soviet era. Both Dana and Asel' admired the Soviet era for its sexual purity. Asel' said: 'We had never heard the word prostitute in the Soviet time. Every woman had a decent job and a good salary. They did not need to get involved in prostitution.'

The women thought that they had a higher degree of autonomy than married women and those women who work in ordinary jobs. They arrange their time as they want. They have very few domestic duties. They get up at two in the afternoon. Then one goes shopping to buy fresh bread, meat and vegetables and cigarettes and another makes some omelette for breakfast. After breakfast one of them washes the dishes and another one hoovers. Then for some hours they chat, mock their clients and ring around to find customers. Around five one of them begins to cook the evening meal which is very simple and is prepared quickly. At six they come to my apartment to watch a soap opera, then they go back to their own apartment to eat the meal, make up and take a taxi to the hotel.

Appreciating the autonomy the job has bestowed on them, they try to make it fun and normal for themselves through joking about their clients and mocking them. Moreover, the girls display their autonomy in the ways they relate to their immediate social environment. Although they had negative images of themselves due to their jobs, they would not allow anybody else to put them down or patronise them. Dana said:

Once I had a Turkish client. He was a good man who walked with me one week but did not sleep with me. He finally asked me, 'Why do you do this?' I told him, 'You are a client, it is my own business.' I do not like it when clients ask why do you do this.

Another example which highlights the women's struggle for autonomy is Dana's reaction to her older sister, who tried to persuade her to stop doing sex work.

A friend of mine had told her that I work. When she asked me, at first I denied it, but when she insisted, I told her the truth. She became sad and angry and asked me, 'Why do you do this? Stop it.' I told her I am a grown up person (*vzroslyi chelovek*), I am 28 years old, I do not need somebody else to endorse what I do (*opravdyvat menia*).

Asel', who was listening to our conversation, turned towards us and angrily said: 'It is true, we are not children, we do not need anybody's permission for what we do.'

Another way the women struggled for autonomy was by asserting their presence in the neighbourhood by breaking the masculinised order of time and place, by their noisy traffic in the evenings, at midnight and early in the morning. I am not aware what people in the neighbourhood thought about them, because I intentionally avoided asking other people questions about them. The women had asked me not to discuss anything about them with other people. But they had been photographed with Kazakh butchers who sold meat in the square and actually received meat from them free of charge.

Another Kazakh man from the south, with whom I had a good relationship and who worked at the cafe there, once told me: 'Do you know Zhulduz?' I said: 'Yes.' Then he added with sympathy: 'She is a good girl.' A third man, a Kazakh who worked in the kiosk where I first met Zhulduz, expressed strong negative feelings about them. Once when I was sitting in the kiosk and talking with him, Zhulduz came to buy something from the kiosk. When she went a way, while following her with his eyes, he said with an insulting voice: 'Prostitute.' Then added: 'She and her friends are prostitutes. They damage our reputation; people will think that Kazakh women are bad (*plokhie*).' I said: 'Maybe they have no other choice.' Pointing to the women who were selling things at the pavement, he said: 'They can trade like them.'

Later I asked the women 'whether they were worried that they might create a bad reputation for their nationality (*natsional'nost'*). Dana answered: 'Prostitution has nothing to do with nationality. Each nation has its own prostitutes. In Jordan you have your own prostitutes. Haven't you?' I agreed, yes we have. 'Austrians have their prostitutes as well haven't they?' I agreed again. 'And the English have their prostitutes, haven't they?' I nodded, yes.

When Dana finished her rhetorical statement, Zhulduz and Asel' confirmed her point of view by saying, 'It is true.'

The women do not hide their jobs from their girl friends. Several of Asel''s former colleagues and classmates visited her. I asked Asel', whether they knew about her job, and she said yes. I asked: 'What is their reaction?' She said: 'They think it is normal (*normal'no*).' I asked her: 'Have they changed their behaviour towards you?' She said: 'Why should they?' They know many girls do this. They say it is your private business (*lichnoe delo*). All four girls, before starting to work, had their own friends who were already working. These friends brought them to the hotel and introduced them to the pimp. Aigula, an old friend of Asel', 22 years old, who visited them regularly, expressed her feelings in the following way: 'Yesterday I met Asel' and Zhulduz. They told me that each had earned $100 the night before. It is twice my monthly salary. It is very exciting. I want to earn money as well but I cannot do it.'

With regard to relatives, while the girls are not worried about letting young women know their job, they hide it very strictly from older women and men. For example Asel' said:

> My cousin (*dvoiurodnaia sestra*) knows about my work. I told her, 'You know there are rich men, foreigners who pay good money for sex; I sleep with them sometimes.' She said, 'It is normal, you are unmarried, you have no husband, if you earn some money from rich men it is good.'

When I asked Asel' whether her cousin herself would sleep with somebody for money, she became offended, and said furiously, 'Never; she is married.' 'But you', I said, 'said to me before that many married women do this.' 'Yes', she answered, 'but they are *Russachki* not Kazakhs (*Kazashki*). A Kazakh married woman will never sleep with anybody other than her husband, but *Russachki* do this. Russachki want many men and never become satisfied with one man.'

Asel''s siblings and parents do not know. They think she is working as a nurse in Almaty. She said: 'My mother would be very sad if she knew it, but my brothers would beat me and bring me back by force to Taldykor- gan.' Dana's mother and her brothers do not know either. 'If my brothers', she said, 'learn it some day, I hope they will kill me, but they will not do this. Instead they will reject me as their sister.' Asel's Kazakh lover does not know either. Asel' told me: 'I have told him the other girls are my sisters. Please don't tell him about my job, or he will beat me.'

In spite of the fact that the girls have justified their work to themselves, they are far from having a happy life. Asel' often complained about having headaches and pain in her legs and back. Dana had two standard sentences which she always repeated about her life: 'My life is a hell' (*Zhizn' moia zhectianka*) and 'I am uprooted' (*zhevio po doveri*).

Zhulduz feels herself alone in the whole world and Alma is often sad. Although they repress their feelings of sadness and despair, on particular occasions these feelings surface strongly. For example on one occasion when I told them about the wedding party of a female friend of one of my female students which I had attended the night before, they suddenly became quiet, sad and depressed and after a while left the apartment.

Although all four women by any measure are strong individuals, they are not able to avoid internalising the social stigma on sex work on the one hand and social streotypes of a 'decent women' on the other. For them the ideal situation was the love of a man and a successful marriage. Even if they felt that their chance for such marriage was marginal, they showed their dream through their strong involvement in the love affair between two main characters in a Mexican soap opera called *Kasandra*. Kasandra and David Luis love each other and want to marry but David Luis, accused of a murder he has not committed, is detained and prosecuted. The prosecutor is a man whom Kasandra had left on the night they were to marry because of her love for David Luis.

The women engage with the serial and in the dramatic moments express very strong feelings of empathy and disgust. For example, when Kassandra is crying, they become sad, and say: 'Oh dearest, beauty, don't cry.' When Kassandra and David Luis meet in prison and kiss each other, the women became very happy and look at them with admiration. When the doctor who is the brother of the prosecutor cures David Luis the girls admire him. When Roberto the prosecutor refuses to be convinced by the doctor that David Luis is innocent, Asel' pointing at him says with an angry voice: 'This man is an idiot. He does not understand that David Luis is innocent.' Asel' says: 'I love Kassandra most because she is kind (*dobraia*) and beautiful. After her I like David Luis.' Through their concern for the love between Kassandra and David Luis, the women actually relive their own past loves and visualise their dreams. Asel' said: 'When I see the love between them I think about my own beloved (*liubimykh*).' Alma said: 'I love David Luis. He arouses me. He is kind and attractive.' The women wish and dream that some day a young, handsome and prosperous man like David Luis might ask for their hand.

But the reality is much harsher. Women who practise sexual strategies successfully are better off than those dispossessed women who avoid it. However, they are continuously exposed to stigma and violence.

STIGMA AND VIOLENCE

In this section I will discuss how the public moral attitudes to sexualised economic strategies instigate and legitimise domestic and public violence against women.

The way different people approach morally sexualised strategies depends on the current sexual ambiguities engendered by the encounter of the so-called sexual revolution (*seksual'haia revoliutsiia*) with Soviet official ideology on sexuality, on the one hand, and the revival of 'ethnic-tradi-tionalist' sexual morality at the other. The sexual revolution which has meant more liberal practices and discourses of sex, on the one hand, and the commercialisation and advertisement of sex on the other, is oriented towards pleasure.[49] The Soviet and ethnic sexual moralities are oriented towards reproduction. Those who adhere either to the sexual morality of the Soviet time or to an ethnic one consider the sexualised strategies corrupt and perverted. Thus, women who practise sexual strategies are stigmatised as deviant from women's idealised roles as wives and mothers. Such stigma in its turn legitimises the use of widespread domestic and public violence against women in general. The violence is particularly justified, because men who have embraced the sexual revolution for themselves have very ambiguous attitudes towards women who practise extra-marital sex. While they adore such women as objects of desire and sources of pleasure they usually share the opinion that such women are moral perverts.[50] Such duplicity from men is related to the particular ways rich men benefit from the sexual revolution. Culturally, the consumerism which is the main life-style of this group of men includes a very strong sexual element. Having young and beautiful women as mistresses and wives has become one of the main symbols of the post-Soviet masculinity. Having women as lovers is not only a matter of prestige for rich men, but also for those who are not wealthy. I communicated regularly with a group of men, of middle income, most of whom were married. One of the main ways they tried to impress me or each other was by telling stories about their success in seducing women or showing their skills in this. Men who were particularly successful, apparently had a better sense of their manhood. The following proverb, recited frequently by both men and women illustrates this: '*muzhchina Kotoryi ne guliaet ne muzhchina*' (a man who is not involved in illicit sex is not a man). When I asked different people about the interpretation of the proverb, most of them said that it is in the nature of men to seek other women than their wives.

Economically, the commercialisation of sex as an important component of the consumerist culture, has become a multi-million dollar business from which a whole range of men benefit: owners of tabloid newspapers, who sell their papers by publishing pictures of nude women, producers and dis-tributors of pornographic films, owners of hotels, casinos and restaurants, and pimps. The presence of women in entertainment places is a necessary precondition for attracting the men who spend money. Moreover, as mentioned before, the post-Soviet poverty of women has forced them to practice sexual strategies, which are considered by the locals as a principal element of the sexual revolution.

Thus, such men use moralising discourses, instigated by the transforma-tion of sex into a commodity, and targeted on women who get involved in extra-marital sex, to impose their terms on women in the relationships of exploitation. From the point of view of women who use sex as an economic strategy, both the Soviet-style sexual morality and its binary opposite, the commercialised sexual revolution, serve in a complementary way the interests of powerful men. The stigmatisation of women who do not conform to the puritan moral norms makes them defenceless against the men who exploit them both sexually and economically. The surge in wide-spread domestic and public violence against women partly legitimised by moralising discourses, is one of the main strategies for such exploitation.

In the following, first I will introduce very briefly some elements of the moralising discourses and then show how such discourses legitimise violence against women.

Let us list the local sexually oriented stereotypes of femininity:

Modest (women, girl) (*skromnaia (Zhenshchina, devushka)*)/ vulgar (woman, girl) (*Vulgarnaia (Zhenshchina, devushka)*); good woman (*normal' naia zhenshchina*)/ bad woman (*plokhaia zhenshchina*); loose woman (bitch) (*suka*); woman (*zhenshchina*)/ girl (*devushka*); a virgin woman (*devstvennitsa*); innocent girl (*nevinnaia devushka*); clean girl (*chistaia devushka*); the old maid (*staraia deva*); wife (*zhena*)/ mistress (*liubovnitsa*); fiance (*nevesta*)/ girl friend (*podrushka*); prostitute (*prostitutka*).

'Modesty', which has a very high positive virtue, is related to a woman's sexual behaviour, bodily expressions and her relations to time and place. First of all, a modest woman does not engage in extra-marital sex. Second, she does not display sexuality through dressing provocatively, walking or laughing loudly in public. She does not drink and smoke in public places, does not attend restaurants and bars without her husband or relatives, does not walk the streets alone at night, and does not speak with strangers. The Soviet state, intervening directly in family relations, modernised the gender regimes (Massell, 1975; Akiner, 1997). An important element of the post-Soviet nationalist rhetoric is the demand for the revival of the 'traditional family' and its values (Akiner, 1997: p. 284). The notion of female modesty is central to this traditionalist discourse. A vulgar woman is one who commits such acts. Actually a 'vulgar woman' is considered to be a bad woman and a 'modest woman' a good one. Another word for a 'vulgar woman' is *suka*. *Suka* is a stigma and attached to women who are allegedly involved in illicit sex. Although literally it means bitch, in practice it is not as strong a stigma as prostitute.

The opposition girl/woman which is constructed with reference to sexuality is important. A girl is an un-deflowered female, and a woman is the opposite. An un-deflowered woman was usually called innocent by many young women I interviewed. She is called clean as well. The innocence and cleanness attributed to a virgin woman imply that a women who has experienced premarital sex has become both sinful and polluted. Her sin is less condemned in religious terms than it empowers the woman with an untamable force. According to men I spoke with, a woman who has sex with a man other than her husband before marriage cannot resist the temptation to taste other men after marriage either.

'Virginity' is a great virtue for an unmarried woman and its loss a great shame for her and her family among all ethnic groups. However, its negative effects are stronger among Asians and Muslims than Europeans. While pregnancy without marriage damages the reputation of a Russian family, the parents of the girl will admit that their daughter gives birth and will raise the child. Both non-Muslims and Muslims said Muslims will consider this a great shame and could beat the woman in question.

Marriage provides the only legitimate framework for sex and gives women the highest status they can achieve: wife and mother. A young woman over 25 who is not married yet, is pressured and usually called 'the old maid'.

Sex outside marriage imposes a stigma on women. My male students, distinguished between a 'girlfriend' and a 'fiance'. While they did not necessarily devalue their girlfriends, they did not trust them. They said that they expect their girlfriends to sleep with other men and usually they will not trust them enough to marry them. On the other hand, they said they could trust their fiance and wives. The young women were well aware of these attitudes.

The same distinction is made between a 'wife' and a 'mistress'. The former is praised and respected as the agent of reproduction and the servant of the practising of kinship and family rituals. The latter is stigmatised as the practioner of illicit sex and a danger to family. The prostitute is represented as a category on the same wavelength, but more evil.

One of the effects of constructing illicit sex as the binary opposite of sex between spouses is the lumping of different types of extra-marital sex together under the category of *guliat'*. *Guliat'*, which literally means to walk, is used as a metaphor for all sorts of illicit sex. For example, when it is said about a woman that 'she has illicit sex' (*Ona guliat'*), depending on the context, the sentence could be interpreted as she is loose, or she is unfaithful to her husband, or she is a prostitute.

This kind of dichotomy goes along with widespread duplicity. In other words, while a considerable number of people seek a variety of sexual pleasures, they still try to do this secretly. Such secrecy is motivated by the following factors: first of all, people keep their sexual affairs secret out of concern for their own reputation (*reputatsiia*). Reputation of a person, which is a high asset in networking, is closely linked to sexual behaviour. A man or woman with allegedly loose sexual behaviour is called *babnik* (lecher, womaniser) or *suka*. However, such labels affect men and women very differently. Women may not trust a *babnik* but his reputation enhances his own sense of his masculinity and wins him prestige among his male friends and acquaintances. On the other hand, a *suka* is depicted by both men and women as a perverted being who cannot be trusted. Although a stigmatised woman may have friends and relatives who do not care about her label, she is exposed to a great moral pressure which may undermine her self-esteem. The second reason people keep their sexual affairs secret is concern for their spouses and families. They simply do not want to disturb the family life or, even worse, cause a split. As the family is one of the main sites for networking, divorce undermines the spouse's access to resources. Again these concerns vary with regard to class, gender and generation. A wealthy man, or for that matter a wealthy woman, is less afraid of divorce. With regard to gender, women are more worried about the fate of the family, and they are afraid of being exposed to physical violence by their husbands, if their infidelity is betrayed. The younger generation are less afraid of divorce, because after divorce they can rejoin their parents. While a young man can easily marry again if he is prosperous, the chances of young divorced women remarrying a prosperous man are undermined, but she can find sponsors or engage in other sexualised strategies.

The third reason people keep their sexual affairs secret is their concern for social order. On one occasion I discussed this matter with a group of men, all of whom, with one exception, had extra-marital relations. All of them insisted that open practice is dangerous and corrupting for society. One of them said: 'If everybody talks openly about his sexual affairs this will create chaos, because then everybody will go around and fuck with everybody else like dogs and this will destroy society. We will be like animals. Nobody will respect anybody else.'

Women who allegedly break the perceived codes of modesty are considered as dangerous to both family and society, and so the use of violence to discipline them is legitimised. Indeed, as young women challenge this type of morality, they are subjected to both domestic and public violence.

Domestic violence, most women told me, which was already a considerable phenomenon in the Soviet era, has intensified as a result of post-Soviet social change. Social and economic problems like the growth of alcoholism and unemployment and the growth of suspicion of parents and husbands against young women's sexual conduct can result in domestic violence. The suspicion is a result of the dynamics between the commercialised sexual revolution on the one hand and the claims to an authentic Soviet sexual morality on the other. To clarify this let us look at the following case.

The reader might remember Aleksander's family (chapter 4). The main problem which disturbed the family peace time and time again was a dispute between Ludmila, the mother, and her two daughters, Natasha and Nastia, over the time she allowed the girls to come home at night. In summer, which was lighter, this time was 10pm and in winter 7pm. But the daughters, particularly the older one, Natasha, an independent and articulate woman, usually broke this rule. When I asked Ludmila about her worries, she answered:

> In the Soviet time it was safe for a young girl on the streets. Now there are businessmen, rich foreigners, Mafioso and hooligans who are looking for young girls in bars, restaurants and streets. Each time they are out I am worried; a foreigner may cheat them by giving them dollars, or hooligans may kidnap and rape them. They are young, they do not understand. I am responsible for their reputation and for marrying them all. Tell me, who will marry a girl, who, excuse me, is not a virgin? It is very difficult to be a mother in these times. Before, it was easier, both girls and boys were simple (*prostye*), they met each other, fell in love and married. But, now boys have become cheaters (*aferisty*). They just want to have sex.

Her daughters disagreed with her. Natasha said: 'My mother grew up in a village, she has not changed her provincial attitudes, she doesn't understand urban life.' Nastia agreed it was dangerous to be outside at night, but recited the following Russian proverb: 'Do not be too afraid of the wolf, or you will stop going to the forest (*volka boiatsia v les ne khodit'*).'

In the same manner, husbands or their families control young wives. Actually, young women helped each other go out with men by providing 'alibis' (*alibi*) in the following way. A girl friend of a young woman, who has a date with a man, rings the latter's mother and asks her to permit her daughter to accompany the first girl to visit a third girl friend. They inform the third girl of the matter in advance. Then the woman goes and meets the man. If her mother rings the third girl she will say, 'They went to buy something from the shop.' Mira, the waitress (above) told me that this method was also used by married women against their husbands. The unmarried, supposedly virgin women, and young married women were much more strictly controlled than divorced young women. In some cases, like that of Mira, the waitress, their lovers had contact with the rest of the family.

However, young women were less afraid of domestic control and violence than public violence, described and analysed in chapter 3. Women see the surge of public violence as a post-Soviet phenomenon. It has seen such a dramatic growth that almost every young woman I spoke with had been exposed to direct sexual harassment ranging from 'minor' ones like verbal abuse or touching to more dangerous ones like being kidnapped, raped or beaten.

The rise of public violence against women has several causes. It is an integral part of the general social chaos, the emergence of the mafia and hooligans, and the surge of violence (chapter 3). The very commercialisation of women's bodies makes them potential targets for violence in a situation where organised violence is an integral part of the appropriation and selling of any commodity. Men, like members of the mafia and police, who are agents of organised violence exploit such women economically and sexually. But as the women above said, women suffer more from the unorganised violence imposed on them by hooligans than that from mafia and police. The public violence against women is legitimised by the morality mentioned above. According to such morality a woman who breaks the moral codes on sexuality, dresses improperly, visits inappropriate places and breaks the gendered rules of time, invites such violence on herself. Moreover, she is depicted as a pervert who must be disciplined or eliminated. This results in the absence of any social pressure on the police and judicial systems, dominated by powerful men, to give any protection to women in public.

CONCLUSIONS

Women's involvement in sexual strategies is motivated partly by poverty and partly by their desires to access expensive goods introduced by the consumerist culture. People's moral attitudes on sexualised strategies are ambiguous. While these women are praised as the sign of a 'modernity' brought about by capitalism, simultaneously they are stigmatised by the 'traditional' morality as perverts and thereby the use of violence against them is instigated and legitimised. The sexual revolution and the so-called traditional Soviet morality, apparently depicted as opposites, are complementary axes of the exploitation of women by powerful men. The women who practice these strategies have ambivalent attitudes towards the social stigma imposed on them. On the one hand they justify their practice with reference to economic needs, sexual freedom and their rights over their own bodies. On the other hand as their ultimate goal in life is to achieve the officially sanctioned roles of wife and mother, some of them have negative feelings about their involvement in sexualised strategies. Sexual strategies and the sexual revolution are considered alien phenomena through negation of which the dispossessed create a sense of belonging to a Soviet imagined community. I will deal with this in the next chapter.

6 CONSTRUCTION OF THE ALIEN: IMAGINING A SOVIET COMMUNITY

In the conclusion of the previous chapter I suggested that notions of prostitution, illicit sex and alien were used negatively to create images of an authentic Soviet identity. Such images are part of the people's responses to wild capitalism (chaos). In this chapter I will explore, from the local point of view, how this was done.

In Almaty I kept hearing people classify people, social manners and goods and territories rhetorically as Soviet (*Sovetskii*), ours (*nashe*), or in opposite terms such as foreigner (*inostranets*), foreign (*inostranye*), abroad (*granitsa*), from abroad (*iz za rubezha*), not ours (*ne nashe*). The conversations in which the meanings of such categories were negotiated were part of and a response to, current political and social change on the macro level.

In spite of my expectations, I found a very strong Soviet patriotism among the majority of dispossessed people, regardless of their ethnic, rural or urban origin. This is not to suggest that there were no anti-Soviet feelings among a part of population. On the contrary, one could observe very quickly that the population was polarised in their attitudes to the Soviet past. The new rich (*novye bogatye*), sections of the intelligentsia and the younger generation of the middle class rejected the Soviet era as tyrannical, boring and monotonous. The rest of the population had positive attitudes towards it. However, this polarisation has not led to a homogenisation or fixation of attitudes at either pole. On both sides, the intensity of feelings expressed in relation to Soviet identity vary with regard to sociological factors such as class, gender, generation, ethnicity, rural or urban backgrounds, personal histories on the one hand, and the situation and active involvement of the speakers on the other.

This plethora of opinion on Sovietness is created by deploying two intertwined strategies of negation and remembering. As I have already touched upon the nostalgia for the Soviet era in chapter 3, let me begin by considering the negative ways of imagining of the Soviet community.

THE NEGATIVE CONSTRUCTION OF THE SOVIET IDENTITY

Negatively, Soviet identity is defined in contrast to a notion of alien (*ne nashe*) which is created from the articulation to each other of notions of an alien person (*inostranets*) and his alleged manners, alien phenomena, and alien goods.

The notion of alien

Although the notion of alien is attributed implicitly to those locals who have allegedly adopted an alien life-style (see below) its explicit representative in the local imagination is the foreigner (*inostranets*), a person who comes from outside the former Soviet territory, is male and is assumed to be rich. He is engaged in some kind of business and propagates prostitution, sexual disease, including AIDS and a consumerist life-style.

This kind of negative homogenising and essentialising view of the foreigner is in fact mostly articulated by the dispossessed. The intelligentsia and rich people have a rather differentiated, yet in a different way essentialising, notion of foreigners. They divide foreigners in an evolutionary manner: civilised (*tsivilizovannye*) and cultured (*kul' turnye i*) Americans and Europeans, semi-civilised Arabs, Turks, and Iranians and other Asians and uncivilised (*netsivilizovannye*) and uncultured (*nekul' turnye*) black Africans.They explicitly express very strong racist attitudes towards Africans. But they usually feel insecure and humble in relation to Americans and Europeans, and make symbolic capital of their association with them as the representatives of culture and civilisation.

I am concerned mainly with dispossessed people's concepts of the foreigner, although I will comment occasionally on those of the intelligentsia as well. In the first sense, the foreigner is contrasted to a Soviet person (*Sovetskii chelovek*),who is considered a member of the Soviet people (*Sovetskii narod*) associated with the Soviet homeland (*Sovetskii Rodina*), i.e, former Soviet territory, the three Baltic republics excepted. While people widely and explicitly conceived the people of other post-Soviet republics as their compatriots, they explicitly excluded the Baltic people from this. When asked the reason, they usually said that those from the Baltic states were always separatist and never became real Soviets (*nastoiashchie Sovetskii*). A young Kazakh woman, a student of mine, is typical: 'People from the Baltic (*Pribaltika*) were different from the rest of us. They never became Soviets from the heart. Even in the Soviet time, they were chewing gum while the rest of us had no idea of a chewing gum.'[51]

Actually when people, regardless of their ethnicity, used the phrase 'our people' (*nashi liudi, nash narod*), they usually referred to the 'Soviet people' (*Sovetskii narod*). The term referred also to another meaning, namely Kazakhstan people (*narod Kazakhstana, Kazakhstanskii narod*), but it was rarely used. For example, when people spoke of the sufferings or the glories of the *narod*, or cursed Gorbachev for betraying the *narod*, they referred to the first meaning of the word. But when they criticised

Nazarbaev for not having done anything for the *narod* they referred to the second one.

Among the dispossessed the rules of trust and reciprocity are applied to Soviets and foreigners in different ways. While a foreigner is depicted as cunning (*khitryi*) and greedy (*zhadnyi*), the opposite attributes are given to a Soviet.[52] Because of this, cheating foreigners or expecting them to pay higher rents for apartments is legitimised.

While the foreigner is perceived as an evil figure, he is sought as a resource as well. Such ambivalence is evoked by fact that he is identified as a male who is rich. As a wealthy person who has access to transnational business networks he is considered a potential resource. But his very wealth combined with his gender, make him a competitive man in the sexual market and thereby a sexual risk.

The foreigner as a resource

The people in my neighbourhood and other places looked to the foreigners not only as a direct economic resource, but also sometimes as a resource for learning languages or access to information or access to networks.

For example, a foreign visitor to the visa section in the police office in Almaty will be surprised by the absence of foreigners (with the exception of a few) among the tens of people who queue there each day. I visited the place on several occasions to arrange my residential documents. On one such occasion, when I stayed there the whole day, of more than a hundred people queuing only three were foreigners: myself, a young Chinese woman and a young German man. The rest were locals who had come to pick up or deliver passports which belonged to foreigners.[53]

The people queuing were young and old men and women from different ethnic backgrounds. The foreigners on whose behalf they were queuing came from all corners of the world, but the majority were Americans, Europeans, Turks, Arabs and Iranians. Moreover, most of these foreigners were businessmen, working in foreign companies, or linked to some local institutions. The foreigners were mainly the locals' employers or their tenants,[54] or were connected to them through the institutions in which the locals worked. In some rare cases the foreigners were either the husbands of a woman in the queue or the husband of somebody's daughter.

As this example suggests, there is an interdependence between foreigners and a wide range of locals, mainly of an economic nature. The dispossessed, elite, immigration authorities, the members of police, tax inspectors, the members of the mafia, hooligans, local businessmen, bar girls and prostitutes see a foreigner as a multiple potential economic resource. The dispossessed try to find a job through, or hire an apartment to, a foreigner. Some may try to marry a daughter to him, others try to get access to grants and scholarships in Europe and the US. Some look to him as a source of information, others try to learn a language from him. The tax and police officers and other corresponding authorities may try to extract bribes or gifts. Some locals will try to establish legal or illicit business links abroad. Members of the mafia and hooligans try to benefit by threatening him or offering him security and sexual services. The bar girls and prostitutes find him a lucrative sponsor or client.

In my neighbourhood two men were working for DHL, and another was a driver for the American embassy. A single mother was working in a Turkish cafe, and Gula, mentioned in chapter 5, was working in a Turkish bakery. Many of my students were working for foreigners as interpreters. People in the neighbourhood and at the university asked me to find for them foreign employers, reliable foreigners who could marry their daughters, or foreign business partners. People were also interested in me because I could provide information about the West. They usually asked about the size of apartments, wages and welfare systems in the West. However, in spite of this search for foreigners, they were suspected and their presence was considered as evil by dispossessed people regardless of their ethnicity.

The foreigner as evil

The foreigner is demonised by the dispossessed. For them, the foreigner epitomises the promiscuous rich man (both local and foreign), who is feared and hated for seducing women, involvement in prostitution and spreading sexual disease; and they associate such promiscuity with an alien life-style of consumerism, which is accused of contaminating the authentic Soviet way of life. The rich promiscuous man is also associated with alien evil forces who allegedly conspired against the *Sovetskii narod*, destroyed the Soviet Union and now establish wild capitalism (*dikii Kapitalism*).

Whenever I was out with a woman, men invariably, and women in some rare cases too, stared, abused us verbally, or sometimes became physically abusive. The male Iranians and Turks with whom I got acquainted had similar experiences. Such behaviour is a very complex phenomenon, related to changing gender images and relations, on the one hand, and local images of foreigners, on the other. The foreigner is assumed to be the representative and partly the agent of all 'evil phenomena'. First of all they are held responsible for the 'emergence' and the growth of prostitution. People claimed that their Soviet society was a pure one (*chistoe*), in which spouses did not cheat each other, where love and family were the main motive for the relation between two persons, and nobody could imagine selling herself. It was said that sex before marriage was not imaginable. But once the foreigners came with their US dollars, promiscuous sex and sexual diseases, they contaminated the local population both morally and physically.

This description of the Soviet era's sexual mores is not completely true. Because forms of sexuality, which were classified as perverted, were practised (Stern, 1981) and prostitution existed, though marginally (Posadskaya, 1992; Waters, 1989; Dobrokhotova, 1984). However, here I am primarily concerned with the purposes and implications of people's rhetoric on sexuality rather than whether their claims are true or false.

The alleged moral corruption and spread of diseases were not only associated with foreigners who were present in Almaty, but with foreign men in general. It was argued that local women who travel, either as suitcase traders or prostitutes, contract sexual diseases abroad (outside the former Soviet territory). This must be understood in relation to two of the main post-Soviet survival strategies mainly adopted by women, suitcase trade and sex work abroad. As a result of the post-Soviet reforms a number of markets have been created in which mainly foreign goods are sold. The suppliers of such goods are partly suitcase traders, overwhelmingly women, who travel to countries like Pakistan, Iran, Turkey and the United Arab Emirates. These women are mainly former professionals like doctors, teachers and engineers and, as mentioned in chapter 3, they have the reputation of sleeping with their trade partners abroad in order to buy goods more cheaply. Another reason for the travel of women to the Emirates and Turkey is prostitution. I have no statistics but according to the locals it is a massive phenomenon. Beller-Hann (1995) explores the way the presence of allegedly Russian prostitutes in Turkey has provoked stigmatising discourses against them, and has influenced local politics. In Almaty the travel of women to the Emirates and Turkey has become a subject for films (made in Russia), songs, newspapers and daily talks. In almost all of these cases the women's presence abroad is associated with illicit sex.

Even those whose close female friends and relatives were involved in the suitcase trade expressed stigmatising attitudes to women who travel abroad, while representing their own friends and relatives as exceptional. But these attitudes were clearly gendered. Men, without exception, had homogeneous attitudes of condemnation towards both women and foreign men alike. Women's attitudes were more mixed, flexible and contradictory. Some women, usually older ones, condemned the travellers. The younger ones expressed empathy, and instead blamed both local and foreign men for women's involvement in transnational prostitution. The two following quotes illustrate such gendered attitudes.

A local Korean man, whose own wife had been involved in trade with Pakistan and was now working for a Turkish company in Almaty, said: '*Chelnoki* (suitcase traders) have created a bad reputation for our women in Turkey and the Emirates. They sleep with everybody for money. Now people in the other countries think that all our women are prostitutes.'

Viktoria, a student of mine, the casino dealer from chapter 5, had made a trip to Pakistan, and her brother and his wife were involved in the suitcase trade with the Emirates. While saying that most of the female suitcase

traders were sleeping with their trade partners she defended this practice in
the following way:

> Our women are responsible for the survival of families, often with two or
> three children. Their husbands earn very little money. For divorced and
> unmarried women it is difficult to find a husband, because those of our
> men who have got money are so rich that they do not know how to
> entertain themselves. They want to change their women every day. When
> a Russian woman meets a foreigner she thinks that God has just helped
> her.
>
> It is easier for a woman than a man to negotiate a deal with a man in
> the Eastern countries. Women may sleep with Arabs sometimes to get a
> better deal and sometimes to earn money. It could be profitable to sleep
> with Arabs, because they are rich people and it is exotic for them to sleep
> with Russian women. But I know about women who stayed with Arabs
> for a long time, not as a wife but a lover, worked for them, slept with
> them. They were exploited by Arabs and not paid so much. But Arabs are
> better than our men here.
>
> Men here can do everything with women. I think it is better in the Arab
> Emirates. They will not really hurt you. But here they can beat you! Here,
> they can even kill you. Sometimes they will not pay you at all.

This brings to the fore an element of conflict of interest between the
foreigner and the local strong men. Although the local strong men benefit
economically from the presence of foreigners in Almaty,[55] they use the
notion of the 'evil foreigner' to control local women. Women are a
threefold resource for these men. As lovers and prostitutes they are a
source of sexual pleasure. As pimps and managers of illegal brothels and
owners of entertainment places they benefit economically from women.
Moreover, wives run their households. A foreigner is a competitive rival,
a threat to his domination over women. The presence of foreign men in
Almaty and women's ability to travel abroad provide those women who
practice sexualised strategies of survival with an alternative source of men
and thereby an ability to manoeuvre against local men. What particularly
makes a foreigner a threat to the local dominant men is both his money
and his vulnerability in the eyes of the local women. Many local women
including prostitutes told me that they felt safer with foreign men. They
thought foreigners were not able to force them into sex without their own
consent or assault them. This positive view did not mean that women
thought foreign men were more women-friendly, but that due to the cir-
cumstances they could not use violence against women. Asel' formulated
this as follows:

The foreign man has no contact with the police and the mafia. He has no local contacts (*sviaz'*) no friends. The police and authorities wait for him to do something illegal, then he must either pay great bribes to them or go to jail. We know police, hooligans and Mafioso, all of whom will be interested to help us against a foreigner, but they will not help us against a local man because they all know each other, and will not fight with each other to defend women.

In spite of the fact that a rich foreign man cannot use violence and is dependent on the local strong men even for his own protection, he is a strong rival for the local dominant men because of his money. This is well illustrated by Asel''s description of her foreign clients: 'They are better, they have green dollars.'

The local strong men deploy the notion of 'evil foreigner' to claim a shared Soviet identity with the local women and thereby establish rights of decision over their bodies. As the bodies of women are considered to be bearers of the collective Soviet identity, contact, or even worse her sexual contact, with the evil and promiscuous foreigner is damaging for such an identity. Relating collective identities to sexuality and the policing of women is a well known phenomenon (at least in the Muslim and Christian worlds) (Ahmed, 1992; Kandiyoti, 1991; McClintock, 1995). But from the women's point of view in Almaty, there are two distinctive features to the local dominant men in this respect. First, their use of the notion of a collective Soviet identity related to an authentic sexual conduct of women is completely cynical. According to most of the women, such men will not hesitate to sell local women to foreigners to make money or acquire other privileges. Moreover, such men are the main beneficiaries of the post-Soviet change and represent a consumerist life-style which includes a strong element of sexual promiscuity. They have no commitment to the images of authentic Soviet sexual morality; rather, they ridicule such notions. They are not opposed to contacts between foreign men and local women in principle, but try rather to mediate themselves between local women and foreign men. I frequently heard stories from both foreign businessmen and locals about how local men introduce beautiful local women to foreigners to get good contracts or establish a relationship or just as pimps. According to the locals, sex is a part of signing any good business deal. Second, their claims on women in relation to foreigners transcends ethnicity which is otherwise partly constructed through the policing of women's trans-ethnic sexual relations. For example, Kazakh men have strong claims on Kazakh women's bodies in relation to men from other local ethnic groups. They make the same claims on the bodies of women of any other ethnic group of the *Sovetskii narod* in relation to foreign men.

The actual targets of the discourse of the evil foreigner are not so much the foreigners as the women seen with them. Although foreigners may be abused occasionally, any such victims are not rich or influential, but are Afghan refugees, students or those who work for NGOs. Businessmen or the professionals of multinationals live in well-protected areas, visit well-protected clubs and are personally protected either by the government or the mafia. Their local women have none of these privileges. The local dominant men try to control local women's relationships with foreigners through both ideology and violence.

The stigmatisation of women's relationships with foreign men is not only a strategy to control their sexuality, but is also intended to prevent them using the economic opportunities offered by the transnational economy to develop their careers, independently of local men. As mentioned in chapter 5, wealth is concentrated in the hands of influential men and women's access to it depends on their relations with such men. Nevertheless, the presence of foreign business and multinationals which are 'manned' mainly by foreign men, and transnational links with abroad, provide some opportunities for women to develop their own economic activities. A woman from my neighbourhood sent tourists to Iran. At the university I met a considerable number of women, both students and teachers of foreign languages, who worked for foreign companies as translators. Jamila, a Kazakh woman, is one of them. Her story is one of success and stigma: Jamila, was in her early forties. When I met her, she worked for an Austrian company and was married to an Austrian. She had divorced her former Kazakh husband. The reason for divorce had been his alcoholism and violence. Jamila had left her job as a university lecturer in the English language in 1990. The reason, according to her, had been that the salary was not enough for her and her daughter to survive. As she could speak English very well, she found a job as a cleaner in an Austrian company. While emptying the bin in the Austrian man's office by chance she read the drafts of letters he threw away, and offered to correct his grammatical mistakes. Once the Austrian discovered her skills in English, he employed her as his secretary. She was then promoted to higher posts. She said: 'As I worked honestly and very hard the Austrians trusted me and consequently promoted me. Many Kazakh young men who tried to please Austrians by introducing girls to them were not trusted. But my brother-in-law believes that I could not get the job or the promotion without sleeping with Austrians.' When I asked her: 'Why does he think so?' Laughing loudly, she answered: 'Because he is a stupid Kazakh.' But Jamila was not angry with him. On the contrary, she had saved this man and his family from poverty. First, Jamila had found him a job in an Austrian company as a driver, for $400 per month, six times more than the average salary. Second, she had exchanged her apartment and their apartment for a larger one and had furnished the latter through Austrians with Austrian furniture. A few days after I met her she found an English tenant for the apartment who rented it for $1,000 per month. Jamila gave all this money to her sister's family. Jamila explained the reason for her generosity towards the family as follows: 'When I left my husband they received me generously and supported me. My sister's husband has grown among Russians in the North. He is not like a Kazakh man. He helped me and now I help them back.' Jamila's leading role in the family economy had bestowed her with a hegemonic authority in family affairs. She had used her authority to subvert this man's former dominance over her sister. She told me: 'He abused my sister before both physically and verbally; he is a stupid Kazakh man; but now I have registered the apartment in the name of my sister, and have told him if he continues to abuse my sister I will throw him out in the street. As he knows that I am serious and that I know good lawyers, he has stopped abusing my sister.'

As this example demonstrates, some women use relations with foreigners, who are overwhelmingly men, to acquire a greater economic role in the family networks and thereby strengthen their own positions. So the women's contact with foreigners undermines not only the sexual monopoly of the local powerful men, but also the authority of local men over women in general. The sexual stigmatisation of such women is an ideologically suitable way to control women's contacts with foreigners because it has, as we will see below, great resonance among the wider population. But as a considerable number of the local women particularly the younger ones, challenge the stigma, the bearers of dominant masculinity resort to violence to reinforce their control. The following example is illuminating.

Once four of us, me, a young Kazakh female colleague, her girl friend and an English man were sitting in a cafe discussing the relation between Kazakhs and Russians. But gradually we felt a growing attention towards us from a group of three Kazakh men sitting at a neighbouring table. Fortunately this did not develop into a dramatic event. But when they were passing by our table on their way out, one of them said in Russian to the women: 'This is shameful (*eto stydno*).' The women who had become afraid did not answer but became silent and to avoid him looked down at the surface of the table. While all of us felt relieved when they left the place, the English teacher said:

> Unfortunately our Kazakh men are uncultured. They come from the south and rural areas here to Almaty. Then they engage in boxing and body building and get involved in violence and different crimes. They treat Kazakh girls as prostitutes. If they invite you to something they expect you to sleep with them. If you avoid it they will tell you: 'I have spent

money on you. I have bought this, and that for you, you must repay it.'
Even if they buy you a bite of chocolate, they will ask you to sleep with
them. If you will not agree to do so, they will force you to do it. If they
see you with a foreigner they think you are a prostitute. They will insult
you and your company, or even attack you physically. But if they feel
that the foreigner is protected by the state or the mafia they will not say
anything, but later they will hit you whenever they find you alone.

As the woman above suggests, the use of violence against women to
control their relations with foreigners is an element of the wider violence
imposed on them by dominant men. The sad aspect of the situation is that
subordinate men and a wide range of women, not only do not question
such violence but conform to the notions of foreigners and honour and
shame which give legitimacy to such violence. Below I analyse their
motives for this.

Subordinated men and the foreigner
The weak men who lack wealth and means of violence, use the notion of
'the evil foreigner' to challenge both foreign and local rich men in the
sexual market. They try to do so by the exploitation of the notion of the
foreigner as the epitome of the rich promiscuous man in general. This
notion of foreigner has to do with the monetisation of the sexual relations.
As described in chapter 5 money and violence play determinant roles in
different types of the post-Soviet sexual relations ranging from marriage to
prostitution. A 'weak man' has no great chances in the Almaty sex market,
unless he is extra handsome or lucky. The reason for his misfortune is that
he does not fit into the image of the post-Soviet gentleman (*dzhentl'men*),
described in chapter 5, who is desired so strongly by the opposite sex.

Although for most of the Almatian men it is impossible to reach the status
of gentleman, because of its high expenses, they are still obliged to provide
their lovers or would-be wives with presents or invite them to restaurants.
All young women I spoke with expected their would-be husbands to do so.
A man who fails to fulfil such expectations is not considered to be a real
man (*nastoiashchii muzhchina*). But this imposed high costs on the ordinary
men. For example, a young Kazakh male student spent the whole of his
monthly scholarship to invite a young Kazakh woman whom he loved to a
restaurant. In another case a young Russian/German worker paid the whole
of his salary buying gold earrings for his girlfriend.[56] But as all men cannot
afford to spend money, their chances of finding a lover or a wife are
undermined. A group of men with whom I communicated complained that
it was expensive for them to find or keep lovers.

This was particularly true of unmarried migrant Kazakh men whose lack
of money resulted in sexual deprivation.[57] But they are not alone in this.

All the poor urban men, regardless of their ethnic origin, are in the same boat. Two Russian young brothers, aged 25 and 28 years old, who were my neighbours, complained that they had not met women for ages because of their lack of money. The younger one was an electrician with a salary of 2,500 tenge ($37) a month and the older one an unemployed former army officer. He had become an alcoholic and was living on his brother's and mother's salary, and they all lived together.

It is not only the poor man's poverty which makes him undesirable but even his style and job. The only sexy job in Almaty today is to be a businessman, foreigner or local. Workers, academicians, officers, and university lecturers are not reckoned to be 'real men' (*nastoiashchii muzhchina*). In order to be seen as attractive one must dress in a suit, put on a tie and shiny shoes. Many young lads without the cash resort to small crimes to provide these. A 19-year-old Kazakh and his half-Tatar half-Russian friend told me that without small crimes, mainly thefts, it is impossible for them to have access to girls. Although they were well aware of the risks of being imprisoned, they said they will continue to do this.

The rich men, locals or foreigners, not only undermine the chances of poor single men to find partners but are a potent threat to those men who already have partners, because they are a strong temptation for the poor men's partners.

What makes poor men's partners less resistant to such temptation is the current ambiguities and instabilities in the relationships between spouses among the dispossessed. A good looking wife in a poverty-ridden family with a disastrous relationship with her husband, may seek to divorce or find a well-off man as a sponsor.

Mira the waitress, from chapter 5, said that it was a common practice among Russian young women to have lovers. Viktoria, from the same chapter said that many married women had sponsors. The loosening of the old sexual morality under the influence of the sexual revolution and temptations of the consumerist culture encourage such women to divorce or find sponsors. To lose one's wife because of poverty is a disaster which may lead to suicide. In the neighbourhood, I knew of two women whose husbands, a construction worker and an electrician, had committed suicide. The neighbours said the reason was that their wives were involved with other men. Both of these women, in their mid-thirties, were broken, alcoholic and very poor. So the rich men not only undermine the single poor men's opportunities to find wives or lovers but rich men may take poor men's partners from them.

To resist the rich man in the sexual field the poor man resorts to the discourses of a moral community of the Soviet *narod,* constructed to question the new rich and post-Soviet change in general. Such a discourse contrasts the Soviet community with the overall notion of the alien (*ne nashi*) in order to bolster the position of the weak men in sexual competition by use of the following strategies. In this discourse sexual promiscuity and consumerist culture are epitomes of the alien.

Related to this, particular moral and sexual obligations are imposed on dispossessed women. They are expected to communicate sexually within the community, otherwise they are shamed for smearing the collective honour of the community. Moreover, their sexual behaviour and social conduct is checked by the morality of modesty described in chapter 5. So the Soviet moral community is based on a sexual morality which is a double-edged sword. While one edge is used for challenging the power of rich men, the other edge is in the service of the dispossessed men's domination over dispossessed women. Again, the claims of identity turn out to be claims on women's bodies by men.

Women's reactions to the obligations imposed on them by the discourse of community vary with generation. Younger women challenge such sexual morality, the burdens of which are imposed on them. But the older women are its guardians. The conflicts between Ludmila and her daughters Natasha and Nastia, mentioned in chapter 5, illustrate such conflicting attitudes. As Ludmila said, mothers are responsible for their daughters' reputation and successful marriage, so they control them very strictly.

The young women resist the Soviet sexual morality because they are attracted to the consumerist culture and use sexual economic strategies to gain access to materially protected lives and consumerist goods. Among the dispossessed, the young women are almost the only group who are more or less attracted to the consumerist culture. Both in the neighbourhood and at the university young women were the main readers of tabloid journals like *Kakadu* and *Speed*, and were the main groups who visited clubs and discos.

Although mothers worry that their daughters will be seduced by foreigners or local rich men they will be happy if their daughter can find a good husband among either group. The marriage of Aleksander and Ludmila's daughter Natasha with a Turk-Bulgar illustrates this. As it turned out her husband was a good and reliable man. This enhanced Natasha's reputation among friends and neighbours as a smart girl who had managed to find a good husband. Her husband's pleasant character also improved the image of foreigners among Natasha's close neighbours and friends. After this event two Kazakh women, both mothers of Natasha's friends, asked me whether I had reliable foreign friends who were willing to marry their daughters.

However, most people believed that the foreign men lured naive local girls into marriage in order to recruit them for brothels abroad. The following comments on Natasha's marriage are typical. A Kazakh man who used to sell things illegally beside Natasha said: 'The Turk will sell her. How could her family let this happen?' He added 'I have read in newspapers that they sell Russian girls in Germany and Turkey.' A half-Russian half-Tatar woman, a street trader who also knew Natasha, said: 'He is right, they sell our girls abroad. I will never let my daughters marry foreigners.' I told this to Natasha's family. Ludmila said that the woman was jealous, because nobody took her daughters.

Although young women were inclined to sexual strategies and consumerist culture, they also shared with older women and men very strong feelings against them as elements of wild capitalism, which had allegedly destroyed the Soviet-era relations between men and women based on trust, love, respect and security. I will now examine the dispossessed's attitudes towards consumerism and wild capitalism.

CONSUMERISM AND THE DISPOSSESSED

I visited the international business club in Almaty on Friday evenings for a good while. My reason for visiting the club was that I had frequently heard the local people saying that 'prostitutes' are responsible for the spreading sexual diseases, including AIDS (*SPID*), which they contract from foreigners. As mentioned, the images of sexual diseases, prostitutes, prostitution and the ways these are related to those of foreigners, constitute components of a wider local discourse on the alien, through which people construct negatively an authentic Soviet 'identity'. As the club was famous for being one of the main places where the foreign men met local women, I began to visit it to meet of some of the alleged culprits.

The club is owned and administrated by Turks and staffed mainly by local young, beautiful women, mostly 'Russians' with some Kazakhs among them. The guests consist mainly of white[58] men from Australia, Europe and America and the beautiful young local women, from any ethnic origin. The male visitors work in embassies or multinationals like Shell, Chevron, Volvo, KLM, Lufthansa, or provide consultancy work for the government, or run their own businesses, or are businessmen who visit Almaty for short periods to exhibit their goods.

The local young women consist of different categories. The first group are the lovers and a few wives of the white men. The second group work as secretaries or interpreters for white men. The third group are those who come here to find foreign husbands, or 'sponsors' (a lover) or find a job. And the last group are young prostitutes.

In addition, one can occasionally meet a few men from the Middle East or South Asia or a few American or West European women. Visiting the club for a while I saw just one black man there; he was from the US.

The guests mix, drink and eat until midnight when the club is closed. Then they drive in their expensive cars, accompanied by their women, home or to Manhattan, a disco in Almaty, or to KIMEP (another disco bar owned and run by an American), or Casino Plaza beside the Hotel Rakhat Palace (Marco Polo) which is run by Turks, or to other similar places.

The business club and other entertainment places mentioned above are part of a wider newly created economic, social and cultural sphere. In the eyes of a rich foreign or local man who has enough money and a beautiful woman in his company, or a superficial and biased Western journalist, this sphere has transformed Almaty from a 'boring' Soviet city to an 'alive and vibrant' one. The shopping centres, business offices, exhibitions centres for foreign goods, fashion salons, restaurants, casinos and hotels which have shaped the new face of the city belong to the private sector. The owners of these businesses are those foreign and local men who mix with a particular type of the beautiful young local women, and lavishly spend money in the numerous entertainment places. The most impressive of these places are the Hotel Rakhat Palace (Marco Polo) built, owned and run by Turks, and the restaurant Dostyk. Turks, Americans, Italians, the local Koreans and other locals have their own share in creating this small Babylon.

Most dispossessed people, young and beautiful women excepted, not only cannot afford to visit these places (with the exception of shopping centres), but associate them with the alien, prostitution and immoral sexual behaviour. The dispossessed stigmatise these places because the men who own, run and visit them have a privileged access to wealth or means of violence, and as a result have access to beautiful women by virtue of their wealth and violence, and people think that such men corrupt social morality and spread sexual diseases. Moreover, these places and the men associated with them symbolise the wild capitalism which has ruined people's lives.

In a sense the dispossessed distinguish clearly between consumption and consumerism. Consumption is oriented towards the use value of the goods due to their physical structures and material substances. Consumerism is related to the prestige/sign values inscribed in them by the genres of fashion and the advertisements which form the social practices of 'distinction' (Bourdieu, 1984). This does not mean that consumption in the dispos-sessed's terms constitutes a natural process stripped of any cultural history. On the contrary, the Soviet type of consumption and sharing of drink and food among the post-Soviet dispossessed are highly ritualised (Humphrey, 1983; chapter 4 in this book) and related to the regimes of the body (chapter 4 in this book; Appadurai, 1997; Bourdieu, 1977). Moreover they constitute elementary forms of reciprocity around which social networks are organised (see chapter 4). What this suggests is that late capitalist consumerism represents a break with the Soviet type of consumption, still prevalent among the dispossessed.

This break is primarily marked by the fact that in consumerism the relation between the prestige values inscribed in the goods by the genres of fashion and advertisement and their material structures and physical properties becomes arbitrary. The prestige goods imported from the West bring a new dimension to the world of consumption: the consumption of signs and images.

Signs and images are consumed in order to create fictions of identity evolving around fictional role models. To drive a Mercedes, to consume expensive Western goods, to spend dollars in restaurants and casinos, to build villas, to buy expensive furniture, to travel to the West, to send children to the Western universities, to have beautiful lovers and American friends are signs of distinction.

In consumerism, through the articulation of the body to Western com-modities and imaginary association with Western celebrities, an identification with the West, mainly the US, is created. The new rich consider the US as the cradle of civilisation, the main terms of its descrip-tion are glamour, wealth and power. The images of a powerful America emanate particularly from two recent historical facts: the USSR is considered to have been defeated by the US and US dollars are practically the main currency in the daily life of the country. So the identification with the West through Western commodities is an identification on the level of fantasy, with the civilised, the glamorous, the wealthy and the powerful.

The notions of America as elegant, muscular and rich correspond to those of the local rich men. Such an identification with glamour and power through the use of sign-commodities are articulated to a new economy of erotics through the media and the market. Indeed, market and media have both become erotic spectacles. They produce and stimulate desires through the glamorous exhibition of sign-commodities. Television, video and the print media offer visual pleasures juxtaposing the pictures of beautiful women and luxurious commodities not only on the covers and front pages of magazines and newspapers, but more spectacularly and nakedly on the inside pages. In this sense the images of commodities including those of women's bodies are consumed as part of the consumption of media (Jameson, 1991: chapter 8). The luxurious shops which offer sign goods and exhibitions, arranged by foreign merchants, stage similar spectacles. A glamorous and desire-provoking space is composed by juxtaposing beautiful perfumed women (sellers), who are fashionably dressed and with the latest make-up on their faces, with sign-commodities beautifully exhibited.

In this way the luxurious shops and other places like expensive restau-rants, business centres, casinos, bars and discos mentioned above, have acquired double functions in relation to consumption: they offer visual pleasures on the one hand and prestigious goods and services on the other.

To summarise the argument, the pluralisation of the market and media, their articulation to each other, and their analogous practices create inter-twined economies of fantasy and erotica articulating representations of the

West as the centre of civilisation, glamour, wealth and power. These notions inform the ideology and the visions of the new rich.

In order to oppose this ideology, the dispossessed associate consumerism and its intertwined fantasy and erotica with foreigners, prostitution, theft and immorality in general. Such attitudes should not be attributed to working people's inertia or inability to adapt to social change. Nor should they be interpreted as showing the dispossessed to be opposed to consumerism on principle. They may enjoy watching soap operas or visiting exhibitions but still oppose consumerism for political reasons. To paraphrase Walter Benjamin, I would say that while the new rich have brought fashion and glamour into class distinctions, the dispossessed bring class distinctions into the world of fashion and glamour. If the new rich uses the sign-commodities to construct their own identity, the working people stigmatise consumerism in order to question the arrogant life-style of the new rich and their alleged foreign associates, whom they consider a bunch of thieves and criminals. Thus, the working people have a complex relationship with Western goods. As they know for sure that such goods, food and drink excepted, are of better quality, than their own, they may buy particular goods, if they can afford them, while refusing the ideological values the new rich ascribe to them.

The dispossessed contrast consumerism with the Soviet culture, claiming that such a culture was authentic and based on higher moral and aesthetic principles. Morally, it is claimed that the Soviet life-style and culture encouraged sexual purity and fidelity, humanism and solidarity. Aesthetically, they claim that their Soviet art was more genuine and of a higher quality. It might be that these claims do not correspond to the 'reality' of the Soviet era and merely express the anger of the dispossessed against the new rich. However it must be noted that working people in Almaty have a more sophisticated taste for art and knowledge of so-called 'high culture' (theatre, classical music, ballet, opera, the classic realist novel and sophisticated films), to which they refer as the authentic Soviet culture, than its counterpart in the West. From the very beginning the Soviet regime used these forms of art as an instrument for agitation and political education and rituals. Given the extension of the state rituals (Lane, 1981) this type of culture came to constitute an important part of Soviet 'mass culture'. Thus, the collapse of the Soviet mass culture is experienced as a tragedy by the dispossessed. Besides the significance of consumerism for cultural struggle the dispossessed dismiss it as part of the new wild capitalism.

WILD CAPITALISM AS AN ELEMENT OF THE ALIEN

On an abstract level the transformation from communism to the 'free' market has democratised access to goods. People have no need of patronage networks in order to access particular goods; if someone has the money s/he can buy the goods. But for the majority of Almatians such democracy and egalitarianism has turned out to be a fiction. Because of the new poverty they cannot afford the prices. The dispossessed think foreigners and the local elite, marked by their corrupt alien life-style (sexual promiscuity and consumerism) jointly represent the forces which have destroyed the Soviet Union and established the wild capitalism, the cause of their poverty. In this way foreigners, the local new rich, their alleged habits (sexual promiscuity and consumerism) and those social conditions which allegedly underpin their privileged positions such as prostitution, the mafia, monetisation of life worlds including sexual relations, and privatisation of the state property are lumped together as alien forces of an evil character.

In this sense the new rich are not only excluded from the Soviet *narod* but also depicted as a traitors (*izmenniki*). The rich men are accused of contaminating the Soviet authentic culture, propagating alien immoral habits and the destruction of the Soviet Union itself. The significance of this latter allegation must be understood, in the context of a widely held conspiracy theory that the Soviet elite led by Gorbachev conspired with foreigners to destroy the Soviet Union. *Perestroika* is considered simultaneously as the greatest treason (*izmena*) and the greatest deception (*obman*). Thus, Gorbachev, admired in the West as a great historical figure, was seen as a great traitor (*izmennik*) and a great deceiver (*obmanshchik*). Without doubt Gorbachev was the most hated person among the ordinary people in Almaty. In this sense the negative feelings about the alien were articulated to a strong nostalgia for the Soviet era.

SUMMARY AND CONCLUSIONS

The articulation of the overall notion of the evil alien to a strong nostalgia for the past creates a sense of a Soviet *narod* whose homeland is the former Soviet territory. The concepts of foreigner, the new rich, sexual promiscuity, prostitution, sexual diseases, authenticity, consumerism, wild capitalism, deception, betrayal, loss of freedom, loss of security, loss of happiness, loss of trust, despair and fear of the future are the main tropes through which such an articulation is shaped.

Both the rejection of the alien and the idealisation of the Soviet past are also reactions to social chaos (*bardak*) (see chapters 1 and 3). They are also part of the dynamics of current ideological 'class struggles'. While the new rich use consumerism to alienate the dispossessed from 'civilisation', the dispossessed alienate the rich from the Soviet *narod* by linking their habitus and economic position to alien forces. Money, sexual promiscuity, consumerism and wild capitalism underpin the privileges of the new rich and also represent the social reality brought about by the post-Soviet change. Thus the negation of such phenomena by the dispossessed evokes a strong romantic image of the Soviet past. From my point of view, this image of the past certainly includes a strong element of forgetting. People are simply unwilling to remember the KGB and economic shortages. Yet we should not conclude from this that people desire the return of a totalitarian political regime or an economy of shortage. Without doubt people are demanding the restoration of the welfare state. However, the distorted image of the Soviet era as a time of happiness, freedom, security and trust stems primarily from the miseries of the present time and lack of any hope for a better future. Most working people, regardless of age, gender, or ethnicity, believed that they have no future. In the working people's construction of time the present and future are judged from the vantage point of the Soviet era (*Sovetskoe vremia*). It almost seems that the flow of time has ceased to exist for them since the disintegration of the Soviet Union. Recall the assertions of the Kazakh teacher cited in chapter 3: 'But now we have nothing. We are corpses. We are moving corpses.'

Paradoxically, by turning their backs on the dark future they expect from wild capitalism and looking backward, people imagine an alternative future which is free of both the evils of the Soviet era and the miseries of the present. Through distorted and romanticised images of the Soviet era people design the contours of a better egalitarian future. While nostalgia becomes an element of utopia, the projection of utopia onto the past provides evidence of its possibility in the future.

In this way people explicitly contrast socialism with capitalism; the former is identified with egalitarianism and the latter is considered as the cause of all the present miseries.

However, the Achilles heel of this egalitarian discourse is its authoritarian attitudes on gender relations. Notions of cultural authenticity defined partly by women's modesty perpetuate patriarchal gender relations. The claims of a shared Soviet identity between men and women, when translated into the field of gender, turn partly into men's claims on women's bodies. Women are discouraged from transgressing the rules of modesty. Or they are stigmatised and violated. Paradoxically, the main beneficiaries of such gender ideologies are a group of powerful men who are excluded from the Soviet community by the ordinary people. They cynically use the popular morality to impose their own terms on women. The dispossessed men resort to gendered notions of a Soviet authenticity because the post-Soviet change such as unemployment, wage cuts, consumerist culture and sexual promiscuity of rich men, both foreigners and local, undermined their masculinity. This observation points to an important aspect of the relation between masculinity and wealth in the post-Soviet conditions. The post-Soviet change has undermined the masculinity of the dispossessed men and enhanced that of the rich men.

The fact that all working people hold the elite and foreigners responsible for the present situation is a key factor in preventing large scale ethnic conflicts emerging out of the present chaotic and desperate situation. The intensification of competition between ethnically based networks for resources, and the post-Soviet ethnicisation of the state have led to an intensification of ethnic tensions, which will be dealt with in the next chapter. But the scale of such conflicts would be larger and their forms much more violent in the absence of a feeling of common Soviet identity between Kazakhs and non-Kazakh. For example, while the tensions between Russians and rural Kazakh migrants represents the peak of ethnic conflicts in Almaty, neither group holds the other responsible for the current situation. Both groups point to the elite. The rural Kazakhs who are more religious and 'traditional' are the most ardent defenders of the Soviet identity because the post-Soviet change has literally ruined their lives.

7   ETHNIC TENSION

In this chapter I deal with ethnic tension but not with all significant aspects
of ethnicity. I do so because the locals considered ethnic tension as an
element of chaos. This tension is primarily caused by the fact that ethnically
based networking, articulated with the Kazakhification of the state, is
pivotal for the distribution of resources. State institutions themselves are
considered as important resources, because access to a high post in such an
institution provides access to various resources through reciprocal exchange
within networks of influence. Indeed, non-Kazakhs blamed Kazakhs for
monopolising state posts and places in higher education. Another sphere of
contest was urban space, notably apartments and markets. There was not a
great competition for jobs in the industrial sector. Owing to the collapse of
industry, wage cuts and salary postponement neither migrant nor urban
Kazakhs were inclined to work in factories. Thus, in this chapter I explore
the Kazakhification of the state and the struggle for urban space.

KAZAKHIFICATION OF THE STATE

In spite of the fact that Kazakhstan has more than a hundred different
nationalities, in the both the Soviet and the post-Soviet eras the republic
has been primarily associated with Kazakhs. In the Soviet era the Kazakh
was considered as the titular nationality and the republic was named after
it. They also enjoyed legal quotas in both higher education and administrative posts. However, the association of the republic with Kazakhs did
not create acute problems for non-Kazakhs, because all Kazakhstan's inhabitants were *de facto* citizens of the Soviet Union. After the dissolution of the
USSR, non-Kazakhs could choose to become citizens of the new state or
'repatriate' to their own 'historical homelands' (*istoricheskaia rodina*).[59]
Most of them are not content with these two alternatives. Aleksander
expressed the paradoxical situation of non-Kazakhs in the following way:
'Here I am a second class citizen (*vtoroe sort grazhdanin*) but in Moldava
nobody is waiting for me.'

The worries of non-Kazakhs are caused by the ritual and administrative
Kazakhification of the newly independent state. First, the Kazakh language
has been declared in the constitution as the state language (article 7.1, p. 7).
Second, the state rituals, holidays and heroes are related to Kazakhs. Third,
the names of streets and places have been changed to Kazakh ones and the

pictures published on currency notes are of Kazakhs. Administratively, non-Kazakhs have been systematically purged from the high and middle ranks of the state apparatus and replaced by Kazakhs. Even in an elected organ like parliament, Kazakhs constitute the majority although they did not constitute more than 42 per cent of the total population at the time of the election. The dominance of Kazakhs in the state institutions is depicted by the non-Kazakhs as a main cause of corruption. They argue that state officials distribute posts in state institutions, credit and places in higher education among their friends and relatives. Non-Kazakhs questioned the legitimacy of such domination by referring to the constitution or to Nazarbaev's speeches, which associate the state with the people of Kazakhstan (*narod Kazakhstana*) and not merely Kazakhs.

Theoretically, the constitution identifies the state with the people of Kazakhstan. However, in spite of this, both the the constitutional status of the Kazakh language and the preface to the constitution open possibilities for an interpretation which may award Kazakhs a privileged position. The constitution begins:

> We, people of Kazakhstan (*Narod Kazakhstana*),
> united by a common historical destiny,
> creating a statehood on the primordial Kazakh land (*iskonnoi Kazakhskoi zemle*),
> conceiving ourselves as a peace-loving civic society, devoted to the ideals of freedom, equality and consent,
> wishing to occupy a deserved place in the world's association,
> realising our high responsibility in front of present and future generations,
> proceeding from our sovereign right,
> accept this genuine constitution.
> (Translated by the author from the constitution, 1995: p. 3. Emphasis added.)

The identification of the state with the people of Kazakhstan, as distinct from the Kazakh ethnic category, is counterbalanced in the prelude to the constitution by the inclusion of the phrase 'on the primordial Kazakh land'. Such inconsistencies and ambiguities, which correspond to both the real domination of Kazakhs in the state and its nominal identification with all ethnic groups, characterise the relation between the state and ethnicity in Kazakhstan. They are interpreted differently by Kazakhs and non-Kazakhs. From the Kazakh point of view the primordial association of the state territory with them is interpreted to mean that non-Kazakhs should accept Kazakh hegemony in the state if they want to stay in Kazakhstan. For example, a Kazakh colleague claimed that ethnic discrimination did not exist in Kazakhstan. I asked him: 'Why, then, are 75 per cent of students in this university Kazakhs?' 'Because', he answered, 'we are in Kazakhstan. If we were in Russia or Uzbekistan, then 75 per cent would be Russians or Uzbeks.'

Non-Kazakhs interpret this ambiguity in a different way. They reject the Kazakhs' primordial claims on the state territory by resorting to a constructionist concept of homeland and depict Kazakhs as usurpers of state power. Moreover, they blame the current chaos on Kazakhs' assumed corruption, ignorance, irresponsibility, laziness and tribal anarchy in running the country. Let us take the example of a Russian family in my neighbourhood. The father is 44 years old and works in a power station. The mother is 40 and works as an engineer, but her factory works at half capacity, and so she works half time and is paid half. The daughter is 21, married and studies French at university. Her husband is a student as well and lives with the family. Although none of them are 'pure' Russian they see themselves as Russians. All of them told me that the Kazakh elite discriminated against Russians. The father said that people were afraid of speaking of the discrimination in official circles. When I asked him whether his Kazakh colleague had nationalist attitudes towards him, he answered: 'No, they are helpless like me. Only those in high positions (*na verkho*) have the power to discriminate. Kazakhs discriminate not only against Russians but against other Kazakhs as well. They come from three different *Zhuz* who struggle against each other.' Then his son-in-law said: 'Kazakhs have large families and lots of relatives. Once one of them gets a high post, he will give all the good jobs to his own relatives.' According to him, the most attractive jobs were in the state apparatus because of the opportunity of taking bribes. The mother in the family said:

> Each Kazakh comes with a lamb on his shoulder from the *Auls* here, bribes another Kazakh at a university with the lamb and gets a place. Then he gives them some more lambs and buys a red diploma. When he has the diploma his father gives some more lambs to another Kazakh and he gets a job for him. But he cannot do the job, because he has not got the knowledge. What he does is sit there and take bribes (*vziatki*).

Her daughter said:

> To be admitted to the university one must either get 5 on all parts of the entry examination or pay a high fee around US$5,000 each year. I had to pass exams in writing, reading, speaking and retelling a story which I heard from a tape recorder. I got 5 in the first three parts. In the fourth part the sound was so low I could hardly hear it. I told the examiner, who was a Russian woman, that the sound was low. She answered that the

sound was very good and that I should listen carefully. As I was not able
to hear adequately, I failed to tell the story in a good way. She gave me
a 2. She was discriminating against me.

I interrupted: 'Why? Wasn't she a Russian?' She replied:

Yes, but she was afraid for her own position. She tried to strengthen her
own position by pleasing Kazakhs. Then I turned to the examination
committee and said: 'I have got 5 from the other parts! Is it logical that I
have got 2 from the listening?' They said no and let me listen again. The
sound was still low, but I managed to get 4. But as they knew that I
deserved more, they gave a 5 and I entered. The Kazakhs were treated
differently. For example, when I was passing the writing part a Kazakh
girl used a dictionary and had her books with her, which is against the
rules.

Such complaints from non-Kazakhs were widespread. A student of mine,
a Tatar woman married to a Kazakh, wrote an essay on ethnic discrimination in Kazakhstan. She read the essay in class and then we discussed it.
The central point in her argument was that Kazakhs discriminated against
others in the public sector, while in the newly created private sector ethnic
discrimination was less due to the logic of profitability (rationality) and the
considerable presence of non-Kazakhs in the sector. She suggested that the
management of the private firms employed people because of their skills,
not ethnicity. All the students, even Kazakhs, agreed with her. Kazakhs
were also blamed for distributing credits among themselves (see chapter
3). An old Russian woman in the neighbourhood told me: 'They borrow
money from abroad and then the money disappears without trace. They give
it to their relatives.' Pointing to her two granddaughters, she said: 'My
grandchildren must pay this money in future.'

I began to speak with my Kazakh friends and acquaintances about the
accusations from non-Kazakhs. All of them confirmed that Kazakhs had a
monopoly over state power. But they argued the real power lay with
networks of the Kazakh elite and that the majority of Kazakhs were more
dispossessed than any other ethnic group. For instance Saken, who worked
with his wife in another Kazakh's kiosk, accepted that the leadership in
Kazakhstan consisted of Kazakhs, but argued that the majority of Kazakhs
were among the poorest people of the country. He said:

Look around for yourself. Russians and others who complain that we
Kazakhs are nationalists have apartments and cars. But the majority of
Kazakhs have nothing. I have been seven years in Almaty, and I still live
in a dormitory. I have no car. Russians say we Kazakhs are lazy. You

see yourself, Amira and I work even at nights, but we cannot save any money. Almaty is a Russian city, most of the Kazakhs here are students, or migrants (*priezzhie*) who either live in dormitories or rent rooms from the urban people. In the *auls* these people come from, people are starving (*golodaiut*). Don't think that everywhere in Kazakhstan people live like in Almaty. In the *auls* life is much more difficult, people survive only on bread and tea and children walk around without shoes.

Roslan, another Kazakh and the owner of one of the kiosks in the neighbourhood, persistently criticised the Kazakh elite's corruption and nepotism. Yet he shared Saken's opinion that the majority of non-Kazakhs, particularly Russians, were much better off than the majority of Kazakhs. While admitting that the state resources were in the hands of the Kazakh elite, he argued that Russians, Tatars, Jews and Koreans dominated the large private trading sector. According to him, most of the wholesale shops, which sold goods to retailers like him, belonged to Russians, Tatars and Jews. And most of the casinos belonged to Koreans. The first three groups, he suggested, knew people in Russia (the Jews also had contacts in Israel), who provided them with goods and credit. The Koreans were supported by South Korea. But Kazakhs had none of these advantages. Moreover, he said, most Kazakhs had grown up in the *auls* and lacked the necessary language skills to get a job in the private sector. Their Russian is not good enough, and unlike Russians, Jews and Tatars they have no knowledge of foreign languages.[60] Kazakhs also lack the professional skills which are necessary to compete with Russians in the labour market created by the new private sector. He mentioned the multinational in which our Russian friend Nikolaevich was working. Their average salary, he said, is $500, ten times more than the average salary of a university teacher. All of them are Russian, but they still complain that Kazakhs take everything for themselves.[61]

The Kazakhification of the state has led to a widespread, albeit mostly unorganised and still passive, resistance among both non-Kazakhs and the majority of Kazakhs against the Kazakh elite. However, such resistance is manifested differently by Kazakhs and non-Kazakhs. While non-Kazakhs oppose the very project of Kazakhification, Kazakhs question the particular ways Kazakhification has been carried through. A relatively successful example of such resistance by the urban population was in the sphere of language policy (see below). Another example of such resistance was the very low participation of non-Kazakhs in the state rituals, the most important of which during my stay was the celebration of the 150th anniversary of Abai Kunanbaev's birthday. In the neighbourhood I found very few non-Kazakhs enthusiastic about the celebration. As Abai was famous as a representative of cosmopolitanism, no one opposed his anniversary as such.

But most non-Kazakhs shared the opinion of a young Ukrainian woman: 'Why should Nazarbaev spend so much money on celebrations while the majority of our people live in poverty?' The third example of such resistance was that people usually refused to use the new Kazakh street names. This was so widespread that although I learned the new Kazakh names of the streets, I now remember Almaty's main streets by old names like Lenina, Kirova, Dzerzhinskaia, Komsomol'skaia and Kommunistich-eskaia. Not only Russians were frustrated by the name change but even non-Kazakh Muslims. An Uigur electrician who lived in the neighbour-hood told me that he had found a temporary job in Dzerzhinsky street. I asked him for the new name of the street. He answered:

> I don't know. Why they should change these names? They say because they were communists. It is not true. They changed the names because they were not Kazakhs. Zhambyl[62] and Kunaev[63] were communists also, but their names have not been removed because they were Kazakhs.

The most important form of such resistance is that the majority of people question the identity of the new state. The elite have refashioned the notion of the Kazakhstani people (*Narod Kazakhstana*) and identify the state with it. Such a strategy, according to a local Russian intellectual, is directed towards three goals: to achieve a legitimacy for the elite, to create the notion of a break with the Soviet past, and to prevent ethnic conflict through the idea that Kazakhstan belongs to all its inhabitants and not merely Kazakhs.

Although the notion of the 'People of Kazakhstan' appeals to the population, the ways they use it challenge the Kazakh elite's use of it. First, people used the notion to locate the people who inhabit Kazakhstan in the wider concept of the Soviet people. In this sense the *Narod Kazakhstana* is understood as a sub-division of *Sovetskii narod*. A woman Kazakh student said 'When we meet foreigners (*inostrantsev*), we are *Sovetskii narod*, but when we meet people from Russia (*liudi iz Rossii*) we are Kazakhstanis (*Kazakhstantsy*).' This statement illustrates in more ways than one how the locals construct the concept of the *narod Kazakhstana*. First, it constructs the two versions of peoplehood in relation to foreigners and in relation to people from Russia. Second, the people of Russia and those of Kazakhstan are implicitly included in the wider Soviet people. Third, the image of the people of Kazakhstan is constructed in contrast to that of people from Russia (*Liudi iz Rossii*), not ethnic Russians (*Russkii*). Why is the Kazakh-stani territorial identity constructed in contrast to Russia and not another post-Soviet republic? To be sure, people have the same feelings of identity and difference towards other post-Soviet republics, with the exception of the three Baltic republics, but Russia plays a central role in their imagina-tion. Moscow was, and is still, considered to be the centre. People strongly

believe that what happened in Moscow determined their fate. This was illustrated by the extraordinary attention they paid to the two rounds of
presidential elections in 1996 in Russia rather than the referendum on the
constitution and the election of the *Mejles* (parliament) in Kazakhstan. The
majority of the people in the neighbourhood, regardless of ethnicity,
watched ORT (Russian state television) and NTV, both broadcast from
Moscow rather than the Kazakhstan national television. They read widely
Moscow's newspapers like *Argumenty i fakty*. Moreover, Moscow and St
Petersburg are still centres of cultural inspiration, particularly for urban
Kazakhs. 'Leningrad and Moscow', said a woman Kazakh university
teacher, 'are our Mecca and Medina.' Patterns of art, fashion, music, mafia
and business which are fashioned in Moscow are imitated in Almaty.

Second, the phrase *narod Kazakhstana* also denotes the dispossessed
people who are assumed to suffer from the mafia, the corrupt elite and the
dikii kapitalism. In this context people (*narod*) is the opposite of the elite
which people call interchangeably the leadership (*rokovodstvo*,
nachal'stvo), bosses (*nachal'niki*), they (*oni*), the top (*verkh*) and the new
rich (*novye bogatye*).

These two uses of the concept of *narod Kazakhstana* by the ordinary
people are different from those used by the elite in two senses: they
represent a continuity with the past through integrating the Kazakhstani
identity in the Soviet identity, and they represent a break with the elite
through opposing the *narod* to the elite, the mafia and the new rich. In this
way they question the ways the elite construct the very identity of the new
state. The Kazakhification of the state and the ways it has been carried out
hamper an identification between the state and the *narod*, imagined from
below. Kazakhification of the state, most Kazakhs told me, has alienated not
only non-Kazaks but also most Kazakhs as well. The state has been monopolised in the name of the Kazakhs by tiny, yet very powerful, rival networks
of the Kazakh elite who formed the higher echelons of the former
communist party (*partikraty*). They have expanded their old power base by
converting to the new market orthodoxy and by restructuring the old state
apparatus. The main characteristic of this restructuring is that it happened
through the rivalries, horse-trading and clandestine deals between the
networks of the old Kazakh communist elite, not through a democratic
process (Masanov, 1996a).

In spite of the constitution and elections the new state has strong authoritarian tendencies (Bremmer and Welt, 1996; Olcott, 1997). In this sense
not only the non-Kazakhs but even the majority of Kazakhs have been
excluded from the state. In Almaty, both urban Kazakhs and rural migrants
complained about the elite monopoly of the state. The main concern of
urban Kazakhs was the language policy (discussed below). The economic
life of the rural migrants had been ruined by the collapse of the Soviet

economy, and they complained the elite did nothing to help them. One of the main reasons for the widespread resentment against the Kazakhification of the state is that a wide range of people link it to the so-called privatisation of state property (chapter 3). There is a widely shared opinion among people that those networks which are linked to state officials and the mafia have monopolised the main resources on such a scale that the resources left for the rest of the population are hardly sufficient for survival. It is argued that those who have links with the mafia and the state officials manage to get rich. The rest are starved and bullied by both the state officials and the mafia.

Those who see themselves as underprivileged by this processes, understand it in two different ways. Underprivileged Kazakhs of both urban and rural origin attribute it to the corruption of the elite and their links with the mafia. Non-Kazakhs, particularly Russians, recognise that the majority of Kazakhs are excluded as well, but associate it rhetorically with Kazakhs in general. The reason for this is that non-Kazakhs think that even the dis-possessed Kazakhs benefit from the state language policy and the support of the state officials in their disputes with non-Kazakhs over urban space. In the following I will deal with these issues.

The language policy

A prime concern with the revival of ethnic languages (*rodnoi iazyk*) was a common feature of the national movements instigated by *glasnost*. In Kazakhstan such concerns, expressed by Kazakh intellectuals like the poet Solemenov, acquired a new urgency after independence. Although knowledge of the Kazakh language did not become a precondition for acquiring citizenship in the new state it became a formal precondition for getting or keeping a job in the state sector. In the beginning the Kazakh elite intended to force the population to learn the language in a short time. But three major problems prevented the success of a short term programme: the lack of the necessary infrastructure, the lack of economic incentives and political resistance.

Although Kazakh schools existed in the Soviet era and in the universi-ties one had the option of studying in Kazakh, the Kazakh language had been ousted by the Russian language in Almaty. Although Kazakh schools dominated rural areas, this was not possible in Almaty, because in rural areas both books and teachers were orientated to a Kazakh-speaking population. In Almaty, the main language of communication at home and at work is Russian, even for the overwhelming majority of Kazakhs. Kazakh is taught as a second language with the help of Russian. There are no good books, good dictionaries or trained teachers for this purpose. Sur-prisingly, although the Kazakh language has become one of the main emblems of the state, the elite do not invest enough money to ensure its dominance. The lack of good teachers and good books means learning

Kazakh is very difficult. Many Kazakhs who put their children in Kazakh schools had to transfer them to Russian schools. The reason was that insufficient language skills made the overall performance of the children worse than those in Russian schools (Dave, 1996).

In addition to the lack of a good infrastructure for teaching the language, the lack of practical incentives is another factor which discourages people from learning Kazakh. While Russian functions as the daily language and the knowledge of English and other foreign languages brings economic advantages, the majority of people have no practical incentives to learn Kazakh. Although a sufficient knowledge of Kazakh is a precondition for occupying high administrative posts, such knowledge in itself does not entitle someone to such posts, because they are monopolised and distributed by the elite.

The resistance of the urban population, including the urban Kazakhs, to the state language policy also hindered its short term success. The Slavic people were the most ardent opponents of the policy, because they considered it a challenge to their cultural hegemony in the city and part of the wider process of Kazakhification. Their attitudes are illustrated by what a young Ukrainian woman, a student of German, said:

> My husband says the Kazakh language is a dead language. It has no future, so why should we waste our time learning a language which is of no use to anybody. When Nazarbaev ordered us to learn the language, neither I nor my husband nor my younger sister paid any attention. We said to each other, if we learn a new language we will learn English or German, or another European language. But my mother was forced to go to Kazakh classes, because otherwise she would lose her position as a chair in the faculty of... But it was so difficult for her to learn the language. She said that the language is not beautiful, it sounds strange. It is a very backward (*ne razvityi*) language which cannot accommodate modern times. Kazakhs force it on us to prove they are the rulers here.

People of Slavic origin were the core of the opposition to the new status of the Kazakh language, but other urban people, including urban Kazakhs, also contested this. The language of most urban people is Russian, and so they assumed the new language policy would discriminate against them. A Korean university teacher expressed this discontent in the following way:

> In the Soviet time 50 per cent of places at the universities were given to Kazakhs and 50 per cent to others. But today 80 per cent of places are given to Kazakhs. You can see this in your own university. The Kazakh[64] sections alone take 50 per cent for Kazakhs. Then from the 50 per cent

which is devoted to the Russian section 30 per cent is taken by Kazakhs and the rest is left for others.

Urban Kazakh attitudes to the language policies are more contradictory, varied and complex than among other groups. They simultaneously benefit and lose. Their ethnic identity combined with their very poor knowledge of the Kazakh language entitles them to privileged positions in the state apparatus. Purging of non-Kazakhs from the high and middle ranks of the state, under the condition that Russian remains the main language in state institutions and life in general, has provided vacant places for urban Kazakhs who have a good command of the Russian language. But at the same time, there are complaints that the Kazakh elite use Kazakh language status as a pretext for monopolising the top posts for their own relatives. Such complaints are made because Russian has become the mother tongue of the urban Kazakhs and their knowledge of Kazakh is below the required level for the top posts in the state. So the urban Kazakhs have a dual position. Confronted with Russians they lean on their claims of knowledge of the Kazakh language to justify their own privileges. But they are unhappy at being deprived of the most powerful offices because of their insufficient knowledge of Kazakh.

The emotional relation of urban Kazakhs to the Kazakh and Russian languages is very complex and contradictory. While many of them regret their lack of knowledge of the Kazakh language and blame it on the Russians' alleged colonial policies, they are more attached emotionally to the Russian language. For example, I was invited to a small family party given by the Kazakh mother of one of my students. She invited her older sister and her family and two men, who were her cousins, with their families. This woman had complained on earlier occasions that because of the Russians' colonial policies they had lost their mother tongue. But during the party, they spoke in Russian all the time and gave their toasts in Russian, and once they got drunk both men and women sang Russian songs. In my university department only two people talked in Kazakh together. When these two addressed others in Kazakh, the latter answered in Russian. Two of my classes, each with 16 male and female Kazakh students, belonged to the Kazakh section. In the Kazakh section, Kazakh was the formal language of instruction. But to my surprise the students, with the exception of two girls who came from Shymkent and Kyzylorda, spoke Russian to each other and all of their teachers, most of whom were Kazakh, also taught them in Russian. I asked the students in one class, 'If you don't speak Kazakh and your teachers do not teach you in Kazakh, why have you joined the Kazakh section at all?' A male student from Almaty, jokingly answered: 'Because we Kazakhs are smart (*khitrye*).' While the rest of class burst into laughter, I asked him to explain it to me. He said:

We want to have as many Kazakhs as possible in the Russian section. But there are others who want to have places there as well, so we keep half of the places for the Kazakh section. In addition, it is good to have in your diploma that you have finished in the Kazakh section. It will help to get a better job in the future.

Then I asked the class whether the rest agreed with him. They did. I then asked, 'Why then don't you speak Kazakh?' The whole class went quiet. Then the girl from Shymkent, one of two girls who spoke in Kazakh, interrupted the silence by saying 'They are ashamed of speaking Kazakh.' I asked others whether she was correct in her judgment. After another moment of silence, a young married woman from Almaty, with an apologetic and embarrassed voice, said: 'Young people in Almaty do not speak Kazakh because they are afraid of being called *Iuzhanin* (Southerner).' The word for Kazakh men[65] from the south who are supposed to command the Kazakh language and have preserved the Kazakh 'traditions' (*traditsiia*) is a very strong social stigma in Almaty (see below). Depicting the Kazakh language as a stigma is a Soviet legacy. The Russian language was associated with civilisation, progress and urbanisation and Kazakh was depicted as a backward tribal language (*ne razvityi kochevoi iazyk*). A woman Kazakh student of mine who had recently learned the Kazakh language with enthusiasm said:

My mother remembers often with regret, how I spoke Kazakh sweetly when I was a little girl and how she encouraged me to forget it. After staying two years with my grandmother in the *aul* from the age of two, my parents took me back to Almaty. My mother says that I had learned to speak Kazakh beautifully in the *aul,* because there everybody spoke in Kazakh. But she became embarrassed and ashamed when I spoke Kazakh with her in shops or other places, so she discouraged me from speaking Kazakh.

The continuity of stigma in Almaty indicates Russian cultural hegemony. Although this cultural hegemony does not result in either political or economic hegemony, it still provides a basis for Russians and other non-Kazakhs to feel at home in Almaty, in spite of the Kazakhification of the state. Yet as mentioned above, the Russian language is not spoken merely by Russians but by almost the majority of the urban population. This has led to the emergence of a new concept of *Russko iazychnoe naselenie* (Russian speaking population) in the language of journalists and intellectuals who challenge the Kazakhification of the state.[66] The concept signifies a block of the population united with the common political interest of defending the rights of the Russian Speaking Population (RSP) against Kazakhification. Although the term had not yet been popularised among ordinary people, it corresponds to their feelings of sharing a common cause against the state language policy on the one hand and the migrant Kazakhs from the rural areas on the other.

Because of the effective resistance of the RSP the elite made some substantial concessions. First, they have practically abandoned their initial demand that everybody should learn the Kazakh language at a stroke or lose their job. Second, the constitution declared the Russian language (article 7.2, p. 7, 1995) the official language of the republic, while Kazakh still preserves its higher status as the state language. The higher ritual status of the Kazakh language is counterbalanced by the Russian dominance in practice. When Nazarbaev began to address the people of Kazakhstan in Kazakh on New Year's Eve, 1996, on the Kazakh national TV a Russian man said: 'He will speak only five minutes in Kazakh, then he will speak half an hour in Russian.'

However, we should not conclude from these concessions that the Kazakh elite have abandoned their long term project of making Kazakh the first language in daily life. This is clear from what two members of the elite, a director of a prestigious institute of the Academy of Science, and the rector of a prestigious university told me. Both men were very optimistic about the future of the Kazakh language. The director of the institute told me that the number of Kazakh schools had grown rapidly since independence and will be increased even more rapidly in the coming years. He was of opinion that as Kazakhs put more and more of their children in Kazakh schools, the infrastructure for teaching the language would be improved. He argued: 'The massive Kazakh migration to Almaty from the *aul* and the Russian emigration, the higher birth rate among Kazakhs and the fact that Kazakh population has a much lower average age than the Russian one promote the future success of Kazakh.' 'If you', he said, 'had come to Almaty ten years ago you could not hear anybody speaking Kazakh. But today you hear it everywhere in the bazaars and the streets. And ten years later the situation will be much more better.'

The rector added two points to his argument. First, the urban Kazakhs have already been warned that the present situation will not be tolerated in future. 'Today the ministers speak Kazakh, but under them there are still many who do not speak Kazakh properly. This situation will not be tolerated a generation on. If their children want to make good careers then they must learn Kazakh.' Second, he admitted that they discriminate positively in favour of Kazakh speakers for admission to university. He hopes that through such policies Kazakh will replace Russian within a generation or two. This has created a great fear among the Russian-speaking population for the future of their children. They suspect that the lack of knowledge of Kazakh will disadvantage them in future.

As the director of the Institute said, the main speakers of the Kazakh language are not merely the Kazakh elite but Kazakh migrants from the south and Kazakhs who live in rural areas and southern parts of Kazakhstan. As I did not carry out any fieldwork among rural Kazakhs my discussion will be confined to migrant Kazakhs from the rural areas and the south. Prior to *perestroika* the migration of Kazakhs from rural areas to the cities was almost negligible. This was partly because Kazakhs preferred to stay in the rural areas with their kith and kin, and partly because of difficulties getting residential permission (*propiska*). However, as a result of the economic policies which accompanied *perestroika*, Kazakh *Kolkhozes* began to stagnate and disintegrate. Consequently, many of those who worked there were forced to migrate to cities to survive. In addition to economic migrants, the students from rural areas and repatriated Kazakhs from other countries came to Almaty. The influx of these Kazakh-speaking Kazakhs into Almaty has introduced a new cultural element and has caused a new social conflict.

Both the presence of Kazakh people and the Kazakh language and 'culture' are asserted more strongly than before. A Russian woman complained: 'Almaty has become a Kazakh city. If you take a bus, the majority of travellers are Kazakhs, before *perestroika* you seldom heard people talk Kazakh, but today you hear it everywhere.' The presence of migrant Kazakhs in Almaty has caused conflicts over apartments and control of public urban space.

The contest over apartments
The apartments had been privatised in 1992. Kazakh migrants, who were often the tenants of the urban Russian speakers, were discontented with this. Before privatisation the state provided apartments, but now they had to purchase their own. One of the main aims of the young women who were involved in prostitution, discussed in chapter 5, was to buy their own apartment. The rural Kazakhs thought that the privatisation of apartments privileged Russians.

Bulat, a Kazakh migrant, who was a tenant of a Russian family said: 'Russians have rooms for their dogs but Kazakhs have no place to live.' Indeed, he left the Russian family because their dog gave birth to puppies and Bulat did not like the smell. He added, 'In the Soviet time they kept us Kazakhs in *kolkhozes* and the Russians occupied apartments in the cities, and now they have become the owners of apartments.' Amira, a kiosk seller, who had lived for seven years with her husband in a student dormitory, told me, 'This is our land (*nasha zemlia*). Russians must leave for Russia and leave apartments for Kazakhs.'

Moreover, migrant Kazakh tenants complained that Russians and other urban people exploited them by charging high rents. Bulat, whose landlord was an unemployed and alcoholic Russian, complained: 'I pay $50 a month to this Russian alcoholic (*alkash*), I feed him and his family. This is half my income.'

On the other hand, non-Kazakhs see Kazakh migrants as a threat to their ownership. The Uzbek woman mentioned in chapter 4 had bought an apartment for her mother, but the mother went to live in Vladivostok with another daughter who was married to a Russian. She wanted to rent the apartment to a friend of mine. Showing me the steel door she said: 'I changed the door, because Kazakhs are looking for empty apartments. When they find one they break in, and then it is difficult to throw them out without paying large bribes to judges.' Although non-Kazakhs rented rooms to Kazakhs, they were usually unwilling to rent a whole apartment to them. A Russian family rented an empty apartment for $130 to a foreigner, but avoided renting it to a young Kazakh man who was prepared to pay $200. When I asked why, the son told me: 'If you rent an apartment to Kazakhs, firstly you are not sure they will pay the rent, and secondly you are not sure that they will leave the apartment when you need it.' Aleksander, mentioned in chapter 4, told a story about a dispute between a Russian colleague of his and his Kazakh tenants who resisted leaving the apartment. As the subject had been brought to a court, the Russian man was fined $1,200 for not having paid the taxes for the rents received. As he could not afford to pay so much money, while Kazakhs were still living in the apartment, he was given a deadline by the tax authorities to get the money, or his apartment would be confiscated. Again a half-Kazakh and half-Russian woman rented her mother's apartment, who had left for Russia, to a Kazakh family. They avoided paying rent for three months, because of a lack of money. She evicted them with the help of another Kazakh man.

The contest for control of public places
Let us start with a detailed example.

It was the evening of 26 June 1996. After writing my diary notes in a Turkish cafe in the centre of the city, I returned to my neighbourhood. But instead of going home to my own apartment I went to the neighbourhood shashlyk bar. The Azerbaijani girl who had closed her bread kiosk and was ready to go home greeted me and asked for the time. I greeted her and said: 'Half past ten.' Then the girl, while greeting an old Russian woman who lived in the neighbourhood and sold things in the evening on the pavement, handed her a loaf of bread. Expressing her gratitude, the old women embraced her and kissed her face. While most of the street traders had already gone home, some were still packing up their things. Passing by one of the kiosks, I greeted the Kazakh woman inside. Greeting me, she asked: 'Where have you been so late?' 'My apartment', I answered, 'was hot. I went to a cafe in the centre to write my notes.'

Then I went around to the second kiosk and turned up into the platform of the Shashlyk bar. Nikolaevich, an acquaintance of mine, a little intoxicated, was sitting with another young Russian man, whom I had not seen before, drinking vodka and talking. Seeing me, Nikolaevich shouted as usual: 'Khelo my friend! how are you? Come here and have a drink.' When I joined them, Nikolaevich introduced his companion to me, as Kolia. Kolia was younger than Nikolaevich and completely drunk. Nikolaevich was talking about a dispute with the blood bank concerning a car accident. Just a few metres from us a young Kazakh man, who had arrived two weeks before from Zhambyl, was preparing shashlyk. Bulat was standing with his arms around Madina, chatting with her and the young Kazakh.

While Nikolaevich was talking, an older Russian man approached us and asked for cigarettes. Handing him a cigarette, Nikolaevich shouted in a friendly way: 'Oh, Iura where have you been?' But Kolia, who did not like the old man or did not like him asking for cigarettes, suddenly raised himself and tried to assault the old man. Iura ran away. Nikolaevich turning towards Kolia, snapped: 'Calm down.' But Kolia, paying no attention to Nikolaevich, chased, caught and began to abuse Iura physically, but mildly. The young Kazakh who was preparing shashlyk ran to help Iura. Approaching them, he aggressively ordered Kolia: 'Don't bother him.' Kolia, without saying anything, obeyed him like a school child, let Iura go and came back to our table. Nikolaevich blamed him and told him: 'Go and bring Iura back here.' Kolia went to bring Iura but Iura would not come. Nikolaevich went himself and brought Iura to our table. Nikolaevich said, 'Joma you write about people, write about Iura's life. For two years he has been homeless (*bomzh*).' Iura, offended by being called a *bomzh*, protested: 'No, I lived with my cousin.' Nikolaevich, paying no attention to Iura's protest, told us the story of how Iura had been a famous sportsman but was thrown out of his house by his wife and her lover, who sold the apartment and moved to Russia.

Meanwhile Bulat and Madina were joined by another Kazakh street trader from the south and moved to a table not far from us. They opened a bottle of vodka. Five southern Kazakh men, who were usually described by other men and women as hooligans or racketeers arrived by car. They parked the car in the corner of the square, sat at a table, opened two bottles of vodka and ordered shashlyk.

Kolia went to the nearby kiosk and bought a bottle of vodka for himself, Nikolaevich and Iura and a can of cola for me. While Nikolaevich was opening the bottle, Kolia took my arm and pointed at the table of five Kazakhs. Laughing, he said: 'Look he fell off the chair!' I turned and saw one of the Kazakhs who rose up from the floor and righted his chair. But I did not stare and quickly turned my face away. After two minutes the man who fell down approached our table and with a polite but a cunning voice said: '*Tovarishch* (comrade, fellow) when I fell down you laughed at me. I want to have words with you.' Then he took Kolia's hand and raised him from his seat and the latter followed him obediently. The Kazakh brought him to the middle of the bar, stood face to face with him and spoke for only a minute, very calmly. Kolia, paralysed and bewildered, kept quiet. Suddenly, the Kazakh grabbed his neck and tried to throw him on the floor. Kolia resisted, but defensively. Within a second the Kazakh threw him on the floor and began to kick him wildly in the face. Suddenly three of the four remaining men from the visiting Kazakhs' table rushed towards them. The fourth remained there and watched. I thought they wanted to stop their friend but instead they joined him in kicking Kolia. In addition to them Bulat and his male companion rushed towards the scene and took part in kicking Kolia as well, while Madina, Bulat's lover, remained at the table watching. Then the young Kazakh man who worked there rushed to stop them. But, confronted with the aggressive reaction of the man who had been offended by Kolia he retreated to his shashlyk place. While the six men were kicking Kolia violently and indiscriminately all over his body, he suddenly lost consciousness and became motionless. The six Kazakhs continued to kick him. The older Kazakh sitting at the table and watching intervened by coming forward and suddenly shouting 'Stop'. All the men stopped at once, and went to their respective tables, leaving Kolia unconscious and bloodstained on the floor.

Nikolaevich and I did not intervene because we were afraid of the Kazakhs. Nikolaevich pretended that nothing had happened and told me: 'Interview Iura, his life is a good case.' Then proceed to tell me: 'Iura became homeless', but Iura interrupted him: 'I have never been homeless.' Nikolaevich said: 'Then tell me why did you live the whole winter in the barracks?' Iura answered: 'Because I had a conflict with my wife.' He took out a bunch of keys from his pocket, showed them to us and said: 'Here are my keys.' Nikolaevich, pointing to the crystal rectangular key-holder, told me with a joking tone: 'Look Joma, this is his credit card.' Neither of us liked his joke. Although Nikolaevich did not intended to insult Iura, he was patronising him. According to the local custom he should not have called him by his first name in the first place, but by the first name and patronymic, because Iura was older than him. Moreover, he should not have talked about Iura's life so nonchalantly. While we were speaking Bulat came to our table and ordered Iura: 'Come with me.' Iura, without protest, followed him to the place where Kolia was still lying unconscious. Bulat ordered Iura to take Kolia's legs. When the latter refused to do so, the former punching him in the face shouted angrily: 'Mother-fucker (*tvoiu mat*) do what I say.' Iura, intimidated, took Kolia's legs and Bulat took his arms and they pulled him from the middle of the platform to the foot of the wall into the darkness. Bulat obviously did not want the police to see Kolia. Then Iura returned to our table and Bulat to his. Then Bulat began to stare angrily at Nicolaevich. As he had a good relationship with me I called him to our table. He greeted me in his humble and friendly way. I greeted him back. Then, pointing to Kolia, who was still unconscious, he asked me: 'Is he your friend?' 'No', I said, 'but please be calm.' He agreed. Bulat went back to his table.

Then, after a while, Iura for some reason went to Kolia who was still lying there motionless. He took Kolia's hand in his and tried to help him get up. After a while Kolia, recovered and, humiliated by the Kazakhs, jumped on Iura and began to beat him. While Iura lay under him trying to resist, nobody went to separate them. Kolia continued to punch Iura. Iura took hold of Kolia's hair and pulled. Kolia was not able to punch any more, so put his hands around Iura's neck and tried to strangle him. At this point, the oldest Kazakh at the hooligans' table went to separate them. The Kazakh man took Kolia's shoulders and tried to pull him back, but he resisted and still had Iura's throat in his hands. Finally the Kazakh held onto Kolia's wrist and twisted his arm hard. Kolia released Iura's throat. Iura, feeling somebody was helping him, kicked Kolia in the chest and got up. While Kolia fell down again on the floor, Iura came to our table and began to drink the vodka which Kolia had bought earlier. Then another young Russian man, an acquaintance of Nikolaevich's and mine, joined us. The Kazakh man who seemed to be the leader of the gang of five told him with an imperative voice: 'Come here! (*idi siuda*)' The Russian man humbly obeyed him at once and went to their table.

In this cruel human drama, different actors and spectators outline some of the main characteristics of the contest for control of public urban space in Almaty. The roles played by each represent their respective attempts to negotiate their positions in the field of power relations in a particular place. First, this control is negotiated through and backed up by the use of brute force. Second, the struggle for the control over urban space is the business of men. This is illustrated clearly by Madina's behaviour. While the men acted in the different moments of the drama, Madina remained a pure spectator. Third, ethnicity is very important in this struggle. Through such struggle the dominant masculinities are articulated to a dominant Kazakh ethnicity, and both are reconfirmed. Fourth, status, wealth and connections with influential individuals play very important roles in such a struggle.

Let us have a closer look at the ways these factors conditioned the degree and significance of each person's intervention. Kolia, by assaulting Iura, transgressed the important local custom that a person must respect those senior in age. However, Iura's marginal status as a homeless person made Kolia's conduct less reprehensible. Iura's lack of respectability was also evident in the way Nikolaevich treated him. Moreover, the fact that Iura was a Russian made him an easy target for Kolia: his insult to Iura was considered an interpersonal affair. If Iura had been a Kazakh, Kolia would never have dared either to bother him, or would have paid a high price. We saw his assumed insult later to a Kazakh provoked a collective Kazakh reaction.

The fact that Kolia turned down Nikolaevich's mediation between him and Iura, but obeyed the young Kazakh who prepared shashlyk, illustrates the same logic. If he had refused the Kazakh's order, the latter would have punched him and other Kazakhs would have joined him. In the square of the neighbourhood and the platform of the neighbourhood's cafe, the Kazakhs' dominance was recognised by the non-Kazakh men, and they were careful not to provoke conflict with Kazakhs. The exception was Akhmet, a Caucasian Bashkir and a so-called Afghan, a veteran from the war in Afghanistan, whom the Kazakhs respected. Kolia by pointing to and laughing at the falling Kazakh man broke the unwritten law (*ne pisannyi zakon*) of Kazakh domination. However, he did this out of drunkenness and carelessness and had no intention of challenging the Kazakh. But the latter, perhaps knowing this, could not leave such carelessness unpunished. By beating Kolia up he saved his own face and reinstated the status quo, which Kolia had challenged unintentionally. The participation of other Kazakhs in kicking Kolia highlights their concern to preserve Kazakh domination.

The differences between Iura, Nikolaevich and I on the one hand, and the two Kazakhs, who did not take part in kicking, on the other, again highlight Kazakh domination. According to the local custom shared between people from all ethnic backgrounds it was the duty of Nikolaevich and I to defend Kolia, because he was sharing a drink with us. But we did not intervene because both of us knew it would lead to a fight with Kazakhs, which neither of us wanted. Thus, we were 'reduced', like Madina, to being purely spectators. Such feminisation was a greater minus for Nikolaevich than for me. First, there was a greater expectation placed on him than me to take part in the local games of masculinity, because he was a native and I a foreigner. Second, Nicolaevich was a Russian and I a 'Muslim'. I had at least exchanged a greeting with all the Kazakhs involved and some of them were my acquaintances. They did not expect me, a Muslim, to fight them for a Russian. But as the fight took an ethnic dimension Nicolaevich was expected to defend Kolia, his co-ethnic. His failure to do so certainly made him a coward (*trus*) in the eyes of the Kazakhs.

Iura's status as a homeless person made him free of any manly and ethnic obligations, because his masculinity had already been degraded. In contrast to the three of us, the two remaining Kazakhs displayed their masculinity through intervention. The young man rushed towards the stage in order to mediate, and thereby enhance his own masculinity. But not being able to counter the threat of the Kazakh who began the fight he retreated to his subordinate position. However, the latter did not consider his intervention an offence, but an act out of proportion to his junior position. It is worth mentioning that if Nicolaevich or I had tried to mediate, the Kazakh would without doubt have considered it an offence and an invitation to fight. The right to mediate and settle the conflict was the monopoly of the senior member of the gang, who was also the boss. He reaffirmed his leadership by intervening in the conflict. Although, the punishment could not be initiated without his permission, he distinguished himself from his protégés by not taking part in the beating and displayed his hegemonic position by stopping the kicking at a stroke.

The collective kicking of Kolia was meant to reaffirm Kazakh collective dominance in the square and on the platform. But such dominance does not imply that all Kazakhs were equally in the control of the place, nor does it exclude the fierce struggle between Kazakhs themselves. Different levels of control were effectively exerted by the police officers, state officials, violent Mafioso gangs, owners of the place and migrant Kazakhs from the south who traded in the illegal market. One could speak of the existence of different layers of Kazakh dominance, in which the same Kazakh individuals took dominant or subordinate positions *vis-à-vis* each other. The police officers, who were mainly Kazakhs, had a daily presence there. They usually ate free in the shashlyk bar, harassed illegal street traders and alcoholics, received bribes from them and from the kiosk owners. Not only non-Kazakhs, but also Kazakhs who were poor and lacked contacts with influential people, were very afraid of them. Bulat dragged the unconscious body of Kolia into the darkness because of such a fear. He explained to me some days later that if the police had seen Kolia's unconscious body he and his friend would have run into trouble, and would have had to pay the police a large bribe to avoid being charged. I asked him why the gang did not care about this. He answered that the gang's leader knew every policeman in the district and the police would not make any trouble for him and his friends for the sake of a drunk Russian (*P'ianyi Russkii*). Officially the cafe and its attached platform, the neighbouring shop and the square belonged to the state. Those in charge of the complex were Kazakhs, who leased it to their own associates. Mafioso, according to the neighbourhood, mainly Kazakhs, were involved in the control of the space, by extracting protection money from the kiosks and the shops around. Hooligans who drank and fought frightened ordinary people. The owner of the place, who was on good terms with the police through serving them shashlyk and was supported by the migrant Kazakhs traders, had considerable control over the place as well. The migrants supported him partly because he himself was a migrant, and partly because his employees were also migrants. However, he could not prevent different gangs from fighting with each other or harassing his customers.

The involvement of such diverse Kazakh forces in control of the place created tension and conflict between Kazakhs themselves, which was resolved either by negotiation or the use of force. The most obvious sign of tension was the frequent fights between different Kazakh gangs. Beside this, the Kazakhs who owned the kiosks and the owner of the shashlyk bar blamed both Kazakh state officials and Kazakh Mafioso for milking them. But one of them, who had a good contact in GSK, did not care about either the police or the Mafioso. An important example of the contest between Kazakhs was the eviction of one Kazakh from the cafe against his will and the leasing of it to another Kazakh. Both the evicted man and the Kazakh who passed the news to me first, were of the opinion that the new owner had contacts with more influential people.

The last group who exerted their dominance over the place were ordinary migrant Kazakhs, from the *auls* or the South. Although these Kazakhs were in a subordinate position to those mentioned above and feared them, they bullied people from other ethnic backgrounds in the illegal street market. The shashlyk man whom Kolia obeyed and Bulat and his friend, who kicked Kolia, were all such ordinary migrants. The relations between the migrants and non-Kazakhs often took unfriendly, and sometimes antago- nistic, forms around the Shashlyk bar and the neighbourhood's illegal market. In both places a clear-cut division existed between the urban population and the migrants. In the cafe-bar this division is illustrated by the drinking circles. Southern and rural Kazakhs drank strictly together and did not admit others. The urban people did not try to join them. While the drinking circles of urban men were open to all ethnic groups, they never invited migrants. Nicolaevich, a Russian, and Serek, an urban Kazakh, were both of the opinion that drinking with rural Kazakhs could lead to conflict because of the assumed improper behaviour of the latter. I personally drank with all of them. However, the rural Kazakhs did not like me to drink with Russians. On one occasion I was drinking with a group of Russians. A former Kazakh miner, who sold beer in the street in the first half of the day and worked as a barman in the shashlyk place for the second half approached me. He took my hand and said: 'You are drinking with Russians; you have forgotten your Muslim brothers,' and tried to pull me away from the group. I excused myself by saying that I was interviewing Russians. On another occasion, I drank first with migrants, in the early evening, because they had invited me to photograph the birthday of a daughter of a migrant family, which was celebrated in the cafe. Later in the evening Nicolaevich and his company arrived and began to drink. Nico- laevich asked me join them for a moment. Knowing the migrants might be offended, I spoke to Bulat, and asked his permission to go to the Russians' table. He agreed. Coming back to the table one of the migrants was so angry that he was about to pick a fight with me. Fortunately Bulat stopped him.

In the illegal market the networks of migrants were separate from the networks of the urban street traders, and the two networks were in conflict with each other for places. There was always a pretext for conflict; somebody had taken somebody else's plastic bag, or stolen his/her customers, or was selling in a place which somebody else claimed belonged to him/her. The migrants usually told the non-Kazakhs to go to their own countries and trade there. The urban sellers were women from all ethnic backgrounds and had their own networks. They defended themselves by saying that they had a right to the market, because they had lived in the neighbourhood for a long time and the migrants were newcomers. However, they were very afraid of migrants, because there were a good number of men among the migrants, they had a stronger solidarity and they reacted collectively. The urban Kazakh women were included in the networks of the urban women who traded in the street. Khaledeh, a woman who was a respected figure among the urban traders, blamed the migrants for swearing (*obozvat'*) at other people in Kazakh, taking other's places, and making the street untidy by not cleaning up after themselves in the evenings.

The antagonism between urban women and migrant Kazakh traders was seen differently by each of these two groups. The former, including urban Kazakhs, considered it part of a wider conflict between the Russian speakers and the Kazakh speakers, or between the city dwellers (*gorodskie liudi*) and migrants (*priezzhie*). The migrants considered it as a conflict between Kazakhs and non-Kazakhs, mainly Russians. For them the city represents Russians and the *aul* represents Kazakhs. The urban population lumped street traders and hooligans together as southern Kazakhs (*Iuzhnye Kazakhi*) or *aul* Kazakhs (*aul'nye Kazakhi*), whom they blamed for crimes. On the other hand, the Kazakh street traders, although subordinate to the violent Kazakh gangs, saw the latter as their ally against the Russian-speaking population. The gangs were usually migrants as well, and their presence in the place provided *de facto* support for migrants against non-Kazakhs. Bulat afterwards told me that he joined the hooligans later in abusing Kolia because Kolia had insulted a brother Kazakh.

The fear of migrant Kazakhs, particularly violent gangs, is a universal phenomenon in Almaty. But their actual presence in a particular place and the extent of their influence varies depending on the type of place, the involvement of the state officials in the place and the involvement of organised mafia in the place.

In the industrial workplaces, where the majority of workers are Russians, both inter-ethnic violence and Kazakh dominance are absent on the shop floor. In the factory where I did fieldwork, although younger male workers had experience of fights with Kazakhs outside the factory they told me this kind of thing did not happen in the factory. Workers from other factories with whom I talked in the neighbourhood, confirmed that hooliganism did not exist in their factories. The absence of such a phenomenon was explained differently by younger and older workers. Younger workers often argued that Russians, unlike Kazakhs, were a peaceful people. The older workers said that they had no cause to fight, that all of them belonged to the same powerless people (*bednye liudi*). This difference probably arises because the ethnic-oriented fights outside the factory were a matter for younger men.

In places like universities, where Kazakhs constituted the absolute majority among both staff and students, Kazakh dominance is achieved through official channels rather than through force. As the people who are in charge of such places are influential Kazakhs and well-connected to the police and other authorities, they are able to eliminate hooligans. The director of the institute with which I was associated was one such well-connected Kazakh. However, in spite of this there are networks of young Kazakh men who bully other students, extract tributes from them and fight with each other. In my university I knew of one such network. They extracted protection fees from a good number of students when they received their scholarships. However, the sphere of influence of the group was limited. Many students did not know there was such a group who taxed students. Some male students said that if somebody asked them for such money, they would not pay and if necessary they would fight back, while the women said they would report it to the authorities or their parents. The leader of the group was afraid of the rector and the other Kazakhs in charge at the university. He pleaded with me: 'Please do not speak with the members of the department about this, they are women, they will panic and call the police.' In addition, the male Russian students were not afraid of them. A group of Almatian students, whose senior member was a Russian sportsman, told me they could fix the gang in two minutes.

In contrast to the university, in our neighbourhood people were very afraid of the hooligans. In the neighbourhoods, I was told, there were two major sources of hooliganism: migrant Kazakhs who lived in the neighbourhoods and those who made raids into the neighbourhoods from outside. The importance of each of these sources varies depending on the presence of Kazakh migrants in a given neighbourhood on the one hand, and the distance from the centre on the other. The elite neighbourhoods such as Samal, around the presidential palace, are usually free from hooliganism. In my neighbourhood, both sources operated. An example of the first source was Jambyl, a man who lived in the same house as me, and bullied Russians in the house with the support of a gang of Kazakh men from outside the neighbourhood.

The ways Jambyl behaved and people's reactions towards him demonstrate the same logic of articulation of a dominant masculinity to the Kazakh dominant ethnicity. In his offences he resorted to a nationalist rhetoric, claiming that Kazakhstan was the land of Kazakhs and Russians must leave it. He justified his claim of dominance in the neighbourhood on the basis that Kazakhs should be dominant in Kazakhstan. He usually said to people: 'I am a Kazakh, I am the master (*Khoziain*).' The fact that he was a Kazakh frightened others into not standing against him. First, as mentioned, he was getting support from a gang of Kazakh men from outside the neighbourhood. Second, his claims on having contacts with the police and the army frightened people. Although most people did not believe him they were of the opinion that in the case of conflict the police and judges would support him because he was a Kazakh.

In addition to the conflicts in the square and the illegal markets, yards and areas close to houses were raided by young Kazakh men from outside the neighbourhood. On one such occasion, when a group of young Kazakh men tried to kill a dog, which belonged to a Russian family, both Kazakhs and non-Kazakhs rushed out of their houses and chased away the intruders. In the suburban areas the tension between Kazakhs and non-Kazakhs was much more visible than in my neighbourhood, due to the high presence of Kazakh migrants there. Bars, cafes, discos, restaurants, streets, parks and markets are the main places of the contest because they are places where two 'objects' of struggle, women and money, circulate. In the entertainment places, which according to the locals are protected by the mafia, the Kazakh gangs keep a low profile. The market places, both legal and illegal, where a considerable number of migrant Kazakhs sell goods alongside others, are one of the main fields of contest. In such places migrants who are not members of the gangs support the dominance of the gangs and benefit from it. Bulat and his friend, both street traders and migrants from the South, kicked Kolia alongside the hooligans for such reasons.

The reasons for the hostilities between the urban population and migrants are described differently by migrants, non-Kazakhs and urban Kazakhs. Migrants find Almaty an alienating and hostile place dominated by Russian culture and language, the bearers of which look down on them and their culture. They interpret the clash between themselves and the Russian-speaking people as an ethnic conflict between Kazakhs and Russians, because for them the *aul* represents Kazakhs and the city, Russians. Second, they have very precarious lives, which make them jealous of the urban people. In addition to the competition for legal and illegal markets, their hostility towards urban non-Kazakhs is motivated by their lack of apartments. And they criticised the urban people for exploiting them by extracting high rents. Bulat complained that he paid half of his income to a 'Russian drunkard' (*Russkii alkash*) who did not work.

Non-Kazakhs argued that the reason for the conflict was the rise of Kazakh nationalism. However, they distinguished between two types of Kazakh nationalism: official nationalism (*ofitsial'nyi natsionalism*) and street nationalism (*bytovoi natsionalism*). The official nationalism was ascribed to state officials and their supposed discrimination against non-

Kazakhs over places in universities and posts in state institutions. Street nationalism was ascribed by both urban Kazakhs and non-Kazakhs to Kazakh-speaking Kazakhs, who were assumed to come from the South and *auls*. However, they linked these two types of nationalism by claiming that the judges and police who were assumed to be Kazakhs, supported hooligans and migrants in their conflicts with non-Kazakhs. The urban Kazakhs I spoke with rejected the nationalism of migrants. This makes a unified Kazakh identity problematic. In the following section I explore this in some detail.

The problems of a unified Kazakh Identity
Usually Russians and other non-Kazakhs distinguished between the urban Kazakhs (*Gorodskie Kazakhi*) and rural Kazakhs (*aul' nye Kazakhi, cel' skie Kazakhi*), and also between Almatian Kazakhs (*Almaatinskie Kazakhi*) and southern Kazakhs (*iuzhnye Kazakhi*). Urban Kazakhs or Almatian Kazakhs were those who had lived in Almaty for a long time, and the latter were migrants from the South and *auls*. The urban Kazakhs were seen by non-Kazakhs as peaceful, civilised (*tsivilizovannye*) and educated (*obro-zovannye*). Moreover, all urban people, including urban Kazakhs on the one side, and the Kazakh migrants on the other, were suspicious of each other. Actually, words like *Iuzhanin* (male southerner), *Iuzhanka* (female southerner), *menbet* (a male nickname), *menbetka* (the female equivalent) have strong derogatory connotations and are used to denote Kazakhs from the South. I heard the word *Iuzhanin* when I discussed the question of marriage with a group of students from mixed gender and ethnic back-grounds. A woman Kazakh said she wanted to marry a Kazakh but not an *Iuzhanin*. Then we began to discuss *iuzhanin*, and I was surprised by the degree of consensus over the concept. They saw *Iuzhanin* as religious, tra-ditional (*traditsionnye*), backward (*nerazvityi*), rich (*bogatye*), cunning (*Khitrye*), Mafioso, violent and patriarchal.

They argued that, while *Iuzhanin* were closer in their culture and manners to Uzbeks, Almatian Kazakhs and Kazakhs from the north (*severnye Kazakhi*) were closer to Russians, who were described in positive terms. I found later that the concept was universally used among the urban population. A Kazakh colleague of mine who came from the north and had spent some of his teenage years in Shymkent told me that *Iuzhanin* denotes one of the darkest aspects of Kazakh culture. He described *Iuzhanin* as dishonest, corrupt and bigoted, characteristics which are often ascribed by the urban Kazakhs to Uzbeks. He said that they were cowards in a fight; several of them fight with one person, and they continue to beat the person, even when he is on the floor. *Menbet* and *Menbetka*, which mean a stupid and backward Kazakh from the *aul*, were originally coined by Russians to insult Kazakhs, I was told by a Kazakh friend. However, during my stay in

Almaty, I never heard Russians using such expressions. They were afraid of being punished by the Kazakhs. On the other hand the urban Kazakhs used the words frequently to describe the assumed stupidity and backwardness of migrants from the *aul*. In response to such attitudes, the southerners and migrants considered the Urban Kazakhs as *mankurts* (ignorant of one's own history and culture) and *chala* Kazakhs (hybrid). The southerners who were fluent in the Kazakh language and had kept and reinvented the Kazakh 'traditions' considered urban Kazakhs to be Russians in soul and Kazakhs in appearance. *Chala*, which was used historically for the children of marriages between Tatars and Kazakhs, is today used by migrants to denote the urban Kazakhs' assumed spurious and unauthentic culture. The migrants have two derogatory words for Russians: '*Ivashka*' for males and '*Russachka*' for females. *Ivashka*, I was told, means more or less a stupid Russian (*Russkii durak*). And *Russachka* means a rude (*neskromnaia*), superficial (*legkomyslennaia*) and sexually loose (*rasputnaia*) Russian woman.

While Kazakhs' negative stereotyping of each other makes a unifying Kazakh identity problematic, both urban and migrant Kazakhs have claims to be 'original Kazakhs' (*nastoiashchie Kazakhi*). The urban Kazakhs usually affiliate *aul* Kazakhs with Uzbeks and thereby deligitimise their claim to an authentic identity. The latter associate the former with Russians. However, *aul* Kazakhs are more consistent in their rhetoric, because the Kazakh language, *aul*, *yurt* and the other symbols of the Kazakh ethnic identity are closely related to their daily cultural practices. The urban Kazakhs have contradictory and complex attitudes towards such symbols. In their contest with migrants and southern Kazakhs such symbols are denounced as the sign of backwardness, while on other occasions they are used as symbols of the national identity and assets of cultural capital. Such contradictory attitudes were displayed by some of the urban Kazakh members of the department of which I was also a member. As they knew I had no taste for exoticism, they usually affiliated themselves with Russian culture, which they considered European and progressive, and disassociated themselves in different ways from the *aul*'s assumed traditional life. In the regular celebration of the birthdays of the members of staff, they did not display anything particularly Kazakh. The only element which represented Kazakh culture was the horse meat (*kazy*), which was consumed without any comment. Then two Belgians came as guest lecturers on behalf of a Tacis programme for a week. The goal of the programme was to select members of staff for a number of scholarships in the UK and Belgium. They tried to entertain the Belgians in the best possible way. They were invited by a high official in the Ministry of Education, a parent of one of the students, to a *yurt* outside Almaty, where they were served lamb, in the Kazakh traditional way. At the university, elements of so-called Kazakh traditional culture were displayed only on ceremonial occasions like the Eighth of March, Nuvroz, the celebration of the 150th anniversary of the birth of Zhambyl,[67] or when they had foreign honoured guests (Indian, German or American ambassadors).

In short, the attitudes of urban Kazakhs towards the symbols of Kazakh traditions are ambivalent. They often dismiss them as the symbols of backwardness but display them in particular situations as symbols of national identity and make cultural capital out of them.

The same ambivalence existed towards the *aul* Kazakhs. As most urban Kazakhs are first, second or third generation migrants, they still have relatives in the *auls*. Given the strong obligations between kin among Kazakhs, their kinship networks transcend the division between the city and the *aul*. For example, many urban Kazakh women, involved in the street trade, had ties with kinfolk in *auls* and were involved in reciprocal exchange with them. The same was true of my women colleagues at the university. Moreover, while the urban Kazakhs support the rest of the Russian-speaking population against the migrant Kazakhs, they distinguished themselves from them by claiming to have a separate Kazakh identity. Such claims were often used for justifying their privileged access to the posts in the state institutions. The contest over the urban space also fragments the Islamic identity.

THE STRUGGLE FOR URBAN SPACE AND THE FRAGMENTATION OF ISLAMIC IDENTITY

> A Soviet Muslim and a Muslim from abroad feel completely at home with each other in whatever country they meet. Both belong to the same 'Milet' (nation), to the same Dar Ul-Islam, and share the same spiritual background which rules their everyday life. (Bennigsen, 1980: p. 2)

The statement above by one of the leading Central Asianists is an example of the standard way the majority of Western scholars invented and essentialised an Islamic identity in Central Asia, not innocently, but often for political purposes related to the Cold War. Many of those who write today about Central Asia follow the same pattern. They continue to represent Islam as an over-arching identity. One of the early findings of my research in Kazakhstan was that notions of an umbrella Islamic identity are an illusion. I discovered very soon that although different Muslim groups were conscious of being Muslim, identification with Islam was subordinate to the contest over resources. Not only did Russian-speaking urban Muslims usually identify themselves with Russians, but most importantly, the more religious Muslims among the Turks, Azaris, Uigurs, Uzbeks and Tadjiks often had a positive image of Russians, while attributing negative attributes to *aul* Kazakhs and southern Kazakhs. On the other hand, Russians' attitudes were more negative to Kazakhs, Chechens apart, than any other Muslim group. The two following cases illustrate such attitudes.

In the first neighbourhood in which I lived, there was a restaurant and a shashlyk bar run by Azaris. All their staff were Azaris and Russians. After a while I asked one of the shareholders, 'Why do you not employ Kazakhs, who are Muslims, instead of Russians?' He answered:

What Muslims? They are thieves (*zhuliki*) and lazy (*lenivye*). The only thing they know is how to take (*brat*). If I employ a Kazakh then his friends and relatives will come here to eat free of charge, he will take my money. If I sack him, he will collect his friends and relatives and attack me. I cannot do anything, the police are on their side. We have no problem with Russians, they are honest (*chestnye*) and hard-working (*try-doliubivye liudi*).

The second case is of a young Russian worker in the factory where I did fieldwork. He was the one who received me most warmly, and befriended me quickly, lunching with me, playing chess with me, introducing me to other workers, asking questions about my projects, and telling me in great detail about whatever I asked him. He was so good-natured that everybody loved him. But there was something strange about him from the very beginning. He had drawn a great swastika with a pen on the arm of his jacket. As he was so nice to me and often joked in a gentle and friendly way with two Uigurs, who worked on the same shopfloor, I was sure that he was not a Nazi. One day I asked him: 'What is this Vas'ka?' He answered: 'You don't know?! This is the emblem of fascists! I am a fascist!' I asked him: 'What does it mean?' 'It, means', he answered, 'that we fight against Kazakhs.' Then he explained to me that they were a network of friends, who called themselves fascists and fought together against Kazakhs, whenever the latter attacked them. Then he told me several stories about their fights with Kazakhs. According to Vasilii, most of the members of his 'fascist' network were of Slavic origin, however they also had Armenians, Tatars and Uigurs among them. I asked him: 'Are you against all Muslims or only against Kazakhs?' Vasilii said: 'Why all Muslims?' Then he added that he had been living with his mother in an Uigur neighbourhood in an Almaty suburb for a long time, and that Uigurs are generous (*shchedrye*) and hospitable (*gostepriimnye*). They invite him and his mother to eat and drink whenever they have a ceremony, and at the Sacrifice Feast (*Korbanat*) the neighbours give a lot of meat to his mother. He said that his best friends are Uigurs and they fought Kazakhs together. The Kazakhs he blamed and fought were young men of his age who had migrated recently from China and Mongolia and who had been housed in the village close to their neighbourhood by the Kazakh government.

According to Vasilii, they moved in groups and if they found you alone they attacked you.

The mutual empathy of non-Kazakh Muslims and Russians and their common negative feelings for *aul* Kazakhs depends on the current ethnically oriented tension over resources, particularly social space. This was evident in the neighbourhood illegal market. The rural Kazakhs occasionally harassed Turks and Tatars and did not allow Tadjiks and Uzbeks to sell in the illegal market. The following example illustrates this.

Once two Kazakh men who sold fruit and vegetables ordered a Turk to move to another place. He refused to obey them and they scattered his tomatoes and cucumbers on the ground. The Turk had no choice but to pack his things and find a new place. I helped him to collect the vegetables and went off with him. He said that the Kazakhs were jealous, because most of the customers bought from him. He sold cheaper and fresher vegetables which he bought from his relatives in Kaskelen. Then he said:

Kazakhs are always like this, they fight for any reason. If five drunk Russians ask me for a lift I will give them the lift, but I will never stop the car for a single Kazakh. I am less afraid of five drunk Russians than a single Kazakh. When I see a Kazakh in the distance I turn away on purpose not to encounter him. They come here from the *aul*, and then tell you, 'I am a Kazakh, you are not. Here is my country, I have nothing. Why do you have a car, why have you got an apartment. Why?' They do not think that I have worked the whole of my life for the car and the apartment. If you say something to them, they will beat you. You cannot complain to the police and courts, because they are Kazakhs, they never prosecute Kazakhs for non-Kazakhs.

Tadjiks and Uzbeks were not only openly harassed by the rural Kazakhs, but by the police as well. The *aul* Kazakhs, both street traders and customers, took fruit and vegetables from them without paying. Police treated them more harshly and the migrant Kazakhs chased them away from the illegal markets. Migrant Kazakhs justified their hostility towards Uzbeks and Tadjiks by claiming that the Uzbeks had chased them away from Tashkent's markets after independence. (In fact, in the Almaty legal markets I met Kazakhs from Uzbekistan whose families lived still in Uzbekistan. They told me they have to trade in Almaty, because Uzbeks do not let them trade in Tashkent.) As a result Tadjiks and Uzbeks were forced to hire places in legal markets and pay much higher fees than the usual 30 tenge each street trader paid to police. Even then they were continuously harassed. I met many Tadjiks and Uzbeks who were trading at *Tastak* and *Zelenyi Bazaar*, markets in Almaty. I kept contact with them until my departure. They sold vegetables, fruit, rice and dried fruit which they brought to Almaty from Tadjikistan and Uzbekistan. They were systematically harassed in both *Tastak* and the *Zelenyi Bazaar*. According to the Tadjiks I knew, every day the police officers take from them a considerable amount of fruit and vegetables without paying. In Tastak bazaar the police regularly robbed Tadjiks two or three times a week. Once the market was closed during the evening and Tadjiks were going home as usual, the police stopped a Tadjik and asked for his papers. Although he had the *propiska* (residential permission), they forced him into the police car, took him to a quiet place, took his money and left him there. Often they abused the victim verbally and physically. In addition to the police, the young Kazakh army conscripts from the other parts of Kazakhstan took fruit and money regularly from Tadjiks and Uzbeks.

Kazakh migrants justified their domination over the urban space by claiming that Kazakhstan was their historical homeland.

CONCLUSIONS

In Almaty, while ethnic competition and tension takes many forms, they are mainly focused on two main resources: the state institutions and urban space. The reason for this is that the social transactions with immediate and in some cases high economic returns are related to these two spheres. The ethnic tensions on the labour market for industrial jobs, which are occupied traditionally by Russians, is very marginal. It is not attractive for Kazakhs, because wages are reduced dramatically, paid irregularly or in kind. The monopolising of higher positions in the bureaucracy and places in higher education by Kazakhs has provoked a strong dissatisfaction among non-Kazakhs. On the other hand this has created a tension between the Russian-speaking Kazakhs and Kazakh-speaking Kazakhs, because the state language policy promotes the interests of the latter in the long run. The tension over urban space is caused by the massive migration of Kazakhs to the cities. This tension is between migrants who speak Kazakh and the urban population who speak Russian. In this tension the Russian-speaking Kazakhs side with non-Kazakhs against migrants. Hooliganism and the use of violence, which are important means of control of urban space, articulate the domination of Kazakh ethnicity to the dominant masculinities among Kazakhs. The gangs of Kazakh men justify their use of violence for control over particular places by claiming that Kazakhstan is their ancestral land. Urban Kazakhs' solidarity with other Russian-speaking people make the picture much more complex. While urban Kazakhs consider Kazakhstan to be their historical homeland they are mostly against hooliganism and the ethno-linguistic nationalism of the state officials. They support non-Kazakhs against hooliganism.

Ethnic hooliganism is a result of the current crisis of hegemony and a by-product of the chaotic mode of domination discussed in chapter 1. While the economic crisis and massive dislocation of rural Kazakhs have created a wide Kazakh lumpen proletariat, the chaotic mode of domination provides a space for this group to engage in hooliganism. Such hooliganism is an important element of the chaos. Non-Kazakhs are of the opinion that the state officials, who are mainly Kazakhs, support hooligans against non-Kazakhs. An important dimension of the ethnic struggle for urban space is the use of violence by Kazakhs against non-Kazakhs and each other. So violence as an important element of chaos, described in chapter 3, relates ethnicity to gender. Urban space is controlled by violent Kazakh men. The ethnic dominance of Kazakhs is equal to the dominance of the strong Kazakh men. In short the hegemonic masculinity and the hegemonic ethnicity reinforce each other. The subjects of violence are not only other men but generally women from any ethnic backgrounds.

Another interesting aspect of this tension is that it usually transcends Muslim/Christian and Slav/Turk divisions. The very dominance of Kazakhs has created feelings of solidarity between non-Muslim and non-Turk ethnic groups on the one hand and non-Kazakh Muslim and non-Kazakh Turk ethnic groups on the other. Another significant observation is that ethnic tension in Kazakhstan is not determined by so-called historical cultural differences, but are dimensions of social struggles for particular resources in the context of the current political and economic chaos. Nor has this conflict among the dispossessed yet developed into the articulated forms of ethnic nationalism represented by some groups of intellectuals. In spite of the ethnic tension between them, the dispossessed among Kazakhs, Russians and other ethnic groups consider themselves to be subdivisions of the same Soviet people. Most people considered ethnic conflict to be a result of the expansion of wild capitalism.

8   CONCLUSIONS IN A COMPARATIVE PERSPECTIVE: WHOSE TRANSITION?

Chaos is depicted by the dispossessed as the intrusion of global, wild capitalism into the territory of Kazakhstan and the effects of such an intrusion. In other words chaos is a particular form of globalisation in Kazakhstan. By globalisation, I mean the restructuring and domination of the world system by North American imperialism (Panitch, 2000). Such globalisation is not only marked by the presence of multinationals, Americanism and the transnational connections of the elite, but the fact that the IMF, the World Bank, the US and the EU are systematically cultivating capitalist values and supervising the transformation to capitalism. The dispossession of millions of people from their basic economic and cultural rights, the emergence of the chaotic mode of domination, the growth of violence and poverty, the monetisation of important aspects of social relations and the emergence and expansion of the sex industry are the most important aspects of this process.

   In contrast to the celebratory and glorious images of globalisation produced by some scholars, for the dispossessed in Almaty globalisation is a story of wild capitalism, chaos, dispossession, loss, tears, horror, violence and fear. All of these are the direct result of the dissolution of the welfare state and the emergence of wild capitalism. The very fact that in Soviet society people enjoyed numerous economic rights makes the transformation to a market economy an immense tragedy. The depth of such tragedy is not understandable unless we agree with the dispossessed that Soviet society had some advantages for them.

   This idea provokes the scorn of mainstream academic and journalistic circles in the West who rush to remind us of Stalinist terror, purges, concentration camps and the lack of political liberties. Yet millions of the dispossessed, who themselves had been subjected to such terror, are nostalgically emphasising that the creation of the welfare state has been a major achievement of Soviet types of societies. The success of the reformed communist parties in elections is a good indicator of such nostalgia. However, those who yearn for the welfare state do not associate it with the political regime of Stalinism and do not wish to see the revival of such a regime.

Indeed, the economic rights of Soviet citizens were not offered to people by Stalinism on a golden tray but the people imposed them on the regime. The Stalinist political regime and the welfare state were two contradictory but not complementary features of Soviet society. The Soviet system emerged as a result of the unacknowledged defeat of the October Revolution by a Stalinist counter-revolution. Stalinists buried the revolution in the name of revolution itself. But they also had to pay a price.

While massively purging and killing genuine revolutionaries they claimed to be the genuine heirs of the revolution and ruled the country in the name of the working class in the following decades. The Stalinists were not able officially to denounce the revolution and the working class because of the relative power and influence of the latter. As a result of this balance of forces, an historical compromise was established between the Stalinist elite and the working class. While the working class conceded hegemonic political and economic powers to the new Stalinist ruling group, the latter made concessions, historically without precedent, to the workers in the sphere of welfare. From its emergence in the 1930s until the mid 1980s, in one sense the short history of the system could be described as that of the rise, expansion and disintegration of the most far-reaching welfare state world history has ever witnessed. Life-time employment, free access to education, cheap access to housing, electricity, central heating, gas, telephone, transport, health-care, sport, books, theatre and numerous other welfare services expanded continuously from the 1930s onwards, the war period excepted (Corrigan, Ramsay and Sayer, 1981: p. 16–18).[68]

These welfare reforms were closely linked to the state ownership of the means of production. This form of ownership also bears the imprint of the paradox mentioned above: while officially it was declared a form of socialist ownership, in practice the surplus products were appropriated and administrated by the elite (Ticktin, 1992). In other words, workers were alienated from the means of production and products. However, the very collectivist guise of property relations was a concession to the working class. This showed itself not only in the various welfare services which were provided by enterprises for their staff, but also in the workers' relations to the means of production and products on the one hand and the labour process on the other. As Alexander, a Russian worker, described in chapter 4 Soviet workers could to a limited extent use instruments of production and products for private ends. More importantly, their control over the labour process was much higher than that of the workers in the capitalist world (Ticktin, 1992).

Another aspect of the social contract between Stalinism and the working class was that the elite's privileges were limited in comparison with those of propertied classes in the capitalist world in three ways: their wealth comprised a lesser proportion of the total national wealth; their privileges were unstable because changes in one's political position inevitably entailed changes in one's privileges; privileges were not transferable through inheritance, although the children of the elite benefited from the privileges in general. Through post-Soviet reforms the elite broke this historical contract at the expense of the labouring masses. In this sense market reforms are a continuation of Stalinism in a new guise rather than a break with it. They finished the unfinished Stalinist counter-revolution. Thus it is no surprise that a majority of today's heroes of the market economy are erstwhile Stalinists.

Once the system sank into a deep crisis in the early 1980s, the renegotiation of the historical compromise between the elite and working class became inevitable. Now radical workers and radical socialists not only wanted to keep the welfare state but wanted to go beyond it. They demanded workers' control over production and the revival of early Soviet democracy (Kagarlitsky, 1988). Indeed, most of the dispossessed I talked with told me that both *perestroika* and *glasnost* had stimulated great expectations for the future. They expected that their living standards would be raised to match those of Western countries and that they would enjoy democracy. However, as the course of events soon revealed, the elite and their Western mentors contemplated something else. They wanted to abolish the welfare state. The failure of radical socialists, the examination of which is beyond the scope of this book, to become a formidable political force (Kagarlitsky, 1990) offered them the opportunity to do this. Thereby, they launched a brutal expropriation of people at a speed without historical precedent.[69]

Low (1997: p. 403), with reference to the global context, argues that cities as the main interfaces between global processes and people's daily experiences are also places of violence, abuse and marginalisation. She relates such brutal experiences to the ways these global processes polarise, gender and ethnicise the cities. Not only does the flexible accumulation of capital lead to the accumulation of wealth on the one hand and accumulation of poverty on the other, but it also creates ethnic ghettos and exposes women and migrants to poverty and violence. In Almaty the polarisation of the population is marked by the disintegration of society as a moral community into networks of the new rich on the one hand and those of the poor on the other. The class positions of these two groups are ambiguous in terms of the relations of production, because both of them acquire important parts of their material resources from outside production. This is partly due to deindustrialisation caused by the collapse of industry and agriculture. Although the sale of raw material and the privatisation of the means of production are important sources of the wealth of the new rich, they mainly acquire their wealth through speculation, bribery, extraction of tributes and monopolisation of commerce. On the other hand the dispossessed do not survive only through their wages, the payment of which is often postponed by several months. They utilise a variety of methods such as cultivating allotments, hunting and gathering, involvement in small scale trade, illegal appropriation of small resources in their workplaces and, most importantly, reciprocal exchanges within their networks.

Both these types of networks are based on marriage, kinship and friendship which more or less acquire an ethnic character. Both appropriate resources illegally, although on different scales. Moreover, they share a morality in which not only do obligations to networks override other commitments, but networks constitute the sole moral community for individuals. In other words society as a moral community of citizens does not exist. To paraphrase Margaret Thatcher, according to current networking mentality: 'Society does not exist. We have only individuals and their networks.' People outside networks are not trustworthy and are feared, but they can be cheated and violated. This morality, combined with the arbitrariness of state officials, the mafia and street gangs, constitutes a strong element of chaos. Practically, what was once called society has disintegrated into a set of networks which negotiate through force and the exchange of bribes and tributes. In spite of sharing these characteristics, these two types differ in several respects.

First, while the new rich glorify the disintegration of society into networks as a step towards a promised capitalist paradise of freedom and prosperity, the dispossessed view it with great regret. While they demand the revival of society as a moral community of welfare, they consider their own involvement in current networking practices a matter of expediency. Second, the networks of the new rich have monopolised the means of violence.

Third, these two types of networks differ in their access to the means of transnational communication and in their cultural orientations as a result and an expression of what might be called an 'uneven' globalisation. In Kazakhstan this is a process whereby particular economic and cultural practices of the prosperous section of the population become part of the so-called 'global ecumene', while the rest are not only excluded from it but dispossessed, marginalised, dominated and exploited by the globalisation process. The new rich in Kazakhstan experience globalisation as an exciting journey from one metropolitan capital to the next, visiting expensive clubs and shopping centres and consuming luxury goods and services. But the rest find it an evil and corrupt process. The dispossessed cannot afford these luxuries. Their communication beyond Almaty has shrunk dramatically because of the simultaneous dramatic rise of the cost of travel, telephone and postage stamps on the one hand and the wage cuts on the other. Indeed, in this sense, while the networks of the new rich have become truly global, those of the new poor have spatially shrunk. Another important dimension of the transnationalisation of the networks of the new rich is their multiple contacts with representatives of multinationals, the IMF, the World Bank,

Western governments, the international banking system and other agencies. Of course the dispossessed are not fully immune from the influence of globalisation, through watching soap operas, experiencing the presence of foreigners, the transnational sex industry, the migration of neighbours, and through the travel of sex workers and suitcase traders to other countries. However, they look on these, watching soap operas excepted, negatively.

A result of the disintegration of the society into these two types of networks is the perpetuation of the current crisis of hegemony. The elite has no moral and ideological authority over the dispossessed. In contrast, the dispossessed consider the elite as a bunch of thieves and criminals. However, from the point of view of the elite, the disintegration of society into networks is a solution to the crisis of hegemony. The multiplicity and arbitrariness of the networks of influence create a great fear among the dispossessed, which pacifies them politically. Moreover, the government officials continuously remind the population that any social unrest will exacerbate the current chaos. Indeed, Nazarbaev says in every speech that stability (*stabilnost*) is the first priority of the republic. People buy this argument to a great extent. Given the ethnic nature of the networks of influence and hooliganism people are afraid that any civil unrest may exacerbate the chaos by instigating widespread ethnic violence. The tragic wars in Chechenia and then in Tadjikistan and the massive presence of refugees from these two places in Kazakhstan reminded people of the consequences of such violence. In such a situation the dispossessed cope with the situation through the networks of survival. However, networking practices among the dispossessed contribute to nepotism and ethnic tension which negatively affects their unification against the elite.

Castells (1997) argues that building communal movements is partly a response of the dispossessed to the exploitative aspects of globalisation. The responses of the dispossessed to uneven globalisation in Kazakhstan include both communal and civic elements. The communal elements are involved in the ways networking practices are related to ethnicity and the civic elements are expressed through the construction of a Soviet identity. The relation of such networks to ethnicity is complex. Although networks acquire an ethnic character and the widespread network-oriented nepotism contributes to ethnic tension, people do not identify networking directly with ethnicity. Ethnicity colours networking mainly through the microprocesses of kinship, marriage and friendship where mutual trust is negotiated and established.

By the construction of an authentic Soviet identity, the dispossessed from all ethnic backgrounds resist economic and cultural globalisation rhetorically. Such an identity is created through demonising the main dimensions of globalisation as an evil alien force. The main elements in local constructions are the alien person, the alien culture and wild capitalism in general. Alien persons are conceived to be male, the agents of wild capitalism, who are rich and promiscuous. They are responsible for the destruction of the Soviet Union and its culture, and the spreading of prostitution, sexual diseases and consumerism. The ways in which the alien person is sexualised and gendered reflects fears about the destabilisation and disintegration of family relations, which constitute the main nodes of networks of survival. The threats to family are imposed by a market-oriented liberalisation of sexuality, bolstered by the dispossession of women which is caused by the transition to a market economy.

In the Soviet era, the 1920s excepted, sexuality was officially taboo. Sex was absent not only from public, popular and intellectual discourses but its practices were subjected to very strict moralistic discourses. One of the results of the Gorbachev reforms was an openness on sexuality. Sexuality was publicised through debates in the media and the circulation of erotic and pornographic material on a huge scale. Moreover, such liberalisation is marked by the massive proliferation of different forms of extra-marital sex. Under the current gendered economic conditions, liberalisation has led to the creation of a huge sex industry not only through the production and sale of pornography but also the massive transformation of women's bodies into sexual commodities. The latter was facilitated by the ways post-Soviet wealth differentiation is gendered. As the new rich consists exclusively of men, the majority of women become dispossessed. The sex market offered young women among the dispossessed the opportunities to deploy the sexual strategies of survival explored in chapter 5.

The tensions between wives and husbands among the dispossessed, caused by unemployment and poverty, might encourage women to practice sexualised strategies. However, the images of women's bodies as sexual commodities have provoked great abuse and violence against them. As in the case of any other commodity, in the post-Soviet chaotic and violent mafia-market, they are appropriated, sold and consumed, often through force. Second, such violence is legitimised by the public stigma inflicted on such women. They are considered as 'perverts' and 'deviants' who should be punished, not as individuals who deserve any moral support. So, in a much broader sense violence and stigma are the two main mechanisms through which the post-Soviet new rich discipline and distribute women's bodies along reproductive and profit-making functions.

The dispossessed link the monetisation of sexuality to another element of the evil alien, namely Western-oriented consumerist culture publicised through the merging of the market and the media. An interesting aspect of anti-consumerist rhetoric is the pride people take in consuming their own Soviet goods (goods produced in CIS). The anti-consumerist rhetoric of the dispossessed is not directed against the use value of the foreign goods or consumption as such, but at the ways these goods and consumerism are used by the new rich as signs of distinction. Conspicuous consumption of luxurious goods is the main way through which the new rich declare their social existence. While opposing this consumerist culture the dispossessed claim nostalgically that their ruined 'Soviet culture' was based on higher humanitarian values. The sexual promiscuity and consumerism of the new rich and foreigners are considered to be elements of chaos (wild capitalism). The dispossessed are of the opinion that prostitution was a part of the wider plot of conspiracy by the elite and foreigners to destroy Soviet society. This nostalgia should not be considered a demand for a full return to the Soviet past. Although people truly demand the revival of the welfare state, they also want democracy and they are critical of the shortage of particular goods under the Soviet regime. Such nostalgia is primarily a criticism of wild capitalism and expresses a demand for an egalitarian society. The nostalgia for the Soviet era is fed by fact that the coping strategies such as networking and sex work are considered to be constituent elements of the chaos rather than solutions to it.

Through the negation of the alien the dispossessed imagine a Soviet egalitarian community. But this sense of community is problematised by gender and ethnic tension. On the gender level the use of sexualised strategies by young dispossessed women and their inclination towards consumerism questions the notions of a Soviet sexual morality. On the other hand the notions of Soviet sexual morality are in the service of patriarchal gender relations and justify the use of violence against women who dare to break the puritanical sexual rules. The feelings of belonging to an imagined Soviet community has helped to contain the explosive expression of ethnic conflicts. The very fact that the dispossessed, regardless of ethnicity, hold the elite and the West responsible for their current miseries prevents them from using each other as scapegoats. However, in spite of this, the competition for resources between networks, the role of the state in this respect and Kazakhification of state and massive migration of Kazakhs to cities have given rise to ethnic tension.

As a Russian woman eloquently pointed out to me: 'The ethnic conflict in Kazakhstan is burning but still not explosive.' People see the emergence of ethnic conflict as an element of chaos resulting from the disintegration of Soviet society and blame this conflict on foreigners and the invasion of the Soviet territory by capitalism. Their view is diametrically opposed to that of scholars who conceive the current ethnic tension as a result of confrontation between different cultures and religions (Smith, 1992).

Let us return to the rhetorical question that is the subtitle of this chapter: Whose transition? What the dispossessed call chaos is celebrated by the elite and the West as a transition to capitalism which is exalted as the natural order of life. This transition is the core element of the globalisation processes in Kazakhstan. Most Western discourses of globalisation, while rightly pointing to the profound technological, economic and cultural changes which have occurred in the postwar period, include a strong element of political rhetoric. On the level of cultural politics, globalisation is celebrated as a diversification of cultural experience and the production of 'rainbow' cultures. On the economic level it has been argued that capital cannot be resisted because of so-called 'flexible accumulation'. Indeed, both of these rhetorics from the point of view of the dispossessed in Almaty reflect the positions and advantages of the new rich and their foreign allies and should be challenged. Globalisation for them is not an experience of rainbow culture or access to the internet, British Airways, clubs in Paris, Rome, London and New York but a hell of abuse, violence, poverty and ruthless exploitation. They call this chaos (*bardak*). World capitalism is depicted as a global brothel. This 'global brothel' and its representatives are condemned by the dispossessed as evil alien forces, responsible for their current social miseries.

To what extent, we could ask, is the present situation in Kazakhstan a legacy of the Soviet era? To what extent is it a product of the new liberal reforms imposed by the US, the World Bank and the IMF? At first sight, the fact that the communist elite, dressed in new clothes, are still in power, and the patronage-based practices of power are very similar to those of the Soviet era, support the claim of apologists of the post-Soviet reforms that the roots of all present evils should be only sought in the misdeeds of the communist past. But comparison with non-socialist countries in the developing world, which have been subjected to IMF restructuring programmes, reveals that the turbulent effect of these reforms in the former Soviet territory share the following aspects of such effects in these countries:

- Economic, and to a great extent political, subjugation to the West, particularly the US, through the macro-economic reforms and debt regulation mechanisms, implemented by the Bretton Woods institutions.
- Social polarisation characterised by the accumulation of wealth on the one hand and poverty on the other.
- Disintegration of the social fabric of daily life while violence, ethnic tension and mass exodus have become defining features of society.
- Privatisation of state property, deindustrialisation, cutting wages, destruction of agriculture, dislocation of educational infrastructures and health-care.
- Dollarisation of prices.
- Formation of a criminal economy, a shadow state and the flight of capital, mainly through money laundering.
- A dual economy: export-oriented economy on the one hand, and the stagnant parts of agriculture and industry, which are not profitable for multinationals, on the other.

It has been argued (Gowan, 1996; Kagarlitsky, 1995; Chossudovsky, 1998) that the emergence of these features in Eastern Europe and the former Soviet Union is a result of the imperialist policies of Western powers. Gowan suggests that the following measures were taken in order to subjugate Eastern Central Europe: breaking up the Comecon regime and separating East Central Europe from the USSR; imposing neoliberal economic policies; and reorienting these economies towards the West. There was a strategy that cooperative states should be rewarded and the disobedient ones should be punished. Burgess (1997) shows that the West pursued a cynical colonial policy in Eastern Europe. Chossudovsky (1998) argues forcefully that the IMF macro-economic reforms, imposed through a regime of conditionalities of debts practised by the World Bank and other international financial institutions, constitute the core of such imperialistic policies. The main goal of these reforms, imposed globally since the 1970s, has been to create a cheap global labour economy. Privatisation of state property, tight budgetary regimes, the closing of factories and redundancy of workers, cutting social welfare, liberalisation of prices and removing tariffs on foreign goods have been some of the main pillars of these reforms.

The debts of developing countries, which have skyrocketed since 1980, were usually serviced through the export of commodities, the prices of which fell dramatically. Thus the debtor countries needed to borrow money from the international financial institutions in order to service existing debts. As the lion's share of the new loans was used to service the previous loans, the amount of debt increased and necessitated newer loans. The World Bank and other international institutions made the giving of such loans conditional upon the implementation of the IMF macro-economic reforms by debtor countries. The countries which refused these conditions were blacklisted. When these reforms were opposed by the population, they were carried out, in most cases, through dictatorial or at least undemocratic methods. Yeltsin gunned the Russian parliament (4 October 1993), with support from the US and Europe, because it refused to ratify the IMF reforms, and Nazarbaev dissolved the Kazakh *Mejles* (1993) for the same reason.

As Chossudovsky (1998) argues, these policies resulted in a worldwide misery, fostering criminal economies, creating crisis and the disintegration of states and promoting violent ethnic conflicts. He shows that the IMF intervention created the famine which led to the disintegration of Somalia by damaging the livestock economy through the privatisation of animal health-care, destruction of food agriculture and tightening the state budget. He also argues that the economic crisis caused by IMF and World Bank intervention was pivotal in instigating the civil war and the subsequent genocide in Rwanda. Rwanda was a weak post-colonial state, mainly dependent on revenues from coffee and tea exports which were used for debt servicing. The fall[70] of coffee prices by 50 per cent between 1987 and

1991 contributed to the creation of famine in rural areas. The IMF-imposed policy consisted of trade liberalisation, devaluation of the currency, lifting subsidies to agriculture, privatisation of state enterprises and the redundancy of the civil servants (Chossudovsky, pp. 115–16). These policies led to sudden increases in the prices of fuel and other basic goods, an increase in the debt burden by 34 per cent (1989–92), bankruptcy of the state enterprises and the crumbling of the public services. As a result of the collapse of education and health-care the numbers of children who enrolled in the schools decreased dramatically and diseases like malaria spread rapidly. All these resulted in an economic crisis, at the peak of which (1992) farmers uprooted 300,000 coffee trees (Chossudovsky, p. 116). In the midst of the civil war the IMF imposed a second devaluation which increased prices further. Although the ethnic conflicts in Rwanda have their roots in the colonial period, the economic crisis was pivotal in their explosion.

Another classic case is the Balkans tragedy. As Chossudovsky (p. 43) has observed, mainstream journalists and politicians in the West have, misleading the public, claimed that either the explosive return of the 'primordial' identities, or the alleged Serbian perverted tendency towards nationalism and hatred, are reasons behind this tragedy. In tandem with these arguments, the decisive role of the Western powers in instigating, monitoring and manipulating these conflicts for their own benefits have been cynically covered up. As Woodward (1995) demonstrates convincingly, the IMF-imposed economic reforms, and the changed international environment of the late 1980s and early 1990s were instrumental in the destruction of Yugoslavia. Her argument is as follows: the 'socialist' Yugoslavia, a prosperous, stable and relatively open society, was a result of the post-war balance of international power. Its political and economic structures were created in response to two basic problems: the crisis of an agrarian economy; and the so-called 'national' question. This stability, Woodward argues, was based on the international relations, the welfare state and the personal security and prosperity of citizens, and the multinational constitutional order. Being a neutral country, Yugoslavia established economic and political relations with first, second and third worlds. Although it was excluded from the economic alliances of the West and the Soviet block, by balancing between these two camps it managed to have trade relations with both, and enjoyed credit from the West. The personal security and prosperity of citizens was guaranteed through a wide range of welfare provisions. Moreover, the Yugoslavian model of self-management provided the workers with an opportunity to have a say in the management of enterprises. However, the welfare system had two important shortcomings: the welfare provisions were offered only by the state enterprises; and unemployment was legal.[71] As a result, employees of the private sector and the unemployed were deprived of these provisions. Therefore, the competition for jobs in the state sector or access to goods and services in short supply resulted in the growth of nepotism, bribery and the black market. However, in spite of these negative factors, most citizens enjoyed reasonable prosperity.

The multinational constitutional order provided political and economic autonomy and equal rights for the constituent republics of the Yugoslav Federation. The federal government was responsible for the army, foreign affairs and the monetary policies while the republics administrated the rest of their economic, cultural and political affairs autonomously. The productive assets were owned by the republics; however, they paid taxes to the coffers of the federal government. The extension of the devolution of powers to republics is well illustrated by the fact that in the 1960s the defence budget, 67 per cent of the total federal budget, was 4–6 per cent of the GNP (Woodward, p. 39). Although the army was the core federal insti-tution, republics had their own devolved civil system of defence. The overall policies of the federal government were determined through consensus by all republics, thus a certain republic could veto any policy it did not favour. The IMF reforms eroded individual security, and triggered a constitutional crisis, both of which contributed to the growth of ethnic nationalism. The flow of loans from the West to Yugoslavia was interrupted in 1979, due to a recession in 1975 which led to a global economic depression in the 1980s (Woodward, p. 47). The government, avoiding resorting to the IMF, implemented an austerity policy, cutting domestic consumption of imported goods and encouraging exports. However, these measures were not sufficient to solve the government's financial difficul-ties. Between 1982 and 1989, successive governments turned to the IMF for new loans. The IMF conditions for such loans, in addition to its famous recipe of liberalisation of prices and radical austerity, included a change in the constitution. It demanded that the consensus-based agreement between republics should be replaced by the rule of majority. The IMF argued that such a change would strengthen the position of the federal government *vis-à-vis* republics, allowing it to impose monetary discipline on them. The austerity policy resulted in the growth of unemployment and inflation, a fall in the GDP and domestic consumption and shortages of particular goods. These eroded the sense of the security among citizens in various republics, which in turn resulted in the growth of ethnic nationalism and religious revivalism.

The staunch Slovenian opposition to the constitutional changes demanded by the IMF unleashed a constitutional crisis which acquired an ethnic expression. Slovenia and Croatia not only opposed the constitutional change but avoided paying taxes to the federal government which were tra-ditionally transferred to less prosperous republics, arguing that they needed their funds for their own republics. As Woodward put it, the political struggle which was instigated by the IMF programme dominated the whole decade of the 1980s (p. 50). The erosion of personal security combined with constitutional crisis created a secessionist nationalism which was encouraged by the international environment of the 1980s. While the Soviet block was disintegrating, the Western powers were less interested in the integrity of Yugoslavia than in carving out spheres of influence in Central and Eastern Europe. The secession of Slovenia and Croatia, supported openly by Germany, unleashed the tragedy which brought war, rape and ethnic cleansing. The main beneficiaries were the Western powers and war lords of various ethnic description. Croatia effectively became a puppet of Germany and the US, and Bosnia (Chossudovsky, 1998) and Kosovo, in effect became a colony of the US. Serbia became the fiefdom of a number of corrupted networks related to the top officials of the Yugoslavian state.

The closest case to Kazakhstan is the destruction of Russia. The market-oriented reforms in Russia, as elsewhere in the former Soviet Union, have created a situation which has been called by some authors (Kagarlitsky, 1995; Chossudovsky, 1998) the 'Africanisation' or 'thirdworldisation' of Russia. Soviet countries have been reduced to this situation through an enormous destruction of education, industrial and welfare infrastructures. Although at first sight the application of such terms to Russia, which still has superpower ambitions, may seem absurd, a closer comparison reveals striking similarities between politicoeconomic processes in Russia and many third world countries. Let us compare the situation in Russia with that in Sub-Saharan Africa. Castells (1998: p. 83) argues that the disintegration of states and societies, the collapse of economies, the rise in violence, including factional wars, massive forced displacement of people, rapid spread of epidemics and poverty, and the emergence of social and political chaos are some of the defining features of Sub-Saharan Africa. These, Castells says, are the results of two interrelated processes: the dual process of selective integration and marginalisation in global capitalism; and the formation of predatory states. The dual processes of selective integration and simultaneous marginalisation means that while few territories and groups are integrated in the economic and cultural flows of 'informational capitalism', the majority of the world population and vast territories are not only deprived of the fruits of the informational technology but are drowned in poverty. Global capitalism, using the informational revolution, has furthered previous social and geographical gaps by the use of informational technology. The current situation in Sub-Saharan Africa illustrates the working of such processes. While tiny numbers of elites in this region are integrated in the financial and trade networks of global capitalism through the export of raw material, imports of consumer goods, international loans, laundering money in the Western banks and buying property in the West, the rest of its economies are ruined and the majority of the population is doomed to misery.

These dual processes are accompanied by the emergence of the predatory state since the 1970s. Castells argues that the predation is qualitatively different from the previous forms of political patronage and corruption, which he terms 'prebendalism'. While in prebendalism corruption could be rampant, the collective interests of the state or class took precedent over the personal interests of this or that circle of power holders. By contrast, in predatory rule, the state is privatised by competing networks of the elite who use its institutions for the accumulation of personal wealth. Moreover, while positions in the state institutions become the main means of pillage, the logic of the accumulation of personal wealth is disconnected from the rest of economy. As Castells puts it, 'What does not make sense from the point of view of the country's economic development and political stability makes sense from the point of view of rulers' (Castells, 1998: p. 98). This results in the decomposition and denationalisation of the state itself, a phenomenon which has been described wrongly by some commentators as re-tribalisation in Africa. This results in a crisis of the state, characterised by military dictatorship and violent conflicts between shifting alliances of various factions of the elite, who fight each other by mobilising sections of the population through patronage networks. On the other hand, the clients of each elite group depend on the latter in order to access resources.

Now let us return to the case of Russia. Both selective integration and marginalisation and predation are significant features of the post-Soviet Russia. The neo-liberal policies advised by the Western advisors such as Jeffrey Sachs and supervised by the IMF and the World Bank created a situation in Russia which is in many ways similar to that in Sub-Saharan Africa. The so-called 'shock therapy' which started in January 1992 had immediate catastrophic effects. While industrial production declined by 27 per cent the Russian economy as a whole was reduced by 50 per cent. Consumer prices increased by a hundred times, real incomes fell by 80 per cent (Chossudovsky, 1998: pp. 225–6), and the value of people's saving was reduced to almost nothing because of inflation. The state subsidies for education, health-care, child-care, culture and art collapsed. The majority of people were impoverished overnight. The Russian parliament and the central bank, realising that the reforms were ruining Russia, started to oppose neo-liberalism by late 1992. In order to neutralise the resistance of parliament against the reform programme, Yeltsin suspended by decree both houses of parliament on 21 September 1993. As the parliament refused to accept the Yeltsin decrees, the latter (with the open support of the G7) launched a bloody *coup d'état*, storming the parliament on 4 October 1993. Although many were killed or injured the Western media applauded Yeltsin, with the ridiculous excuse that the parliament was a remnant from the Soviet time, forgetting the fact that the same parliament had stood behind Yeltsin against the *coup d'état* of the hardliners two years earlier in

August 1991. After abolishing the parliament, Yeltsin changed the constitution in a way which gave him enormous power, which was used to facilitate the implementation of the IMF policies. As a result, and in the wake of the South East Asian crisis, Russia became completely bankrupt in the autumn of 1998.

The overall results of the neo-liberal reforms, using Castells' terminology, were selective integration and simultaneous marginalisation on the one hand, and a predatory rule on the other. Let us look at each very briefly. The Soviet economy was uneven. It consisted of a technologically advanced defence section of the so-called military-industrial complex industry, on the one hand, and a relatively backward (in comparison with the West) light industry and agriculture on the other. The reforms introduced a qualitatively new form of unevenness to the Russian economy and society. Now the economy consists of two sectors: one based on the US dollar and the other on barter. Most of Russian industry and agriculture, which were declared by reformers to be uncompetitive in the international markets, have been ruined. Gas, oil and base metals, which are demanded in the international markets, have been monopolised by the networks of the former *nomenklatura*. Enterprises in the marginalised sector are closed down or utilise a small part of their capacity; they are often unfunded and involved in barter with each other. The export-oriented sector sells a considerable part of its products in the international markets in dollars; much of this income goes to personal offshore bank accounts (Chossudovsky, 1998; Haynes and Glatter, 1998). In tandem with economic polarisation, a social polarisation has occurred. While a tiny elite has accumulated legendary wealth, the majority of the population is condemned to misery. Unemployment, alcoholism, extreme poverty, suicide and a fall of the life expectancy are parts of daily life in Russia.

> ... we can simply quote UNICEF's monitoring reports lamenting 'the demographic implosion', 'appalling' numbers of excess deaths (1995); the 'staggering' fall in life expectancy for males (1996) which is now lower than in India; the 'tragic rise' in deaths of young people including through suicide (1998) and so on. ... Thus between 1990 and 1997 the rise of mortality over the 1989 levels has led to between 2.6 and 2.9 million excess deaths attributable to the transition. It can similarly be estimated that the cumulative fall in births has been of the order of 4.5 to 5 million in the same period. (Haynes and Glatter, p. 64)

The decline of the economy in general, the collapse of industry, the destruction of agriculture and the collapse of infrastructures have ruined most of the Russian regions. The only goods Russia can sell in the international market are weapons, oil and base metals. As the Russian share of the world arms trade has fallen from 35 per cent to 10 per cent (Haynes and Glatter, 1998: p. 51), the main source of hard currency is the sale of raw material. The major share of the dollars earned from the sale of these goods is transferred to secret bank accounts in the West. Although the flight of capital started before the dissolution of the USSR, after the reforms it reached dramatic heights. Various estimates suggest that hundreds of billions of dollars have been taken out of Russia since the demise of the USSR. On the other hand, lacking sufficient cash reserves, the majority of enterprises and households are involved in barter. 'Barter rose from 6 per cent of industrial output in 1992 to 9 per cent in 1993, jumping with the drive to stabilisation to 17 per cent in 1994, 22 per cent in 1995, 35 per cent in 1996 and an estimated 41 per cent in 1997' (Haynes and Glatter, p. 58). This social polarisation fits in well with what Castells has called selective integration and marginalisation in the world economy. The new rich are closely linked to Western financial institutions,[72] and launder their money in Western banks, profit from the import of Western goods and buy houses in luxurious suburbs in the West. By contrast, the majority of Russians have lost their privileges of the Soviet era.

The new ruling networks which come from the Soviet-era *nomenklatura* have acquired a predatory character. In 1995, 74 per cent of the government and 75 per cent of Yeltsin's close associates came from the old elite (Haynes and Glatter, p. 65). Corruption and nepotism were rampant in the Brezhnev era. Both the rulers and the ordinary people, although on different scales, appropriated, illegally, state property for private ends (Grossman, 1985; Ledeneva, 1998). Moreover, the rulers enjoyed enormous privileges. However, the Soviet state was not a predatory one. The interests of the state and party were more important than the personal interests of particular sections of the ruling elite. The predatory rule began with *perestroika*. During this period the elite used a number of predatory methods to plunder the state wealth, including the following: stealing the reserves of hard currency; stealing the Soviet gold stock; smuggling out metal, oil, gas and weapons; buying oil, gas and metal very cheaply from state enterprises in roubles and then selling them abroad for ten times the purchase prices in dollars; illegal import of goods and selling them on the black markets; and creating import monopolies (Handelman, 1995; Chossudovsky, 1998: pp. 228–9). The fortunes collected through these dealings were legalised in May 1988 (Chossudovsky, 1998).

After 1992 the privatisation of state property became a main means of predation.

A ministry would be abolished and in its ruins a business concern would be created in the form of a joint-stock company (same building, same furniture, same personnel); the minister would resign; the controlling parcel of shares would pass into the hands of the state, the rest would be distributed between the leadership of the ministry; as a rule, the second or third figure in the abolished ministry would become the head of the concern. (Kyrshtanovskaya, quoted in Haynes and Glatter, 1998: pp. 65–7)

Gazprom, one of the largest companies in the world, was privatised by Viktor Chernomyrdin, the last Soviet gas minister and later the prime minister, the same way. Lukoil and Yukos, the first and second largest oil producing companies, were formed through this method as well (Haynes and Glatter, p. 67). Moreover, while the most profitable enterprises were privatised, they not only avoided paying taxes to the state coffers, but used their connections with state officials to get credit and use the infrastructure free of charge. Anatoly Chobias, the Russian agent of IMF's and World Bank's policies, admitted the predatory nature of privatisation as follows:

... they steal and steal. They are stealing absolutely everything and it is impossible to stop them. But let them steal and take their property. Then they will become owners and decent administrators of this property ... the 'Mafia' had benefited from privatisation it was time to legitimise it. (quoted in Haynes and Glatter, 1998: p. 56)

Another method of predation was the use of the newly created banking system for financial speculation in foreign currencies and dealing government bonds, money laundering and stealing money from loans the government borrowed from abroad (including those from the IMF and World Bank). The fact that the numbers of banks grew from a few to 2,500 in 1994 (Haynes and Glatter, 1998: p. 56) is suggestive. When the government failed to repay the credit from the banks which had financed its budget deficit in 1995, the banks auctioned the best of the state enterprises, such as the energy sector, to themselves. This tightened the grip of so-called financial/industrial 'oligarchs' over the Russian economy. According to Berezovsky, one of these oligarchs, seven such oligarchs controlled half of the Russian economy in 1996 (Haynes and Glatter, p. 57).

Another form of predation is racketeering. In the Soviet era, there were criminal rings who had their own code of moral conduct and belonged to a particular subculture. Racketeering had existed in the Soviet Union since the 1970s (Handelman, 1995; Humphrey, 1999). However, as in the case of Kazakhstan, discussed in chapter 3, the enormous growth of racketeering in Russia is mainly related to expansion of private business (Handelman, 1995; Humphrey, 1999). Again as in Kazakhstan, the practices of racketeering involve negotiation, cooperation and violent clashes between various networks of racketeers on the one hand and the state officials on the other (Handelman, 1995; Humphrey, 1999). The convertibility of violence, contacts and money to each other is the rule which articulates their mutual relations.

Although the criminal activities and the culture of the Russian mafia have received a lot of publicity at home and abroad, racketeering is economically a less significant predatory method than those mentioned above, which are practised by the top members of the elite and often have a legal cover. However, its importance lies in the fact that it is conceived by the public as the obvious and spectacular epitome of all forms of predation. The street racket symbolises the oligarch or the statesman (Berezovsky, Yeltsin and Chernomyrdin, and so on). The metaphorical and actual links between the government and the mafia, the statesman and the racketeer are aspects of a chaotic mode of domination which emerged in the form of fragmentation and criminalisation of the Russian state. This situation which was a result of the confluence of the disintegration of the Soviet state and implementation of neo-liberalism was both an instrument and a consequence of the newly emerged predatory rule. Now not only the state property was stolen but the state itself was privatised. The privatisation of the state occurred on two fronts: first, the state institutions and their resources were used for private ends; second, part of the erstwhile state functions such as policing cities and taxation (now called protection fees) were transferred to informal networks of the mafia and private security agencies (covered racketeers) which were closely related to the police. Privatisation resulted in the formation of and triggered a fierce and violent rivalry between: networks of racketeers; networks of oligarchs/politicians in the centre; and the networks of predatory rule in the regions. Although the racketeers and the private security forces are not formally governmental organisations, in practice they are part of the state coercive apparatus in its broad sense. Let me elaborate on this. Gramsci (1971), Poulantzas (1983) and Althusser (1994) dealing with the ideological and hegemonic aspects of state argued that state permeates governmental and non-governmental domains. They suggested that the hegemony of the ruling classes is provided through inter-linked practices within both governmental and non-governmental institutions, which constitute the ideological apparatus of the state. Political parties, family, church, media and what in the bourgeoisie ideology is depicted as civil society, are various elements of such an apparatus. But in Russia there is a crisis of hegemony, which means that domination cannot be achieved through ideological means. This is not to deny that governments may temporarily acquire legitimacy, through demagogy and launching various spectacles using the media. The spectacle of democracy and capitalism staged by the predatory elite in the early years of Yeltsin's rule and that of the strong man staged by Putin, through waging a brutal war, have earned the incumbent government's legitimacy, but this is far from hegemony of the networks of predatory rule. These networks cannot achieve hegemony, not only because of their internal incoherence and violent rivalries, but more importantly because predation, which is their main method of collecting wealth, is conceived by the wider population as theft. So the coercive apparatus of the state is the main instrument of the subjugation of the dispossessed.

To accommodate predatory rule, the coercive apparatus of the state has undergone remarkable changes. First, coercion is practised by both governmental organisations and a myriad of non-governmental networks which are linked to each other in a random and chaotic manner. Moreover, coercion has become a direct element of the accumulation of wealth. The non-governmental coercive organisations (the mafia and the private security firms) are part of the coercive apparatus of the state, because they contribute to the domination of predatory rule over the population. The random and chaotic articulations of and tension between, over-centralised arbitrariness of top governmental officials, epitomised by presidential rule, and centrifugal arbitrariness of various networks of influence, epitomised by the activities of the mafia, resulting in a chaotic mode of domination, are the two sides of the same coin: the coercive apparatus of the state. The fact that both the mafia and private security companies have recruited a good number of their members from former army, KGB and police officers illustrates the link between the public and private sectors of the coerceive apparatus. Indeed, these two sectors are articulated to each other by the practices of predatory networks which control both. It is worth repeating that the basic rule of predation is the exchangeability of money, violence and contacts. The partial privatisation of the coercive apparatus and the concommitant commodification of coercion represent a radical transformation in the political and economic systems. That is, although the commodified coercion is a market element (by the virtue of being a commodity) it plays a regulatary role *vis-à-vis* it. In other words, while political power has been the midwife of the post-Soviet market economy and controls, to a great extent, the economic transactions, power itself has become a commodity. This is an important feature of the chaotic mode of domination. The vast Russian territory and its federal structure have given an enormous scale to the post-Soviet chaos, resulting in great fear and insecurity among the population. Therefore, the images of a strong man, a great 'bully' who could bring the smaller bullies under a centralised rule and thereby restore some kind of order have become popular among Russians. Whether Putin will be able to offer a Bonapartist solution to this situation is a matter for the future. This situation is not a peculiarity of Russia and other post-Soviet countries, the same parameters could be identified among many third-world countries such as Nigeria, Zaire, Mexico, Colombia, Peru and Pakistan.

However, by comparing Kazakhstan, Russia and the former Yugoslavia with Sub-Saharan Africa I do not conclude that Western policies are the only reason behind the current post-Soviet chaos. Nor do I mean that the situation in Russia and Kazakhstan is identical with that in Sub-Saharan Africa. My aim was to establish the global context of the post-Soviet change. Within such a context, the direction of change is contingent upon a complex struggle between external and internal forces which may subvert the context itself.

NOTES

1. A rich suburb in Almaty.
2. For a story of this failure see Kagarlitsky (1990).
3. *Kazakhstan Economic Trends* reports, 'A number of Kazakh opposition groups, including "Azamat", the communist party and the labour movement, prepares for the establishment of a so-called "people's front". The co-chairman of the opposition movement "Azamat", Mr. G. Abyseitov, accuses the government of rolling back democratic reforms and establishing a totalitarian regime in the Republic.' (April–June 1998: p. 70).
4. A previous Kazakhstan prime minister.
5. The story of dispossession, similar to events in England under the stage of so-called primitive accumulation of capital (Marx, 1906), as Marx put it, 'is written in letters of blood and fire' (p. 786). While the peasant/artisan in Marx's story was dispossessed from his rights to land/means of production or from his bonds to community the post-soviet citizen is dispossessed from his/her rights to services and social guarantees provided by the state.
6. She does not mention Marx, but her definition of the dispossessed is evidently similar to that of the proletariat in Marx.
7. *Bomzh*, which literally means homeless, is applied today to everybody living in extreme poverty.
8. As with any classification ours is to some degree arbitrary. For example, sex workers perceived themselves to be poor rather than average. While the money a relatively young and 'good looking' sex worker may earn a night is many times more than the salary of an industrial worker, there were broken sex workers who were very close to the extremely poor group. On the other hand, the level of income of street traders is usually higher than that of the urban working class and in addition at the end of each day they have cash in their hands, while the payment of worker's wages is postponed for several months or is partly paid in kind. But workers have apartments, usually cars, and often *dachas* (village cottages with land allotments), which contribute to their wealth. On the other hand some workers like those of the construction industry had relatively high wages which were paid on time, because of the construction boom. Moreover, such a classification doesn't include people's potential access to resources through their networks (see chapter 4).
9. I heard that middle-aged rich women hired young male prostitutes, but this was on a very limited scale. Although child prostitution does exist it is very difficult to map its extension.
10. The formation of ethnic, national, regional and territorial identities are gendered by assigning different roles to men and women (Yuval-Davis, 1993; Greenfield, 1995; Verdery, 1996a; Krohn-Hansen, 1997; Nagel, 1998). Moreover, such identities are authenticised through the construction of particular notions of women's sexual behaviour (Mosse, 1985; Kandiyoti, 1991; Ahmed, 1992; McClintock, 1995).

11. A pseudonym, as with all other names which refer to local people.

12. As they were not willing to answer my questions themselves, I did not ask other people questions about them.

13. According to an Irish man I met in Almaty, until 1985 there was an Irish community of ten thousand people in Kazakhstan. After *perestroika* most of the Irish emigrated to America. According to him these Irish were descendants of Irishmen who deserted the British army, then helping the Whites against the Bolsheviks during the civil war (1918–1921). In the 1930s, like many other ethnic groups, they were exiled by Stalin to Kazakhstan.

14. Although this figure does not represent the exact number of the families who lived in the neighbourhood, but the number of those I asked about their ethnicity, the two figures according to my estimation do not differ dramatically.

15. The increase of the importance of Kazakhstan in the Soviet Union was related to three factors. First, Kazakhstan provided a great deal of material for the European part of the Soviet Union; second, the Soviet Union major space station was located in Kazakhstan; third, Kazakhstan became important militarily. Almaty was the centre of the Soviet Army in Central Asia and considerable numbers of Soviet atomic missiles were stationed in Kazakhstan.

16. The first two were built by Turks and the third by the French.

17. According to I. Svanberg, Kunaev and his associates had monopolised 247 hotels, 414 guest flats, 84 cottages, 22 hunting lodges and 350 hospital beds for their personal use (1990).

18. For an example of the patterns of cooperation between bureaucrats and the mafia in the post-Soviet context see S. Handelman (1995). In Kazakhstan the same mechanisms are at work, but with the major difference that in Kazakhstan the control of the state officials over the mafia is much stronger than in Russia. Thus, armed clashes between different factions of the mafia are not as widespread as in Russia.

19. For reasons behind the expansion of prostitution, see Bridger et al, (1996). Although the book is on Russia, the economic and social problems, identified as the causes of prostitution, are similar to those in Kazakhstan.

20. For the scale and reasons behind suicide in Kazakhstan see Buckley (1997).

21. They mark the results of exams in two ways. In some subjects the results could be passed (*zache*t) or failed (*ne zache*t). In other subjects they are graded with marks (*ottsenka*) from 0 to 5.

22. State secret committee (*Gosudarstvennye sekretnye komitet*).

23. In chapter 5 I will describe an example of such dramatic violence experienced by Asel, a sex worker.

24. According to the official figures unemployment was 4.1 per cent for the labour force in January 1996 (Istileulova, 1996: p. 42). Although it is very difficult to estimate the real figures for unemployment, it seemed to me that they are much higher. Workers who still worked or had been sacked told me that most of the plants had cut their work force by a half or one third. In addition to this many factories were nominally open but workers were on unpaid leave.

25. In the Soviet era telephones were almost free.

26. I frequently use the terms Soviet workers, Soviet people and not Kazakhstan people, because locals themselves speak in those terms, their self-identity is still in a Sovietian framework.

27. When people used the pronoun 'we' to denote a collective identity, they usually referred to the 'Soviet people', unless we were speaking explicitly of

Kazakhstan or a particular ethnic category. In the latter cases the pronoun referred to the people of Kazakhstan or the ethnic group in question.

28. In the anthropological literature the genealogy of the concept of network is traced back to Radcliffe-Brown (1940) or Barnes (1954). After them a variety of authors have developed the concept further (Wolf, 1966; Mayer, 1966; Mitchell, 1969, 1974, 1987; Hannerz, 1980, 1992).

29. For a sophisticated view on shortage in the command economies see Kornai (1992: pp. 228–301).

30. In the Soviet economy, there was a system called *Val* in which the performance of each production unit was measured according to the gross volume of products in terms of the total number or weight of the products, and was accordingly rewarded. Each enterprise tried to maximise its own rewards through maximising gross volume with less consideration to the actual use value of products. Thus, depending on the measuring method, they produced either very small or very large goods which were not properly usable. So the shortage was partly a result of surplus unusable products. For this reason the Soviet economy was called an economy of waste (Ticktin, 1992: pp. 10–11).

31. *Khrushchevskii dom,* a Khrushchev house, denotes the five-storey cement blocks which were built in the late 1960s and early 1970s as result of a housing policy launched by Khrushchev.

32. In this book I use the symbol $ meaning US dollar. The reason for using it so often in this text is that the local people almost always measured both their incomes and expenditures in US dollars. Those who could save, saved in US dollars as well. Its exchange rate to the tenge, the local money, changed steadily during my stay in Almaty. On my arrival, 15 July 1995, it was 55 tenge; it increased to 70 tenge in October 1996.

33. Sahlins (1972: pp. 193–6), with regard to the degree of altruism or instrumentalism involved, classifies reciprocity as three types: general reciprocity; balanced reciprocity; and negative reciprocity. In the first type, altruism dominates and in the third, instrumentalism.

34. I have borrowed this phrase from Humphrey and Hugh-Jones (1992: p. 1).

35. The importance of this figure can be estimated with regard to the fact that the average salary in Kazakhstan in the same period was 5,000 tenge.

36. As the Soviet economy was an economy of shortage most people had a considerable surplus of money which they saved.

37. On the factory shop floor where I did fieldwork, without exception all apprentices were the children of those who worked or had worked there. At the university department of which I was a member, all staff had been recruited through connections.

38. *Borshch* is a Russian food.

39. *Beshpermak* is a Kazakh food.

40. It is not my intention to give the impression that Kazakh and Russians always speak negatively about each other. In many cases both of them express positive attitudes about each other. For example many Russians admire Kazakhs for being a hospitable people (*gostepriimnye narod*) and many Kazakhs conceive of Russians as a cultivated people (*kul'turnyi narod*).

41. Women are usually not associated with alcoholism.

42. The Tacis programme is organised by the EU in order to recruit university lecturers from the former Soviet bloc and train them in the EU.

43. She was obviously wrong, because unions existed formally, although they had lost most of their erstwhile welfare functions.

44. I usually spent hours each day in one of these places writing my diary notes. Amused by what I was doing and seeing me as a potential sponsor they usually came to my table or I went to their tables. By buying them a couple of Danish or Dutch beers, luxurious and favourite drinks, I could speak with them for hours.

45. I had no students from the second year.

46. In Almaty, the mafia is called 'M Organisation'.

47. The Russian word *otdykhat'* has two usages in the local language: literally it means, to rest or to have a holiday, but it is used as a metaphor for having casual and illicit sex.

48. According to the Kazakh tradition, when an unmarried woman has a problem she must take advice from her brother's wife, who is seen as her sister.

49. The post-Soviet sexual revolution shares its pleasure orientation with the libertarian one which was practised in 1920s in the Soviet Union, or advocated by authors like Reich (1972) and Marcuse (1966), or that which was practised by the proponents of the so-called the counter-culture, in the 1960s in the West. But it is radically different from them in that it has come primarily to be identified with the commercialisation and advertising of women's bodies and sexualities through the market and the media.

50. A young, beautiful, well dressed and perfumed woman is adored in Almaty not only for the passions and desires she may stimulate or satisfy, but also because her body and correspondent stimulations and satisfactions are symbols of the new consumerism. She is the the jewel in the crown in hotels, restaurant, business centres and other similar places. She is invited to restaurants, receives flowers and expensive presents, and her beauty is praised. But for enjoying these privileges she pays a high price: she is stigmatised and exposed to violence.

51. Chewing gum was a rare and expensive good in the Soviet time and treated as luxurious and a symbol of the West.

52. These kinds of glorified positive images of a Soviet person do not correspond to the actual ways the local people treat each other with mistrust and chicanery.

53. As people push and elbow each other, officials are impolite and often offensive, and one must stand for hours before coming forward to the desk. Foreigners who are businessman or in touch with local institutions send locals to arrange their affairs.

54. People usually try to rent their apartments to foreigners for more money.

55. The local influential people benefit economically from the foreigners' presence in Almaty, as their business partners, or by receiving money from them as bribes, or protection fees against the mafia, or visitors to places of entertainment, or buyers of sexual services.

56. They could afford it because both lived with their parents.

57. Sexual deprivation due to gender, class and race is a universal phenomenon, yet unnoticed and undiscussed.

58. In this context 'white' denotes the colour of skin.

59. Both notions of repatriation and historical homelands are official words. From the point of view of most non-Kazakhs I talked with, both of these terms were misleading because they considered Kazakhstan as their homeland.

60. He did not consider Russian a foreign language.

61. I visited the work place several times. All the people who were working there were Russians with the exception of a half-Uzbek half-Tatar woman and a Chechen man. Once, sitting in Nicolaevich's office and drinking tea with him

and a Russian colleague of his, I told them, teasing, 'You Russians get $500 here while my Kazakh colleagues at university earn only $50, and you still call Kazakhs nationalists.' His colleague, smiling, told me the $50 is their nominal salary. Their real incomes (*dokhodi*) come from bribes they receive from students and is much higher than our salaries. I teased them further: 'Why have you not got a Kazakh here?' Nicolaevich, smiling, told me 'Because they are lazy, they do not like to work hard, they prefer to sit in a governmental office and collect bribes.'

62. A Kazakh poet.
63. The general secretary of the communist party in Kazakhstan (1962–86).
64. The universities in Kazakhstan usually have two sections for each department: a Kazakh and a Russian section. In each the language of instruction is either Kazakh or Russian.
65. The equivalent word for women is *Iuzhanka*.
66. I learned the concept and its meaning from N. Masanov, a Kazakh social scientist, in an interview I had with him.
67. A famous Kazakh poet in the Soviet era.
68. I first read this article in1983. Then, I denounced it as a revisionist opinion. To the credit of its authors and to my humiliation most of the post-Soviet dispossessed, particularly workers, have a similar understanding of the achievements of Soviet society.
69. Mainstream journalism and academics in the West have not hesitated to cover up one of the largest brutal expropriation of the masses in history either by pouring scorn on the dispossessed's protests by associating them with the so-called red-brown monsters (communist-fascist), or by some superficial and marginal remarks on corruption of the post-Soviet elite. From the point of view of the dispossessed masses, the corruption of the post-Soviet elite is not separable from the transition to the market economy. Opposing crony capitalism to a civilised and moralistic capitalism is a new form of charlatanism invented by the defenders of capitalism. Indeed, the only morality capitalism knows is profit-making. Plunder, murder, imperialism, wars and torture are just a few 'romantic' methods capitalists have not hesitated to use in order to secure profit. In Europe (both Eastern and Western) capitalist brutality was partially harnessed by the working class movements after the Second World War. However, the so-called 'flexible mechanisms of accumulation' have offered capital the opportunity to return to its earlier forms of brutal and extreme exploitation with the implementation of monetarism.
70. The retail prices were 20 times more than that which was paid to farmers (Chossudovsky, 1998: p. 111).
71. In the Soviet bloc at the time, unemployment was illegal.
72. The presence of the Russian tycoon, Boris Berezovsky, at Rupert Murdoch's recent wedding is an iconic example of the close connection between the Russian lumpen mafia-bourgeoisie with the Western ruling elites.

BIBLIOGRAPHY

Aganbegyan, A. (1988) 'New Directions in Soviet Economics', *New Left Review*, 169, pp. 89–96.

Ahmed, L. (1992) *Women and Gender in Islam*, New Haven and London: Yale University Press.

Akiner, S. (1983) *Islamic People of the Soviet Union*, London: Kegan Paul International.

—— (1997) 'Between tradition and modernity: the dilemma facing contemporary Central Asian Women', in M. Buckley (ed.), *Post-Soviet Women: From The Baltic to Central Asia*, Cambridge: Cambridge University Press.

Allworth, E. (1967) 'Encounter', in E. Allworth (ed.), *Central Asia: Century of Russian Rule*, New York and London: Columbia University Press, pp. 1–59.

Althuser, L. (1994) 'Ideology and Ideological State Apparatus', in S. Zezek (ed.), *Mapping the Ideology*, London: Verso.

Anderson, B. (1991) *Imagined Communities*, London: Verso. (First edition 1983.)

Appadurai, A. (1986) *The Social Life of Things*, Cambridge: Cambridge University Press.

—— (1990) 'Disjuncture and Difference in Global Cultural Economy', *Public Culture*, 2: 2.

—— (1997) *Modernity at Large: Cultural Dimensions of Globalisation*, Minneapolis and London: University of Minnesota Press.

Armstrong, J.A. (1992) 'The Autonomy of the Ethnic Identity', in A. Motyl (ed.), *Thinking Theoretically about Soviet Nationalities: History and Comparison in the Study of the USSR*, New York: Columbia University Press, pp. 23–43.

Ashwin, S. (1996) 'Forms of Collectivity in a Non-Monetary Society', *Sociology*, 30: 1, pp. 21–39.

—— (1999) *Russian Workers*, Manchester: Manchester University Press.

Attwood, L. (1996) 'Young people, sex and sexual identity', in H. Pilkington (ed.), *Gender, Generation and Identity in Contemporary Russia*, London and New York, Routledge, pp. 96–120.

Barnes, J.A. (1954) 'Class and committees in a Norwegian island parish', *Human Relations*, 7, pp. 39–58.

Basilov, V.N. (1987) 'Popular Islam', *Journal of Institute of Muslim Minority Affairs*, 8: 1, pp. 7–17.

Batunsky, M. (1994) 'Russian clerical studies in the late 19th and early 20th centuries', *Central Asian Survey*, 13: 2, pp. 213–35.

Beller-Hann, I. (1995) 'Prostitution and its effects in Northeast Turkey', *The European Journal of Women's Studies*, Vol. 2, pp. 219–35.

Benjamin, W. (1973) *Illuminations*, London: Fontana.

Bennigsen, A. (1980) 'Soviet Muslims and the World of Islam', *Problems of Communism*, XXIX: 2, pp. 38–51.

Bentley, G.C. (1987) 'Ethnicity and Practice', *Comparative Studies in Society and History*, 29: 1, pp. 24–55.

Berliner, J.S. (1957) *Factory and Manager in the USSR*, Cambridge, Mass: Harvard University Press.

Bettelheim, C. (1979) *Class Struggle in the USSR*, Vol. 1, Tehran: Pezhvak.

—— (1980) *Class Struggle in the USSR*, Vol. 2, Tehran: Shabahang.

Bettelheim, C. and Chavance, B. (1985) 'Stalinism as the Ideology of State Capitalism', *Andiche-Rhai*, 5, pp. 264–91.

Bettelheim, C. and Sueezy, P.M. (1975) *Socialism or State Capitalism*, Tehran: Chappakhsh.

Block, M. (1986) *From Blessing to Violence*, Cambridge: Cambridge University Press.

Bourdieu, P. (1977) *Outline of a Theory of Practice*, Cambridge: Cambridge University Press.

—— (1984) *Distinction*, Cambridge, Mass: Harvard University Press.

Brass, P. (1992) 'Language and National Identity in the Soviet Union and India', in A. Motyl (ed.), *Thinking Theoretically about Soviet Nationalities: History and Comparison in the Study of the USSR*, New York: Columbia University Press.

Bremmer, I. (1993) 'Reassessing Soviet-nationalities Theory', in I. Bremmer and R. Taras (eds), *Nations and Politics in the Soviet Successor State*, Cambridge: Cambridge University Press, pp. xvii–xviii.

—— (1994) 'Nazarbaev and the North: State Building and Ethnic Relations in Kazakhstan', *Ethnic and Racial Studies*, 17: 4, pp. 619–35.

Bremmer, I. and Welt, C. (1996) 'The trouble with democracy in Kazakhstan', *Central Asian Survey*, 15(2), pp. 179–99.

Bridger, S., Kay, R. and Pinnic, K. (1996) *No More Heroines? Russia, Women and The Market*, London and New York: Routledge.

Bromley, Y.V. (1984) *Theoretical Ethnography*, Moscow: Novka Publisher.

—— (1990a) 'Ethnic Process in the USSR', in M-B. Olcott (1990) (ed.), *The Soviet Multi-Ethnic State*, New York: Sharpe, pp. 53–62.

—— (1990b) 'Improving National Relations in USSR', in Olcott (1990), pp. 62–72.

Brubaker, R. (1994) 'Nationhood and the National Question in the Soviet Union and Post-Soviet Eurasia: an institutionalist account', *Theory and Society*, 23: 1, pp. 47–78.

Buckley, C. (1997) 'Suicide in Post-Soviet Kazakhstan', *Central Asian Survey*, 16(1), pp. 45–52.

Burgess, A. (1997) *Divided Europe*, London: Pluto Press.

Butler, W.E. (1993) *Foreign Investment in Kazakhstan*, London, Moscow: Interlist.

Caplan, L. (1981) 'Morality and Polyethnic Identity in Urban South India', in A.C. Mayer (ed.), *Culture and Morality*, Delhi: Oxford University Press, pp. 63–83.

Castells, M. (1996) *The Rise of Network Society*, Oxford and Massachusetts: Blackwell.

—— (1997) *The Power of Identity*, Oxford and Massachusetts: Blackwell.

—— (1998) *End of Millennium*, Oxford and Massachusetts: Blackwell.

Chossudovsky, M. (1998) *Globalisation of Policy*, London: Zed Press.

Chylinski, E.A. (1984) *Soviet Central Asia*, Esberg: South Jutland University Press.

Clarke, S. (1992) 'Privatisation and the Development of Capitalism in Russia', *New Left Review*, 196, pp. 3–27.

Clarke, S. and Kabalina, V. (1995) 'Privatisation and the Struggle for Control of Enterprises', in D. Lane (ed.), *Russia in Transition*, New York: Longman.

Cliff, T. (1980) *The State Capitalism in the USSR* (Persian translation), Tehran: Unknown.

Clover, C. (1998) 'Bold Steps to Independence', *Financial Times Survey*, Kazakhstan, Wednesday 17 June 1998, p. 1.

Clover, C. and Corzine, R. (1998) 'One flag over two economies', *Financial Times Survey*, Kazakhstan, Wednesday 17 June 1998, p. 1.

Cohen, A. (1966) 'The Politics of the Kola Trade', *Africa*, 36, pp. 18–36.

—— (1974) 'Introduction: the lessons of ethnicity', in A. Cohen (ed.), *Urban Ethnicity*, London: Tavistock, pp. ix–xxii.

—— (1981) *The Politics of Elite Culture: Exploration in the Dramaturgy of Power in a Modern African Society*, Berkeley: University of California Press.

Connell, R.W. (1996) 'New Directions in Gender Theory, Masculinity Research, and Gender Politics', *Ethnos*, 61 (3–4), pp. 157–76.

Conquest, R. (1993) 'Forward', in I. Bremmer and R. Taras (eds), *Nations and Politics in the Soviet Successor States*, Cambridge: Cambridge University Press.

Cornwall, A. and Lindisfarne, N. (1994) *Dislocating Masculinity*, London and New York: Routledge.

Corrigan, P., Ramsay, H. and Sayer, D. (1981) 'Bolshevism and the USSR', *New Left Review*, 125, pp. 45–60.

Cox, T. (1993) *The Badi: Prostitution as a social norm among an untouchable caste of West Nepal*, Kathmandu: Asian Ethnographer Society Press.

Dallin, D.J. (1951) *The Soviet New Empire*, New Haven: Yale University Press.

Dave, B. (1996) 'Language Shift and Identity Change', *Post-Soviet Affairs*, 12: 1, pp. 51–72.

Demko, G.J. (1969) *The Russian Colonisation of Kazakhstan 1869–1916*, Bloomington: Indiana University Press.

Dienes, L. (1987) *Soviet Asia*, London: Westview Press.

Dittman, K., Kengerer, H. and Hirschhausen, C. (1998) 'Much Ado About…Little: Disenchantment in Kazakh and Caspian Oil and Gas Sectors', *Kazakhstan Economic Trends*, July–September 1998, pp. 33–56.

Diugai, N.N. (1998) 'Balance of Payments of the Republic of Kazakhstan: External Payment Position and Prospects', *Kazakhstan Economic Trends*, January–March 1998, pp. 17–34.

Dixon, A. (1994) *Kazakhstan: Political reform and economic development*, London: Royal Institute of International Affairs.

Dixon, S. (1990) 'The Russians: the Dominant Nationality', in G. Smith (ed.), *The Nationalities Question in the Soviet Union*, London: Longman.

Dobrokhotova, V. (1984) 'Woman Worker', in T. Mamonova (ed.), *Women and Russia*, Oxford: Blackwell.

Dombrovsky, Y. (1991) *The Keeper of Antiquities*, London: The Harvill Press.

—— (1996) *The Faculty of Useless Knowledge*, London: The Harvill Press.

Dragadze, S. (1980) 'The Place of Ethnos in Soviet Anthropology', in E. Gellner (ed.), *Soviet and Western Anthropology*, New York: Westview Press, pp. 161–70.

Drobizheva, L.M. (1980) 'Ethnic Sociology of Present-day Life', in E. Gellner (ed.), *Soviet and Western Anthropology*, New York: Westview Press, pp. 171–80.

—— (1991) 'The role of Intelligentsia in developing national consciousness among the people of USSR under Perestroika', in *Ethnic and Racial Studies*, 14: 1.

—— (1992) 'Perestroika and Ethnic Consciousness of Russians', in G.W. Lapidus, V. Zaslavsky and P. Goldman (eds), *From Union to Commonwealth: Nationalism and Separatism*, Cambridge: Cambridge University Press, pp. 98–113.

Dunlop, J. (1993) 'Russia: Confronting the Loss of Empire', in I. Bremmer and R. Taras (eds), *Nations and Politics in the Soviet Successor States*, Cambridge: Cambridge University Press, pp. 43–72.

Easton, P. (1989) 'The Rock Music Community', in J. Riordan (ed.), *Soviet Youth Culture*, Bloomington: Indiana University Press, pp. 83–102.

Eberwen, W. and Tholen, J. (1997) *Market or Mafia*, Brookfield USA and Singapore and Sydney: Ashgate.

Einhorn, B. (1993) *Cinderella Goes to Market*, London and New York: Verso.

Eisenstat, N. (1992) 'Centre periphery relations in the Soviet Empire', in A. Motyl (ed.), *Thinking Theoretically about Soviet Nationalities: History and Comparison in the Study of the USSR*, New York: Columbia University Press.

Elias, N. (1978) *Civilising Process*, Vol. 1, Oxford: Blackwell.

Eller, J.D. and Coughlan, R.M. (1993) 'The Poverty of Primordialism: The Demystification of Ethnic Attachments', *Ethnic and Racial Studies*, 16: 2, pp. 183–201.

Enloe, C. (1986) 'Ethnicity, State and the New International Order', in J.R. Stack (ed.), *The Primordial Challenge, Ethnicity in the Contemporary World*, New York: Greenwood Press.

Epstien, A.L. (1978) *Ethos and Identity*, London: Tavistock.

Fardon, R. (1995) 'Introduction', in R. Fardon (1995) *Counterworks, Managing Diversity of Knowledge*, London and New York: Routledge.

Fischer, M. (1986) 'Ethnicity and the Post-Modern Art of Memory', in J. Clifford and G. Marcus, *Writing Culture*, Berkeley: University of California Press, pp. 194–233.

Focault, M. (1978) *The History of Sexuality*, Vol. VI, New York: Random House.

Fox, R. (1990) *Nationalist Ideologies and the Production of National Cultures*, Washington: The Association of American Anthropologists.

Furtado, C.E. and Hechter, M. (1992) 'The Emergence of Nationalist Politics in the USSR: A Comparison of Estonia and Ukraine', in A. Motyl (ed.), *Thinking Theoretically about Soviet Nationalities: History and Comparison in the Study of the USSR*, New York: Columbia University Press, pp. 169–204.

Geertz, C. (1963) 'Primordial Sentiments and Civil Politics in the New States', in C. Geertz (ed.), *Old Societies and New States*, New York: Free Press.

Gellner, E. (1983) *Nations and Nationalism*, Oxford: Blackwell.

—— (1988) *State and Society in Soviet Thought*, Oxford: Blackwell.

—— (1992) 'Nationalism in the Vacuum', in A. Motyl (ed.), *Thinking Theoretically about Soviet Nationalities: History and Comparison in the Study of the USSR*, New York: Columbia University Press, pp. 243–54.

Gledhill, J. (1996) 'Putting the State Back in Without Leaving the Dialectics Out: Social Movements, Elites and Neoliberalism', *http://les.man.ac.uk/sa/jgepubs.htm*

Gowan, P. (1996) 'Eastern Europe, Western Power and Neo-Liberalism', *New Left Review*, 216, pp. 120–40.

Gramsci, A. (1971) *Selections from the Prison Notebooks*, London: Lawrence and Wishart.

Grant, B. (1995) *In the Soviet House of Culture: A Century of Perestroika*, Princeton: Princeton University Press.

Greenfield, K. (1995) 'Self and Nation in Kenya: Charles Mangua's Son of Woman', *The Journal of Modern African Studies*, 33: 4, pp. 685–98.

Grosby, S. (1994) 'The Verdict of History: Inexpungeable Tie of Primordiality – A Response to Eller & Coughlan', in *Ethnic and Racial Studies*, 17: 1, pp. 164–71.

Gross, J.A. (1992) *Muslims in Central Asia*, Durham: Duke University Press.

Grossman, G. (1985) 'The Second Economy of the USSR', in C.R. Littler (ed.), *The Experience of Work*, Hampshire: Gower Publishing Company, pp. 252–61.

Handelman, S. (1995) *Comrade Criminal*, New Haven and London: Yale University Press.

Hannerz, U. (1980) *Exploring the City*, New York: Columbia University Press.

—— (1992a) 'The global ecumene as a network of networks', in A. Kuper, *Conceptualising Society*, London: Routledge.

—— (1992b) *Cultural Complexity: Studies in the Social Organisation of Meaning*, New York: Columbia University Press.

Harris, N. (1990) *National Liberation*, London: Penguin Books.

Hastrup, K. and Olwig, K.F. (1997) 'Introduction', in F. Olwig and K. Hastrup (eds), *Siting Culture: The shifting anthropological object*, London and New York: Routledge.

Haynes, M. and Glatter, P. (1998) 'The Russian Catastrophe', *International Socialism*, 31, p. 88.

Hechter, M. (1975) *International Colonialism: The Celtic Fringe in British National Development*, London: Routledge.

Hobsbawm, E. (1994) *Nation and Nationalism since 1780*, Cambridge: Cambridge University Press.

Hobsbawm, E. and Ranger, T. (eds) (1983) *The Invention of Tradition*, Cambridge: Cambridge University Press.

Humphrey, C. (1983) *Karl Marx Collective*, Cambridge: Cambridge University Press.

—— (1991) '"Icebergs" barter, and mafia in provincial Russia', *Anthropology Today*, 7: 2, pp. 8–13.

—— (1995) 'Creating a culture of disillusionment: Consumption in Moscow, a chronicle of changing time', in D. Miller (ed.), *Worlds Apart: Modernity through the prism of the local*, London and New York: Routledge.

—— (1996) 'Myth making, narrative and the dispossessed in Russia', *Cambridge Anthropology*, 19: 2, pp. 70–92.

—— (1999) 'Russian protection racket and the appropriation of law and order', in J. Heyman (ed.) *States and Illegal Practices*, Oxford: Berg.

Humphrey, C. and Hugh-Jones, S. (1992) 'Introduction', in C. Humphrey and S. Hugh-Jones (eds), *Barter, Exchange and Value*, Cambridge: Cambridge University Press.

Huntington, S. (1997) *The Clashes of Civilizations and the Remaking of the World*, London: Simon & Schuster.

Istileulova, E. (1996) 'Unemployment and the social security system in Kazakhstan', *Kazakhstan Economic Trends*, Fourth Quarter 1996, pp. 41–54.

Jameson, E. (1991) *Postmodernism or cultural logic of Capitalism*, London and New York: Verso.

Kagarlitsky, B. (1988) 'Perestroika: The dialectic of change', *New Left Review*, 169, pp. 63–93.

—— (1990) *Farewell Perestroika*, London: Verso.

—— (1992) *The Disintegration of the Monolith*, London: Verso.

—— (1995) *Restoration in Russia*, London: Verso.

Kandiyoti, D. (1991) *Women, Islam and State*, Basingstoke: Macmillan.

Kaplan, R. (1996) *The End of the Earth: a journey to the dawn of the 21st century*, New York: Random House.

Kapur, P. (1994) *The Indian Call Girls*, New Delhi: Orient Paperbacks.

Keesing, R. (1987) 'Anthropology as Interpretive Quest', *Current Anthropology*, 28, pp. 161–76.

Kellas, J. (1991) *The Politics of Nationalism and Ethnicity*, London: Macmillan.

Khazanov, A. (1983) *Nomads and the Outside World*, Cambridge: Cambridge University Press.

—— (1995) *After the USSR, Ethnicity, Nationalism, and Politics in the Commonwealth of Independent States*, The University of Wisconsin Press.

Konstitutsiia Republiki Kazakhstan, 1995.

Kornai, J. (1992) *The Socialist System*, Oxford: Clarendon Press.

Kreindler, I. (1983) 'Ibrahim Altysarin, Nikolai Il'minski and the Kazakh National Awakening', *Central Asian Survey*, 2: 3, pp. 99–116.

Krohn-Hansen, C. (1997) 'The Construction of Dominican State: Power and Symbolism of Violence', *Ethnos*, 62 (3–4), pp. 49–78.

Lane, C. (1981) *The Rites of Rulers: Rituals in Industrial Society – The Soviet Case*, Cambridge: Cambridge University Press.

Latin, D., Petersen, R. and Slocum, J.W. (1992) 'Language and the State: Russia and The Soviet Union in Comparative Perspective', in A. Motyl (ed.), *Thinking Theoretically about Soviet Nationalities: History and Comparison in the Study of the USSR*, New York: Columbia University Press, pp. 129–68.

Leach, E. (1964) *Political Systems of Highland Burma*, London: Athlone Press.

Ledeneva, A. (1998) *Russia's Economy of Favours*, Cambridge: Cambridge University Press.

Lemarchand, F. (1986) 'Ethnic Violence in Tropical Africa', in J.R. Stack (ed.), *The Primordial Challenge: Ethnicity in the Contemporary World*, New York: Greenwood Press.

Liber, G. (1991) '*Korenzatsiia*: Restructuring Soviet nationality policy in the 1920s', *Ethnic and Racial Studies*, 14: 1.

Lomnitz, L.A. (1977) *Networks and Marginality*, New York: Academic Press.

Low, S.M. (1997) 'Theorising the city; Ethnicity, gender and globalisation', *Critique of Anthropology*, 17 (4), pp. 403–9.

MacDuffie, M. (1995) *The Red Carpet*, London: Cassell & Co Ltd.

Mandelbum, M. (1994) *Central Asia and the World*, New York: Council of Foreign Relations Press.

Marcus, G.E. (1995) 'Ethnography in/of the World System: The Emergence of Multi-Sited Ethnography', *Annual Review of Anthropology*, 24, pp. 95–117.

Marcuse, H. (1966) *Eros and Civilisation*, Boston: Beacon Press.

Marx, K. (1906) *Capital: A Critique of Political Economy*, New York: The Modern Library.

Masanov, N. (1996a) 'Kazakhskaia politcheskaia I intellektualnaia elita: klanovaia Prinadlezhnost' I vnytrietnicheskoe copernichectvo', *Vestnik Evrazii*, 1: 2, pp. 46–61.

—— (1996b) *Eitnopoliticheskii Monitring v Kazakhtane*, Almaty: Tsentr Monitoringa Mezhoeinicheckikh otnoshenii v Kazakhstane.

Massell, G. (1975) *The Surrogate Proletariat*, Princeton: Princeton University Press.

Matley, M. (1969) 'Agricultural Development', in E. Allworth, *Central Asia, a Century of Russian Rule*, New York: Columbia University Press, pp. 266–308.

Mayer, A. (1966) 'The Significance of Quasi-Groups in the Study of Complex Societies', in M. Banton (ed.), *The Social Anthropology of Complex Societies*, London: Tavistock.

McClintock, A. (1995) *Imperial Leather: Race, Gender and Sexuality in the Colonial Contest*, London: Routledge.

Miller, D. (1995) 'Introduction', in D. Miller (ed.), *World Apart: Modernity through the prism of the local*, London and New York: Routledge.

Mitchell, J.C. (1969) 'The Concept and Use of Social Networks', in J.C. Mitchell (ed.), *Social Networks in Urban Situations*, Manchester: Manchester University Press.

—— (1974) 'Social Networks', in *Annual Review of Anthropology*, Vol. 3, pp. 279–99.

—— (1987) *Cities, Society and Social Perception*, Oxford: Clarendon Press.

Molyneux, M. (1990) 'The "Woman Question" in the Age of Perestroika', *New Left Review*, 183, pp. 23–49.

Mosse, G. (1995) *Nationalism and Sexuality: Middle-Class Morality and Sexual Norms in Modern Europe*, Madison, WI: University of Wisconsin Press.

Nagel, J. (1998) 'Masculinity and Nationalism: gender and sexuality in the making of nations', *Ethnic and Racial Studies*, 21 (2), pp. 242–69.

Nahaylo, B. and Swoboda, V. (1990) *The Soviet Discussion*, London: Hamilton.

Olcott, M-B. (1981) 'The Emergence of National Identity in Kazakhstan', *Canadian Review of Studies in Nationalism*, 8: 2, pp. 285–300.

—— (1987) *The Kazakhs*, Stanford: Hover Institution.

—— (1993) 'Kazakhstan: a Republic of Minorities', in I. Bremmer and R. Taras (eds), *Nations and Politics in the Soviet Successor State*, Cambridge: Cambridge University Press.

—— (1997) 'Kazakhstan: Nursultan Nzarbaev as strong president', in R. Taras (ed.), *Postcommunist Presidents*, Cambridge: Cambridge University Press, pp. 106–29.

Olwig, K.F. (1997) 'Cultural sites: Sustaining a home in a deterritorialized world', in K.F. Olwig and K. Hastrup (eds), *Siting Culture: The Shifting Anthropological Object*, London and New York: Routledge.

Oraltay, H. (1994) 'The Alash Movement in Turkistan', *Central Asian Survey*, 4: 2, pp. 41–51.

Ornan, Y. (1994) 'Economics and Nationalism: The Case of Muslim Central Asia', *Central Asian Survey*, 13: 4, pp. 491–505.

Ozhegov, S.N. and Shvedova, N. (1996) *Tolkobyi Slovr' Russkogo Iazyka*, Moscow: Az'.

Panitch, L. (2000) 'The New Imperial State', *New Left Review*, II, 2, pp. 5–20.

Pilkington, H. (1994) *Russian Youth and its Culture*, London: Routledge.

—— (1998) *Migration, Displacement and Identity in Post-Soviet Russia*, London and New York: Routledge.

Poliakov, S. (1992) *Everyday Islam: Religion and Tradition in Rural Central Asia*, New York and London: M.E. Sharpe.

Posadskaya, A. (1992) 'Self-Portrait of a Russian Feminist', *New Left Review*, 195, pp. 3–19.

Poulantzas, N. (1983) *Fascism and Dictatorship*, Tehran: Pezhvak.

Radcliffe-Brown, A.R. (1940) 'On social structure', *Journal of the Royal Anthropological Institute*, 70, pp. 1–12.

Reich, W. (1972) *The Sexual Revolution*, London: Vision Press.

Ribakova, T. (1998) 'Export Performance of the Economy of Kazakhstan', *Kazakhstan Economic Trends*, January–March 1998, pp. 35–56.

Richards, P. (1996) *Fighting for the Rain Forest*, Oxford: James Curry.

Richards, P. and Peters, K. (1998) 'Why fight: voices of youth combatants in Sierra Leone', *Africa*, 68 (2), pp. 183–210.

Richmond, A.H. (1984) 'Ethnic Nationalism and Post-Industrialisation', *Ethnic and Racial Studies*, 7: 1, pp. 5–16.

Rigi, J. (1995) *Russians National Identity in Kazakhstan*, Unpublished Research Report.

Rogers, A. and Vertovec, S. (1995) 'Introduction', in A. Rogers and S. Vertovec (eds), *Urban Context*, Oxford: Berg, pp. 1–33.

Sahlins, M. (1972) *Stone Age Economics*, London: Tavistock.

Scheremet, W. (1996) 'Industrial Relations and Wage Bargaining in Kazakhstan', *Kazakhstan Economic Trends*, Fourth Quarter 1996, pp. 28–54.

Shils, E. (1957) 'Primordial, Personal, Sacred, and Civil Ties', *British Journal of Sociology*, 8: 2, pp. 130–45.

Shreeves, R. (1992) 'Sexual revolution or "exploitation"? The pornography and erotica debate in the Soviet Union', in S. Raj, H. Pilkington and A. Phizacklea (eds), *Women in the Face of Change*, London and New York: Routledge, pp. 130–46.

Smith, A.D. (1996) *The Ethnic Origin of Nations*, Oxford: Blackwell.

—— (1991) *National Identity*, London: Penguin Books.

—— (1992) 'Ethnic Identity and Territorial Nationalism in Comparative Perspective', in A. Motyl (ed.), *Thinking Theoretically about Soviet Nationalities: History and Comparison in the Study of the USSR*, New York: Columbia University Press, pp. 45–65.

Smith, G. (1999) 'Introduction', in G. Smith (ed.), *The National Question in the Soviet Union*, London: Longman.

Stern, M. (1981) *Sex in the Soviet Union*, London: WH Allen.

Suny, R. (1992) 'State, Civil Society and Ethnic – Cultural Consolidation in the USSR: The Roots of the National Question', in G.W. Lapidus, P. Goldman and V. Zaslavsky (eds), *From Union to Commonwealth: Nationalism and Separatism*, Cambridge: Cambridge University Press.

Svanberg, I. (1990) 'Kazakhs', in G. Smith (ed.), *The National Question in the Soviet Union*, London: Longman.

Ticktin, H. (1992) *The Origin of Crisis in the USSR*, New York: Sharpe.

Trotsky, L.D. (1930) *My Life*, London: Thornton Butterworth.

Turner, B. (1994) *Orientalism, Post-modernism and Globalism*, London and New York: Routledge.

Van den Berge, P. (1981) *The Ethnic Phenomenon*, New York: Elsevier.

Verdery, K. (1996a) *What Was Socialism, and What Comes Next?*, Princeton: Princeton University Press.

—— (1996b) 'Whither "Nation" and "Nationalism"?', in G. Balakrishnan (ed.) *Mapping the Nation*, London and New York: Verso, pp. 226–34.

Verk, V. (1996) 'Uzhel' "mgnovennoe prozrenie"?', *Karavan*, 30 September 1996, No. 192 (487).

Waldingar, R.H. (ed.) (1990) *Ethnic Entrepreneurs*, London: Sage.

Waters, E. (1989) 'Restructuring the "Woman Question": Perestroika and prostitution', *Feminist Review*, No. 33, pp. 3–19.

Watson, P. (1993) 'The Rise of Masculinism in Eastern Europe', *New Left Review*, 198, pp. 71–82.

Wheeler, G. (1960) *Racial Problems in Soviet Muslim Asia*, London: Oxford University Press.

Williams, B. (1989) 'A Class Act: Anthropology and race to nation across ethnic terrain', in *Annual Review of Anthropology*, Vol. 18, pp. 401–4.

Williams, R. (1977) *Marxism and Literature*, London: Oxford University Press.

Wolf, E. (1966) 'Kinship, Friendship and Patron – Client Relations in Complex
    Societies', in M. Banton (ed.), *The Social Anthropology of Complex Societies*,
    London: Tavistock.
Woodward, S. (1995) *The Balkan Tragedy: chaos and dissolution after the Cold
    War*, Washington DC: Brookings Institution.
Wurzel, U.G. (1998) 'Natural Resources, Geostrategic Interests and Necessity of
    A New Economic Policy for Kazakhstan', *Kazakhstan Economic Trends*,
    July–September 1998, pp. 16–32.
Yuval-Davis, N. (1993) 'Gender and Nation', *Ethnic and Racial Studies*, 16: 4.
Zabelina, T. (1996) 'Sexual violence towards women', in H. Pilkington (ed.),
    Gender, Generation and Identity in Contemporary Russia, London and New
    York: Routledge, pp. 168–86.

INDEX

Compiled by Auriol Griffith-Jones